A FAN'S GUIDE: FOOTBALL GROUNDS
ENGLAND AND WALES
DUNCAN ADAMS

D1350513

First published in Great Britain in 2012 by The Derby Books Publishing Company Limited,
3 The Parker Centre, Derby, DE21 4SZ.

© Duncan Adams, 2012

ISBN 978-1-78091-071-0
Printed and bound by Oz Graf in Poland.

A FAN'S GUIDE: FOOTBALL GROUNDS
ENGLAND
AND WALES
DUNCAN ADAMS

PUBLISHING

Welcome to the 2012-13 edition of 'A Fan's Guide: Football Grounds – England & Wales'. This book covers every ground in the Barclays Premier League and npower Football Leagues, plus the Cup Finals and Play-offs venue; Wembley Stadium. Inside you will find a host of information useful to the travelling supporter. Not only are there practical details, such as directions to the grounds, but other information to make your day more enjoyable, such as pub listings. Plus there are also a number of excellent colour photos of all the stadiums. As a member of the Ninety Two Club (for more details about the Club see below), I have personally visited each of the venues so that you get a real feel as to what it is like to visit the stadium.

It is particularly pleasing this season to include the New York Stadium, the new home of Rotherham United. After leaving their Millmoor ground and moving to the Don Valley in Sheffield, some supporters feared whether the Club would ever return to their home town or even worse go out of business. But they have defied the odds and come back stronger with a striking looking new stadium in the centre of Rotherham. Welcome also to Fleetwood Town, whose Highbury Stadium is bound to become a fan's favourite for an away trip. Plus there is a welcome return to the League for York City. Bootham Crescent and York itself has always been one of my favourite away days.

Although I have strived to make sure that every detail is as up-to-date as it can be, things can change over the course of a season; for example, a pub will close or another open, so please bear this in mind. I hope you find this guide useful and informative. But remember this is only a guide and should be treated as such. If you find that things have changed, or you feel that you can give better directions or provide useful additional information then please feel free to e-mail me at:

duncan@footballgroundguide.com

Remember this guide is for football fans by football fans, so feel free to have your say. Wherever possible I'll strive to include your comments in future editions. To see the latest updates to the Guide remember to visit:

www.footballgroundguide.com.

As a Birmingham City supporter and member of the Campaign For Real Ale (CAMRA), I like nothing more than enjoying a good pint of real ale or traditional cider before a game. CAMRA produce a 'Good Beer Guide' each year. If there is a pub near to a particular football ground that is listed within the CAMRA Guide, that I have visited, then I have endeavoured to mention it, in the 'Where To Drink' Section.

I hope you enjoy the book and that it will improve your away trips, as well as perhaps wetting the appetite to visit a ground that you hadn't thought about visiting before.

Duncan Adams

Record attendances

One note about Record attendances listed within the book. These are for the current stadium that the Club now currently plays in (except Rotherham United as they have moved to a new stadium). Bigger record attendances that may have been set at a previous ground are not listed in the Guide.

Also in some cases you may notice that the record attendance set is larger than the current capacity. This is due normally to when the grounds had larger terraced capacities, rather than current all seated capacities.

The Ninety-Two Club

The Ninety-Two Club was formed in 1978 with just thirty-nine founder members to commemorate their achievement of seeing a first team, competitive match at each of the Ninety-Two grounds of the then Football League; (now the Premiership, Championship, League 1 and League 2.) The Club currently has nearly 1,200 registered members with around 800 still active.

Secretary Mike Kimberley says: "Having followed Crystal Palace since 1968, my first away game was at Brighton in 1976 and I completed my last ground at Brunton Park, Carlisle in 1996. I have currently seen first team competitive matches at 141 different League grounds. Before a visit to a new ground I always consult "The Football Ground Guide" website as I find the information invaluable when planning a trip. I am pleased to see that it has once again appeared in print form. I travelled around 25,000 miles to complete the original Ninety-Two grounds and anybody embarking on this long journey will find it both a testing but ultimately gratifying experience."

You may find further details on the internet at www.ninetytwoclub.org.uk

Or write to: The Ninety-Two Club, 153 Hayes Lane, Kenley, Surrey, CR8 5HP

Special Thanks

To Owen Pavey for providing a number of great photographs and for his support over the years as well as Han van Eijden. To Tim Rigby for providing a photo of Shrewsbury Town and his beloved Molineux. Thanks also to Torquay United FC for a photo of the new Bristow's Bench Stand and to Thomas Mapfumo of European Football Statistics for providing the average attendance information. I am also indebted to Simon Inglis and his book 'The Football Grounds Of Great Britain' for some of the historical information contained within this Guide.

Thanks also to my wife Amanda & daughter Sian who have both had to put up with me on many occasions disappearing on a Saturday to watch another game somewhere around the country. Plus to my Mother Joan Adams for her continual confidence in me.

The Guide has been compiled based on not only my personal visits to the grounds but the feedback of many supporters who have visited them in recent seasons, giving an all-round independent view of each of them. Without this feedback this book would not have been possible, so a big thank you to everyone who has contributed.

Ground Name: The Crown Ground
Capacity: 5,057 (2,000 seated)
Address: Livingstone Road, Accrington,
Lancashire, BB5 5BX
Main Telephone No: 0871 434 1968
Ticket Office No: Same as main number

Year Ground Opened: 1968
Pitch Size: 111 x 72 yards
Team Nickname: The Reds, Stanley
Home Kit Colours: Red & White
Official website: www.accringtonstanley.co.uk

What's The Ground Like?

Although the ground is on the smallish side, it is set in a picturesque area, with views over fields and hills behind the Coppice Terrace at one end of the ground. On one side of the ground is the Main Stand, which at first glance looks like one stand, but in fact it is comprised of two small stands; the Main & Thwaites Stands. They sit on either side of the halfway line, with an open gap between the two. Both are all seated covered stands and have a row of floodlights at the back of them. To compensate for the fair slope of the pitch which runs up along the ground from the Coppice Terrace to the Sophia Khan End, the Thwaites Stand has fewer rows of seats than the Main Stand. Both these stands also have an unusual array of tubular steelwork, running across the top of them.

Opposite is a very small covered seated area, called the Whinney Hill side. This former terrace had seating installed before the start of the 2009 / 10 season, in order that the Club could meet Football League stadium criteria of having a minimum of 2,000 seats (further seating was also installed into the Sophia Khan End). Behind this stand is a relatively new housing development, which overlooks the ground, meaning that some residents can see the game for nothing. Both ends are fairly new looking affairs, of which the home end, the Sophia Khan Stand is covered, while the Coppice Terrace opposite is open to the elements. The Sophia Khan Stand looks a little odd, with terracing at the rear, but with seating at the front, especially when you consider that the stand is quite a small structure. Another unusual aspect of the ground is that it has a total of eight floodlight pylons, with three on either side of the ground and another being located at one end.

What Is It Like For Visiting Supporters?

Away fans are mostly housed in the Coppice Terrace at one end of the ground, where up to 1,800 fans can be accommodated after this area was recently extended. If demand requires it then part of the Whinney Hill side can also be allocated. This small stand has a mixture of seating and terrace and has the benefit of some cover, unlike the Coppice Terrace which is open to the elements. Adam Hodson a visiting Stockport County fan adds; 'As it was raining I decided to head for one of the 200 or so seats in the Whinney Hill stand. I found that there is very little leg room between the rows of seats, of which there are only four. I was though located very close to the playing action as I sat in the front row'.

While Shirley Lawrence a visiting Swindon Town supporter tells me; 'We had a pleasant day at the Crown Ground. Before the game we went to the Crown Pub which was crowded, but as they had six staff serving, we were able to get our drinks relatively quickly. Inside the ground there was not much atmosphere due to the away end being uncovered. Although we had over 800 supporters who were in good voice, the noise just wasn't carried around the ground'.

Where To Drink?

There is a Club Bar at the ground, however, this is for home fans only. The nearest pub is the Crown, which is just behind the ground on the main Whalley Road. This pub welcomes all fans, has some Accrington Stanley memorabilia, and displays scarves and pennants given by visiting fans. A little further down Whalley Road (five minutes walk in the direction of the motorway), is the Greyhound pub, which is a Sam Smith's house.

John Schmidt, a visiting Darlington fan adds; 'If you go from the ground to the main road and head towards the town centre, then a five minute walk away, down on the right is the Grey Horse pub, It is only a small pub but served decent real ale. This area also seemed to be good for street parking'.

Directions & Car Parking

Leave the M6 at Junction 29 and take the M65 towards Blackburn. Continue past Blackburn towards Accrington and leave the M65 at Junction 7. Then take the left-hand exit at the roundabout onto the A6185 towards Clitheroe (this is in the opposite direction to Accrington). At the first set of traffic lights turn right onto the A678, towards Padiham, and then at the next traffic lights, turn right onto the A680 towards Accrington. After about half a mile along the A680 you will pass the Crown pub on your left. Take the next left into Livingstone Road and then an immediate left for the Club car park. The car park is of a reasonable size and is free, however, as you would expect it fills up pretty quickly. Otherwise street parking.

By Train

Accrington railway station is about a mile away from the ground. Leave the station and travel down the slope towards the large viaduct roundabout in the centre of town. Take the Milnshaw Lane exit at the opposite side of the roundabout alongside the Perry's Peugeot dealership. After approximately 100 metres this road then joins Whalley Road. Bear left up the hill and follow Whalley Road for about a mile, passing the hospital, a set of traffic lights and then a mini-roundabout. Take the next right after the mini-roundabout junction into Livingstone Road. The football club is approximately 100 metres on the left on Livingstone Road. Thanks to Rob Heys for providing the directions.

Programme
Official Programme: £3

Record & Average Attendance
Record Attendance: 4,368 v Colchester United, FA Cup 3rd Round, January 3rd, 2004.
Average Attendance: 2011-12: 1,785 (League Two)

Ground Name: Goldsands Stadium
Capacity: 12,060 (all seated)
Address: Dean Court, Kings Park, Bournemouth, Dorset, BH7 7AF
Main Telephone No: 01202 726300
Ticket Office No: 01202 726338

Year Ground Opened: 1910 (pitch rotated 90 degrees in 2001)
Pitch Size: 115 x 71 yards
Team Nickname: The Cherries
Home Kit Colours: Red & Black Stripes
Official website: www.afcb.co.uk

What's The Ground Like?

The stadium was literally built in 2001 in a matter of months. It comprises three permanent stands situated on both sides and at one end. The South End is currently open and unused. However, in the past it has seen the presence of a temporary seated stand and this may return again at some point. All three stands are of roughly the same design and height and are quite smart looking, with the Main Stand having a row of executive boxes to its rear. Each is a covered single-tiered stand, with good views of the playing action with perspex windshields at each side. The stand roofs have perspex panels allowing more light to reach the pitch. When the new stadium was built the pitch was rotated 90 degrees from its old position. So if you ever visited the old ground, try figuring out where the old Brighton Beach End was located! Originally known as Dean Court the ground was renamed the Goldsands Stadium in 2012 under a corporate sponsorship deal. The stadium is completed with a set of unusual looking floodlights that are situated in the open corners.

What Is It Like For Visiting Supporters?

Away fans are located on one side of the East Stand, which is situated at one side of the pitch. The normal allocation for this area is 1,500 seats, but this can be increased to 2,000 if required. The stand is shared with home supporters and offers a good view of the playing action. The facilities are okay and normally there is a good atmosphere. I had a fairly relaxing visit to the stadium with no problems experienced.

Where To Drink?

There is the Legends Bar located at the stadium which allows in away fans in family groups. The 1910 Supporters Bar which is located upstairs above is for home fans only.

Although the Queens Park Hotel on Holdenhurst Road (alongside the A338 Wessex Way) has reopened, it is now unfortunately for home fans only. Around a 10-15 minute walk away is the Sir Percy Florence Wetherspoons outlet on Christchurch Street, in nearby Boscombe. Away fans are welcome at this pub, but no colours are allowed. Next door to Wetherspoons is the Mello Mello bar which also admits away supporters (and with colours). Otherwise alcohol is available to visiting supporters inside the stadium.

Directions & Car Parking

Follow the A338 towards Bournemouth. The ground is situated on the left of the A338 in the outskirts of town. You should be able to spot the tops of the ground floodlights on the left. Otherwise leave the A338 via the slip road which is signposted Kings Park/Football traffic. You will then reach a small roundabout at which you take the second exit into Kings Park Drive. The entrance to the stadium and car park are down this road on the left. The car park at the ground is of a good size, however, please note that this costs 50p per hour, otherwise you may find yourself with a penalty ticket for your trouble.

By Train

The nearest train station is Pokesdown which is roughly a mile from the ground and is around a 15 minute walk away. However, most trains arrive at Bournemouth Central, which is around a half an hour walk to the stadium. Either try to get a train to Pokesdown or grab a cab. If you do arrive at Pokesdown Station (which is served by trains from London Waterloo), then exit the station (there is only one exit) and turn right down the main Christchurch Road (A35). Proceed for about 400 metres and then turn right into Gloucester Road. Dean Court is located down the bottom of this road. Thanks to Andy Young for providing the directions from Pokesdown Station.

If you arrive at Bournemouth Central, then leave the station by the South exit, thereby facing an Asda Supermarket. Turn left and walk down to the main Holdenhurst Road. Turn left (going away from the town centre) and then keep straight on along Holdenhurst Road for around 25 minutes, reaching the Queens Park pub (recommended by this Guide). Continue straight on past the pub until you reach a roundabout at which you turn right into Kings Park Drive. The ground is down the bottom of this road on the left. Alternatively you can catch a Yellow Number 33 bus to the ground, normally a half hourly service. Come out of Station again by the South exit, facing Asda and turn left until you get to a Texaco Garage. There is a bus stop with shelter on the same side of the road. Ask the driver to be let off near Kings Park Drive. Please note that if you decide to use the same service coming back, take a yellow number 2 bus as this is a circular service. Thanks to Richard Barnes for supplying the directions from Bournemouth Central.

Programme & Fanzine

Official Programme: £3
View from the tree Fanzine: £1

Record & Average Attendance

Record Attendance: 10,375 England v Poland, Under-19 Friendly, February 6th, 2007.
For a Bournemouth match: 10,008 v Southampton, League One, March 12th, 2011.
Before the ground was re-developed: 28,799 v Manchester United, FA Cup 6th Round, March 2nd, 1957.
Average Attendance: 2011-12: 5,881 (League One)

Ground Name: The Cherry Red Records Stadium
Capacity: 4,850 (Seating 2,265)
Address: Jack Goodchild Way, 422a Kingston Road, Kingston Upon Thames, Surrey, KT1 3PB
Main Telephone No: 020 8547 3528
Ticket Office No: Same as main number

Year Ground Opened: 1989
Pitch Size: 110 x 75 yards
Team Nickname: The Dons or The Wombles
Home Kit Colours: Blue & Yellow
Official website: www.afcwimbledon.co.uk

What's The Ground Like?

Kingsmeadow is a small but tidy stadium that has seen investment in recent years since AFC Wimbledon took over the lease from Kingstonian FC, who still groundshare with the Dons. On one side is the Paul Strank Stand. This covered, all seated Main Stand looks fairly modern, having recently been extended. It accommodates 1,265 spectators and although only eight rows high, it is free of supporting pillars, resulting in uninterrupted views of the pitch. Surprisingly the team dugouts are not located in front of this Main Stand, but opposite in front of the John Smith's Terrace, which leads to a procession of players and club officials, at half and at full-time. This terrace is partly covered to the rear and has open flanks to either side.

At one end is the Tempest End Terrace (aka the Athletics End, from the Athletics Stadium that sits behind), where the majority of the home supporters stand. This newish looking covered terrace is located quite close to the edge of the playing area, giving a reasonable view of the game. Opposite is the Kingston Road End Stand. A former terrace, this was replaced with a new covered, 1,000 seat capacity stand, in 2012. In

addition the stadium has a set of four rather plain looking floodlights.

What Is It Like For Visiting Supporters?

Away fans are housed in the John Smith's Terrace at one side of the pitch. If the away following is expected to be fewer than 600, then one side (towards the Kingston Road End) is allocated and hence the terrace is shared with home supporters, although adequately separated. For larger followings then more of the terrace can be allocated, with the maximum allocation being 700. This small shallow terrace is partly covered to the rear, with open standing areas on each side. In addition a number of seats are made available in the new Kingston Road End, adjacent to the John Smith's Terrace.

Please note that the away terrace is not accessible by going through the main entrance into the stadium car park. Away fans should instead continue going along Kingston Road (keeping the main entrance on the right) and take the next right into Jack Goodchild Way. Outside the stadium near the main entrance is a handy chip shop while a bit further along is the amusingly named 'Fat Boys Cafe'. I also noticed outside the

Main Stand a vendor displaying and selling the largest array of different football badges, that I think I have ever seen.

Where To Drink?

There are two large bars located inside the main Paul Strank Stand. Away supporters are generally welcome to frequent the bars, however, for the bigger games, and/or when it is all ticket, the bars are reserved for home fans only. On my visit I felt that the inside of the bar that I frequented, was a bit dim and drab looking, but with a real ale on offer from a local brewery and a barbecue selling burgers and hot dogs outside, its plus points outweighed the negative ones!

Nearby pubs include the Duke of Wellington and the more basic Prince of Wales, both located on Kingston Road between New Malden and the ground. Otherwise, you can drink in Kingston or New Malden town centres and get a bus to the stadium (or a long walk!). The 131 bus passes the ground and goes through both town centres. If in Kingston, catch a bus heading to Tooting Broadway; if in New Malden, catch a bus heading to Kingston.

Directions & Car Parking

From Outside London:

M25 Junction 10, take the A3 northbound into London. At the exit for New Malden/Worcester Park, turn off and take the left into Malden Road (A2043) towards Kingston. Follow this to the next roundabout. Take the first exit into Kingston Road (A2043 still) and Kingsmeadow is one mile on the left.

There is limited parking available at the ground and, for Saturday games, to be sure of a space you need to arrive before 2.15 pm at the latest. Parking in adjacent streets can be tight as it is a residential area.

By Train

The nearest station to the ground is Norbiton, which is about a 15 minute walk away. The station is served by trains from London Waterloo via Clapham Junction and Wimbledon.

Leave the station via the back exit (Westbound platform), and take the first left onto Norbiton Avenue. At the end of the avenue, turn right into Gloucester Road, and at the end of Gloucester Road turn left into Cambridge Road. The main entrance to Kingsmeadow is 400 yards down on the right, with the away entrance a little further on past this on the right-hand side and is well signposted. Thanks to John Woodruff for providing the directions

Dave Nathan adds; 'New Malden station is also in walking distance of the ground. This may be a preferred route for away fans as there are better pubs in New Malden namely Bar Malden and the Glasshouse both outside New Malden station and The Fountain at the Fountain Roundabout. Come out of New Malden station and follow the High Street to the left, and proceed up to the Fountain Roundabout. At the roundabout turn right into Kingston Road towards Kingston (or jump on a 131 bus) and the ground is a good mile on the left after passing under the railway bridge and Homebase on your right. This will take about 25 minutes to walk'.

Programme & Fanzines

Official Programme: £3
Wise Men Say Fanzine: £1
WUP Fanzine: £1

Record & Average Attendance

Record Attendance For an AFC Wimbledon game at the stadium: 4,722 v St Albans City, Blue Square South, April 25th, 2009.
Average Attendance: 2011-12: 4,295 (League Two)

Ground Name: The EBB Stadium at the Recreation Ground
Capacity: 7,100 (Seated 2,000)
Address: High Street, Aldershot, Hampshire, GU11 1TW
Main Telephone No: 01252 320 211

Ticket Office No: Same as main number
Year Ground Opened: 1926
Pitch Size: 117 x 75 yards
Team Nickname: The Shots
Home Kit Colours: Red & Blue
Official website: www.theshots.co.uk

What's The Ground Like?

The interior of the ground hasn't changed a great deal since the days of Aldershot FC who alas went out of business in 1992. A new Club was born shortly after named Aldershot Town, who took over the Recreation Ground and have successfully risen through the lower leagues and now find themselves firmly back in the Football League.

The ground itself is set in a pleasant setting with plenty of trees visible around its perimeter. This is particularly so at the High Street End of the ground which is an open end. Some of the trees there are almost as tall as the floodlight pylons of the ground. This end doesn't have any terracing as such, but merely a narrow path that runs along behind the advertising hoardings. On one side is a two storey green portakabin that serves as a Police Control Box, otherwise this end is unused for spectators. Opposite is the East Bank. This is a covered terrace that has a barrel-shaped roof and a number of supporting pillars running across the front of it. On one side is the North (Main) Stand, which was built in the late 1930s. This partly covered stand (to the rear), is

slightly raised having small sets of steps in front of it, so fans can access it. It once was all terrace, but a number of seats have now been added to the middle portion of the stand, with terrace still present on either side. Opposite is the South Stand, which is another covered seated stand, which looks a lot more modern than its age suggests (it was built in 1929). This stand only runs for around half the length of the pitch, sitting astride the halfway line. The ground benefits from an impressive set of floodlights.

What Is It Like For Visiting Supporters?

Away fans are housed in the South East corner of the ground. This comprises 212 covered seated places which are available in the South Stand and space for a further 1,320 standing supporters in the East Bank Terrace and a portion of open terrace extending around to the South Stand. The East Bank is shared with home supporters and there are a number of supporting pillars, which could obstruct your view. Although the East Bank is showing its age, at least it does allow a good atmosphere to be created. Despite the club having done significant work to improve facilities for away supporters, they remain pretty basic.

Robin Carder informs me; 'Travelling fans are also reminded that the Away turnstiles (11 and 12) are not at the front of the ground but via the park entrance accessed off Redan Road (Hill). The walk from the High Street entrance to the Away turnstiles can take 10 minutes so allow plenty of time, and factor in potential queues due to there being only two turnstiles. The only access to away supporters permitted via the front entrance is for disabled supporters who now have two dedicated wheelchair bays in the away seats. Please enquire with the club for more information'.

Where To Drink?

Although there is a Club house at the ground, this is for home supporters only. The closest pubs to the ground are The Beehive and the Crimea, Otherwise, the ground is just a short walk away from Aldershot Town Centre where there are plenty of pubs to be found. If you have a bit more time on your hands then you may want to try the La Fontaine pub on Redan Road. Although located on top of a hill, it does look down onto the football ground and serves Fullers beers.

If driving into Aldershot along the A323, then located nearby is the White Lion pub in Lower Farnham Road. This pub has up to six hand pulled ales and is listed in the CAMRA Good Beer Guide.

Directions & Car Parking

Leave the M3 at Junction 4 and take the A331 towards Farnborough/Aldershot. Continue towards Aldershot passing the North Camp turn off. At the next junction (Aldershot South) turn right at the roundabout towards Aldershot Town Centre (A323). Keep straight on this road and after going under a railway bridge, the ground is visible on your right.

There is little parking available at the ground itself. Most fans tend to park in one of the many pay & display car parks, situated around the town centre.

By Train

Aldershot station is less than a 10 minute walk away from the ground. Upon leaving the train station, go down the station approach and turn right into Windsor Way. Continue down Windsor Way passing the Holy Trinity Church on your left. The road bends to the left and leads into Victoria Road. Turn right along Victoria Road and at the bottom of the road you will see floodlights of the Recreation Ground in front of you. Thanks to Ben Smith for providing the directions.

Programme

Official Programme: £3

Record & Average Attendance

Record Attendance: For Aldershot Town 7,500 v Brighton, FA Cup 1st Round, November 18th, 2000.

Average Attendance: 2011-12: 2,865 (League Two)

Ground Name: Emirates Stadium
Capacity: 60,432 (all seated)
Address: Highbury House, 75 Drayton Park,
London, N5 1BU
Main Telephone No: 020 7619 5003
Ticket Office No: 020 7619 5000

Year Ground Opened: 2006
Pitch Size: 115 x 74 yards
Team Nickname: The Gunners
Home Kit Colours: Red & White
Official website: www.arsenal.com

What's The Ground Like?

Arsenal moved the short distance to the Emirates Stadium in 2006, after 93 years of playing at one of the most historic grounds in the country; Arsenal Stadium (better known as Highbury). The stadium was designed by HOK Sport (who also designed Stadium Australia in Sydney, which was used for the Olympics) and built by Sir Robert McAlpine Ltd. The stadium cost £390 million to build. With a capacity of over 60,000 the stadium is huge in comparison to Highbury and is the largest football ground in London. It is the only stadium that I know of in this country, that is four-tiered. The lower tier is large and shallow, set well back from the playing surface as a cinder track surrounds the playing area. A small second tier, which is called the Club tier, has seating, but is only eight rows high. Inside it has a number of lounges/restaurants, earning it the nickname the 'prawn circle'. This Club tier slightly overhangs the bottom tier.

The third tier is even smaller, being entirely comprised of executive boxes, some 150 in total and fits entirely under the large fourth tier. This fourth tier, known as the upper tier, has been designed in a semicircular fashion and is topped by an impressive looking roof. This includes a lot of visible white tubular steelwork and perspex panels to allow more light to get to the pitch. The roofs though do not follow the semicircular shape of the stands but in fact run across the top of them and even dip down towards them giving them a strange look. Two excellent looking large video screens situated in the North West & South East corners, below the roof line, complete the stadium.

What Is It Like For Visiting Supporters?

Away fans at the Emirates Stadium are housed in the lower tier of the South East corner. The normal ticket allocation for away supporters for a Premier League match is 3,000. Although supporters have big padded seats and plenty of leg room, the lower tier of the stadium is quite shallow (unlike the upper tiers which have plenty of height between rows), meaning that the view might not be as good as you would expect from a new stadium.

Entrance to the stadium is by a 'smart ticket', whereby rather than giving your ticket to a turnstile operator, you enter it into a ticket reader to gain entry. The concourse inside is not that spacious, but just about adequate. There is quite a good choice of food on offer (such as Fish & Chips) although a little on the pricey side. However, with no proper queuing system in place at the food and drink outlets, then it can turn into a bit of a scrum to try and buy anything. There are plenty of flat screen televisions on the concourse to keep you entertained, plus there is a betting facility.

I have been to the Emirates a couple of times now. The first was for an international friendly, where I had tickets for the upper tier of the stadium. I was very impressed all round with the stadium and had a great day out. The second visit was as an away supporter seated in the visiting section. On this visit I was less impressed with the Emirates. The whole occasion just seemed as it was one big corporate event rather than a football match. Plus the view was not that great and afterwards you almost questioned if the stadium did indeed hold 60,000, as the large gaps in the corners below the stadium roof, gave the illusion that it is smaller than what it is. The away fans are also located very close to the home fans, which led to a fair amount of rather unsavoury banter.

Where To Drink?

The traditional pub for away supporters is the Drayton Arms, which is located near to Arsenal tube station and Drayton Park railway station. This Courage pub overlooks the new stadium and is only a few minutes walk away. However, as you would expect it can get extremely busy on matchdays, with drinkers spilling outside onto the pavements. Otherwise alcohol is available inside the stadium.

Directions & Car Parking

Leave the M1 at Junction 2 and onto the A1, following the signs for City (Central London). Keep going on the A1 for around six miles, until you see Holloway Road Tube Station on your right. Take the next left at the traffic lights into Hornsey Road and the stadium is about a quarter of a mile further down this road.

There is little parking at the stadium itself or in nearby streets. An extensive residents only parking scheme operates around the stadium on matchdays. It's probably better to park further out of London around a London Underground station such as Cockfosters and get the tube to the stadium.

By Train/Tube

The nearest London Underground tube station to the Emirates Stadium which is open on matchdays is Arsenal tube station which is on the Piccadilly line. It is only a few minutes walk from here to the stadium. On exiting the station turn right and follow Drayton Park Road around to the left. Then take one of the large bridges over the railway line to the stadium. Other tube stations in walking distance of the stadium are Finsbury Park on the Piccadilly Line and Highbury & Islington on the Victoria Line.

Otherwise you can take an overland train to Finsbury Park Railway Station from London Kings Cross. It is then about a 10 to 15 minute walk from Finsbury Park to the stadium. Drayton Park Station which is situated right by the stadium is closed at weekends.

Programme & Fanzine

Official Programme: £3

The Gooner Fanzine: £2

Record & Average Attendance

Record Attendance At The Emirates: 60,161 v Manchester United, Premier League, November 3rd, 2007.

Average Attendance: 2011-12: 60,000 (Premier League)

Ground Name: Villa Park
Capacity: 42,785 (all seated)
Address: Villa Park, Trinity Road,
Birmingham B6 6HE
Main Telephone No: 0121 327 2299
Main Fax No: 0121 322 2107

Ticket Office No: 0800 612 0970
Year Ground Opened: 1897
Pitch Size: 115 x 72 yards
Club Nickname: The Villans
Home Kit Colours: Claret & Blue
Official website: www.avfc.co.uk

What's The Ground Like?

Although the stadium has been completely rebuilt since the late 1970s, it has some individuality, as the four stands each have their own design, making it one of the more interesting in the League. At one end is the Holte End. This is a large two-tiered structure which replaced one of the largest covered terraces in the country. Opened in the 1994-95 season it has a capacity of 13,500 seated supporters. At the other end is the North Stand, which is older (being built in the late 1970s), but still modern looking. This is two-tiered, with a double row of executive boxes running across the middle. On one side of the pitch is the Doug Ellis Stand, which again is two-tiered and is roughly the same height as the other two stands. This stand was opened prior to the 1996 European Championships, for which Villa Park was a host venue. Opposite is the latest edition, the impressive looking Trinity Road Stand. Opened in 2001 it is three-tiered, with a small tier at the front and then two larger tiers above, which are separated by a row of executive boxes. Although at the time many fans were disappointed to see the old Trinity Road Stand demolished, I think its replacement

gives the ground a more overall balanced look, because the new stand, although the largest at Villa Park, has roughly the same roof level as the other three sides. There are also two large video screens installed in opposite corners of the ground.

An unusual feature is that between the Trinity Road & Holte End Stands is a pavilion type structure that was built at the same time as the Trinity Road. This three-tiered building is used for corporate hospitality. On the other side of the Holte End is another similar looking structure that is used for police control. The only disappointment with Villa Park is that the corners of the ground are open.

What Is It Like For Visiting Supporters?

Away supporters are located on one side of the Doug Ellis Stand, towards the North end of the stadium. Up to 3,000 fans can be accommodated in this area, split between both the upper and lower tiers of the stand. The concourse at the back of the upper tier is particularly tight and easily becomes crowded, whereas there is more space behind the lower section. There is a fair selection of food available and it is the first football ground that I have visited that offers meat products that are Halal. There are wide screen televisions on the concourse, showing past encounters between the teams before kick-off. There are also betting facilities available. Entrance to the stand is gained by entering your match ticket into an electronic reader.

A visit to Villa Park is normally an enjoyable experience, with the stewards normally taking a relaxed and friendly attitude. One concern though, is that there is very little separating the home and away fans and this could lead to possible future crowd problems.

Where To Drink?

There are a number of pubs in the vicinity of Villa Park, but most of them on match days are either members only or have bouncers on the door. However, Dave Cooper recommends the following for away fans; 'The Witton Arms (formerly the Cap and Gown), is not a bad pub, to which half the pub is given to away fans (there is even a separate entrance for visiting fans). It is only two minutes walk from the away entrance, right on Witton Island, however, it does charge £2 per person to gain entry'.

If you arrive a bit earlier then you may wish to visit the historic Bartons Arms, located about a 15 minute walk away on High Street Aston (A34). This Grade II listed building, is one of Birmingham's finest pubs, with superb Victorian decor, serving Oakham ales and Thai food is also on offer. It is a regular entry in the CAMRA Good Beer Guide. Please note that alcohol is not available to away fans inside the stadium.

Directions & Car Parking

The ground can be seen from the M6, if you are coming from the North side of Birmingham. Leave the M6 at Junction 6 and take the slip road sign posted Birmingham (NE). Turn right at the island (the fourth exit), the ground is well signposted from here. However, to be on the safe side, turn right at the second set of traffic lights (there is the King Edward VII pub on the corner) on to Aston Hall Road. This road will take you down to the ground. Mostly street parking (don't be surprised though if you are approached by kids wanting to 'mind your car'), although this is not as plentiful as it once was due to a local residents only parking scheme now in place in the streets around the Witton roundabout area.

By Train

The nearest stations are Aston and Witton which are served by trains from Birmingham New Street. Witton station is nearer to the away section and is only a few minutes walk from the ground. As you come out of the station turn left and continue down to a roundabout. Turn left at the roundabout into Witton Lane and the entrance to the away section is down this road on the right. Aston station is about a ten minute walk away from Villa Park.

Programme & Fanzine

Official Programme: £3
Heroes & Villans Fanzine: £2

Record & Average Attendance

Record Attendance: 76,588 v Derby County, FA Cup 6th Round, March 2nd, 1946.
Average Attendance: 2011-12: 33,873 (Premier League)

Ground Name: Underhill Stadium
Capacity: 5,500
Address: Barnet Lane, Barnet, EN5 2DN
Main Telephone No: 020 8441 6932
Ticket Office No: 020 8449 6325

Year Ground Opened: 1907
Pitch Size: 115 x 75 yards
Team Nickname: Bees
Home Kit Colours: Black & Amber
Official website: www.barnetfc.com

What's The Ground Like?

Underhill has recently seen some much needed investment with the building of a new South Stand at one end of the ground. The stand which was opened in 2008, is covered and has a capacity of 1,000 seated spectators. The Main Stand situated on one side of the ground is quite small and straddles the halfway line, running barely half of the pitch. This stand which was built in 1964, is seated with a capacity of 800. On the North side of the Main Stand is a small terrace, while on the other side is a small all seated Family Stand. Opposite is the East Terrace. This covered terrace runs the full length of the pitch and is given to away supporters. It has an unusual looking box like structure on its roof, which includes a television gantry.

At one end is the North Terrace. This end is so small that it has a large mesh fence at the back of it, to prevent footballs hitting the houses that sit on the other side of Westcombe Drive. On one side (situated towards the East Terrace) is small temporary covered stand, which is given to away supporters. The most striking feature of the ground is the relatively new club office building which sits at one corner of the ground, beside the South Stand. Although the slope of the pitch is not as bad as it once was, it is still fairly noticeable, running down the length of the pitch from North to South.

What Is It Like For Visiting Supporters?

Away fans are mostly housed on one side of the covered East Terrace, towards the North End of the ground. This area accommodates around 1,000 supporters. If demand requires it then the open North Terrace can also be allocated, increasing the allocation to 1,500. In addition around 200 seats are made available in the small temporary stand located in the North East corner. Normally a relaxing and enjoyable day out, although when you view the slope of the pitch, you almost think that it must be an optical illusion, as it is at quite an angle. As a matter of interest you may hear the home fans singing that Beatles classic 'Twist & Shout' from time to time, which is still popular with the Bees fans!

Where To Drink?

Jim Prentice informs me; 'there are a number of good pubs around Underhill. A favourite with away fans is The Old Red Lion, just behind the north entrance to Underhill. Situated up in the town at the top of Barnet Hill are the Moon Under Water and the King John, and down the bottom of the hill (under the London Underground bridge) are the Queen's Arms and The Weaver. Away fans are welcome in all of these pubs on the whole – Barnet fans are generally friendly and welcoming'. Steve Smith adds: 'if you come into New Barnet railway station, then opposite is a Wetherspoons pub called the Railway Bell, which has a good selection of beer'. There is a supporters club at the ground, but this is for home fans only.

Directions & Car Parking

Leave the M25 at J23. Take the A1081 towards Barnet. Follow this road for about three miles. Continue towards Barnet as the road becomes the A1000. The ground is at the foot of Barnet Hill near to the junction with Station Road (A110). Street parking or there is a car park at High Barnet Underground Station (£3), which is well signposted around the area.

By Train/Tube

The nearest London Underground station is High Barnet which is on the Northern Line. There is only five minutes walk down Barnet Hill to the ground (although it is a fair hike back up the hill after the game!). Alternatively you can take a quicker overground train to New Barnet railway station, which is around 15 minutes walk away from the ground. This station is served by trains from London Kings Cross and is a shorter journey time than the tube, taking around 20 minutes from Central London.

Anthony Hammond adds; 'Coming out of New Barnet station turn right and then left into Station Road. Walk up to the traffic lights opposite the Odeon Cinema and turn right onto Barnet Hill (A1000). After going under a railway bridge, you will be able to see the ground behind the Old Red Lion pub on your left. Alternatively you can get a bus from New Barnet Station; the 84, 384 or 107 buses run every 15 minutes or so from New Barnet to Underhill'.

Programme

Official Programme: £3

Record & Average Attendance

Record Attendance: 11,026 v Wycombe Wanderers, FA Amateur Cup, February 23rd, 1952.
Average Attendance: 2011-12: 2,266 (League Two)

Ground Name: Oakwell
Capacity: 23,009 (all seated)
Address: Grove Street, Barnsley, S71 1ET
Main Telephone No: 01226 211 211
Ticket Office No: 0871 226 6777

Year Ground Opened: 1888
Pitch Size: 110 x 75 yards
Team Nickname: The Tykes or Reds
Home Kit Colours: Red & White
Official website: www.barnsleyfc.co.uk

What's The Ground Like?

Approximately three sides of the ground were redeveloped in the 1990s. On one side is the particularly attractive two-tiered covered East Stand running along one side of the pitch. Opened in March 1993, this stand has a capacity of 7,500. Opposite is the classic looking West Stand, part of which dates back to 1904. It was made all seated in the mid 1990s, but is only covered at the rear. On its roof is perched an ugly precarious looking television gantry which obscures a probably more attractive gable. At the Pontefract Road End (now named the CK Beckett Stand) is an all seated, covered stand for home supporters, which has a capacity of 4,500. This stand was opened in 1995. The other end, the North Stand, was previously an open terrace, but is now a relatively new single tier, covered stand, housing 6,000 fans. This is the most recent addition to the ground being opened in 1999 and has greatly enhanced the overall look of Oakwell. The North Stand is shared between home and away supporters. The amount of seats given to away supporters varies according to demand. An unusual feature of the stadium is a purpose built stand for disabled supporters. This is a three floor structure that sits at the corner between the East & South Stands. There is also an electric score-board at one corner of the North Stand, on top of a security control room. The teams come out from one corner of the ground between the North and West Stands.

What Is It Like For Visiting Supporters?

Away fans are housed in the new North Stand, where the facilities are good. The normal all-ocation for away supporters is 2,000 tickets although, if demand requires it, then the whole of this stand can be allocated (6,000). I found this club to be particularly friendly from the car park attendant to the programme seller. Even the PA announcer had a sense of humour (although a little optimistic), when he announced that perhaps the visiting fans would like to come up again to see the next Barnsley home game, so that we could see a decent game of football! However, I have reports of fans getting hassle at Barnsley (especially in the town centre) and stewards acting a little heavy-handed, although I've never personally had any problems. It is advisable to keep colours covered especially around the town centre.

Where To Drink?

Neil Tubby, a visiting Norwich City fan, recommends the Dove Inn on Doncaster Road. This pub which is listed in the CAMRA Good Beer Guide, is an outlet for the Old Mill Brewery. It is only a five minute walk away from the ground down Oakwell Lane and is happily frequented by both home and away fans. Further along Doncaster Road (on the right after the Primary School on the left) is the Barnsley East Dene Working Mens Club, which is happy to admit visiting supporters (including accompanied children) without entry charge. You can also leave your car there at a cost of £1.50. Located between the Dove Inn and the Working Mens Club is a handily placed cafe.

Gary Holding a visiting Blackburn supporter adds; 'A few minutes walk from the away end is the Metro Dome – an all in one leisure centre, which has a bar inside which serves good food and ale'. Drinking in the town centre is generally not recommended, especially near the Bus & Train Stations, although on my last visit I had a hassle free pint (or two) in the Joseph Bramah (Lloyds No.1) Wetherspoons in the centre of town, but I should point out that I wasn't wearing colours. Alcohol is available in the away stand when the whole stand is allocated to away fans. Unfort- unately if the stand is split between home and away supporters, then there is no beer for away fans as the only bar on the concourse is situated on the home side.

Directions & Car Parking

Leave the M1 at Junction 37 and take the A628 towards Barnsley. Stay on this road (the ground is well signposted) and you will eventually see the ground on your right. There are a couple of car parks located at the ground, but they are mainly for permit holders only. In between the ground and the MetroDome is a car park for visiting sup-porters, called Queens Ground, which costs £3 Cars, £6 Mini Buses and £10 Coaches.

Otherwise you can try parking at the MetroDome itself (although it can be slow to get out of after the game has finished) or street parking.

By Train

Barnsley railway station is about a 10 minute walk away. This station is served by trains running between Sheffield & Leeds.

From the train station turn left away from the town centre and head towards the bridge that the dual-carriageway runs over. Go under the bridge and turn left up the slip road and then take the first road on the right and head towards the Metro Dome leisure complex at the top of the hill. Oakwell is now clearly visible.

Thanks to Ian Ambler & Bryn Williams for providing the directions.

Programme

Official Programme: £3

Record & Average Attendance

Record Attendance: 40,255 v Stoke City, FA Cup 5th Round, February 15th, 1936.

Average Attendance: 2011-12: 10,332 (Championship League)

BIRMINGHAM CITY

Ground Name: St Andrews
Capacity: 30,016 (all seated)
Address: St Andrews Ground, Birmingham B9 4RL
Main Telephone No: 0844 557 1875
Ticket Office No: Same as main number

Year Ground Opened: 1906
Pitch Size: 115 x 75 yards
Team Nickname: The Blues
Home Kit Colours: Royal Blue & White
Official website: www.bcfc.com

What's The Ground Like?

Approximately three quarters of the ground has been rebuilt since the mid 90s. One large two-tiered tiered stand, incorporating the Tilton Road End and Spion Kop, completely surrounds half the pitch and replaced a former huge terrace. The new Tilton Road End was opened for the start of the 1994-95 season, with the new Spion Kop following in 1995. At the back of the Spion Kop Stand, which runs along one side of the pitch, are a row of executive boxes, as well as a central seated executive area which also incorporates the Directors 'box'. The other newish stand, the recently renamed Gil Merrick Stand (previously known as the Railway End) was opened in February 1999. It is a large two-tiered stand and unusual in having quite a small top tier, which overhangs the lower area. Again there is a row of executive boxes in this stand, housed at the back of the lower section.

Only one 'old' stand, the former Main Stand, which was opened in 1952, now remains of the former St Andrews. This is a two tier stand running along one side of the pitch and has a row of executive boxes running across its middle. This stand is the smallest at the stadium and is looking particularly tired among its more modern neighbours. This stand which is now known as the Garrison Lane Stand also houses the press area, television gantry and has the team dugouts located in front of it. The team dressing rooms are situated within the Gil Merrick Stand, which results in the teams entering the field of play from one corner of the stadium between this stand and the Garrison Lane Stand. Also in this area is a large video screen that was erected at the start of the 2009-10 season.

What Is It Like For Visiting Supporters?

Away supporters are housed on one side of the Gil Merrick Stand, which is at one end of the stadium in the lower tier. The normal allocation is 3,000 tickets, but this can be increased to around 4,500 for cup games (when the whole of the lower tier is allocated). There are Birmingham fans housed above the away supporters, as well as to the other side of the stand (fans are separated by plastic netting). The facilities and the view from this stand are pretty good.

John, a visiting Burnley fan informs me; 'The beer inside the ground was drinkable and the Balti pies were delicious! On the downside, the seat I had been allocated was in Row 21 seat 002 which was right up against the wall. I've had more legroom on a package tour flight to the Canaries! What really annoyed me was a small section of the City fans who spent the entire game screaming abuse and gesturing to the away fans'.

Where To Drink?

Most of the pubs near to the ground can be quite intimidating for away supporters and are not recommended. However, there is the Brighton pub on the Coventry Road which does tolerate away fans in small numbers. This pub is about a 10 minute walk away, going past Morrisons on your left. Simon, a visiting Chelsea fan adds; 'On our last visit to St Andrews, we managed to find a friendly pub within proximity of the ground. The pub is called The Cricketers Arms and is about 10 minutes walk, maybe less. To find the pub (with your back to the away section) walk along the road ahead of you going away from the ground (not the road going right up by the stadium, but the road going towards Morrisons). Walk through Morrisons car park heading towards the store then join the road next to it, which is called Green Lane. The pub is 30 seconds from there on the left'. Otherwise it may be best to drink in the city centre or inside the ground itself.

Directions & Car Parking

Leave the M6 at Junction 6 and take the A38(M) (known locally as the Aston Expressway) for Birmingham City Centre. Continue past the first turn off (Aston, Waterlinks) and then take the next turn off, for the Inner Ring Road

Turn left at the island at the top of the slip road and take the Ring Road East, signposted Coventry/Stratford. Continue along the ring road for two miles, crossing straight across three islands. At the fourth island (there is a large McDonalds on the far left-hand corner) turn left into Coventry Road going towards Small Heath. Birmingham City's ground is about a quarter of a mile up this road on your left. The ground is well signposted on the Inner Ring Road.

There is a small car park directly outside the entrance to the away end, but availability of space for cars is determined by how many away coaches are expected as they park in the same car park, which may mean for certain games that there is no space available for cars at all. There is though plenty of street parking off the left-hand side of the ring road. There are some local schools and firms that offer parking facilities for around £5.

By Train

The nearest station is Bordesley, which is about a 10 minute walk away from the ground, but is only served by trains from Birmingham Snow Hill and Birmingham Moor Street. Normally scheduled trains do not stop at Bordesley, so they don't show up on national timetables searches.

If you arrive at New Street Station in the city centre, either walk to Moor Street station (five minutes) take a taxi (about £6) or embark on the 20-25 minute walk to the ground.

Otherwise you can take the No 58 or 60 bus from the city centre.; No: 58, 60. These can be caught near to Moor Street Railway Station on Queensway. Look for bus stop ME (58 & 60).

Programme & Fanzine

Official Programme: £3

Made In Brum Fanzine: £1

Record & Average Attendance

Record Attendance: 66,844 v Everton, FA Cup 5th Round, February 11th, 1939.

Average Attendance: 2011-12: 18,883 (Championship League)

Ground Name: Ewood Park
Capacity: 31,367 (all seated)
Address: Blackburn, Lancashire, BB2 4JF
Main Telephone No: 0871 702 1875
Ticket Office No: 0871 222 1444

Year Ground Opened: 1890
Pitch Size: 115 x 76 yards
Team Nickname: Rovers
Home Kit Colours: Blue & White
Official website: www.rovers.co.uk

What's The Ground Like?

The ground is quite impressive, having had three new large stands built during the 1990s. These stands are at both ends and at one side of the ground. They are of the same height and of roughly similar design, being two-tiered, having a row of executive boxes and similar roofs. The ends are particularly impressive, both having large lower tiers. The only downside is the open corners, although there is a huge screen at one corner by the away end, which shows an excellent pre-match programme and among other things, the teams emerging from the dressing rooms and onto the pitch. There is also an electric scoreboard at the Darwen End of the ground.

The Riverside is the only undeveloped stand, running down one side of the pitch. This is a smaller single-tiered stand and is not as pleasing to the eye as its more modern counterparts. In fact it looks older than what it is having been opened in 1988. It contains a fair number of supporting pillars and is partly covered (to the rear). Just to highlight how much the ground has changed, this was at one time the 'best' stand at Ewood Park. One other interesting feature of the ground, is the fact that the pitch is raised. This means that

players have to run up a small incline, while taking throw-ins and corners. Outside the stadium behind the Ronnie Clayton Blackburn End (named after the former Blackburn Rovers legend) there is a statue of former club owner Jack Walker.

What Is It Like For Visiting Supporters?

Away fans are housed in the Darwen End, where the facilities provided are good. However, the spacing between the rows of seats leaves a lot to be desired, being quite tight. The Darwen End is shared with home supporters, but if demand requires it the whole of the stand can be made available. Normally the away allocation is for three quarters of the stand, at just under 4,000 tickets, which are split between the whole of the upper tier and part of the lower tier (with the lower tier being allocated first). If you have not bought a ticket in advance, then you need to buy one from the away supporters ticket office at the ground as you can't pay on the turnstiles. The ticket office is located on the corner of the Darwen End and the Jack Walker Stand.

On the concourse the food available includes pies and other baked products that are made by the Clayton Park company, located nearby in

Accrington. The refreshment areas are opened 90 minutes before kick-off and close 15 minutes into the second half. I found the Blackburn fans both friendly and helpful, plus coupled with the relaxed stewarding, has made it so far for me, four pleasant visits to Ewood Park.'

Where To Drink?

The traditional haunt of away fans, the Fernhurst, has recently been refurbished and is now part of the Hungry Horse chain, however, it is currently closed on matchdays. This leaves very little choice for visiting supporters, as most pubs near to the ground do not admit away fans. There is the Golden Cup pub which is further on past the Fernhurst (going away from the ground) on Bolton Road and is tucked in by the motorway bridge. However, this Thwaites pub is quite small, gets rather crowded and it is a good 20 minute (mostly uphill) trek from Ewood Park.

If you are arriving at Mill Hill station, then you might want to give the Navigation pub a try. It is a Thwaites pub which sits on one side of a canal and on my visit had a good mix of home and away supporters. It is about a five minute walk away from the station. As you exit the station turn left and proceed straight on up the road in front of you. As you approach a bridge going over the canal, the pub can be seen just over on the right.

While just around the corner from the entrance to Blackburn Railway Station is a Wetherspoons outlet called the Postal Order. Alcohol is also served within the ground.

Directions & Car Parking

From The North

Use Motorway M6 to junction 30, to the M61 – leave junction 9 then onto the M65 towards Blackburn – leave the M65 at Junction 4 (A666) and follow signs towards Blackburn. Ewood Park is about one mile down the road on the right hand side.

From The South

Use Motorway M6 to junction 29, then onto the M65 towards Blackburn – leave the M65 at Junction 4 (A666) and follow signs towards Blackburn. Turn right at the first set of traffic lights and Ewood Park is about one mile down the road on the right-hand side.

From The East

Use Motorway M62 onto M66/A56, then onto the M65, head towards Blackburn – leave the M65 at Junction 4 (A666) and follow signs towards Blackburn. Turn right at the first set of traffic lights and Ewood Park is about one mile down the road on the right-hand side.

Various private car parks are available in the area around the ground, costing in the region of £5.

By Train

The closest station is Mill Hill which is around a 15 minute walk away from Ewood Park. It is served by trains from Blackburn and the journey only takes a few minutes. Blackburn station itself is at least a couple of miles from the ground and hence a good 25-30 minute walk away. Blackburn station is served by trains from Manchester & Leeds.

Programme & Fanzine

Official Programme: £3

4000 Holes Fanzine: £1

Record & Average Attendance

Record Attendance: 62,522 v Bolton Wanderers, FA Cup 6th Round, March 2nd, 1929.

Average Attendance: 2011-12: 22,551 (Premier League)

Ground Name: Bloomfield Road
Capacity: 16,750 (all seated)
Address: Seasiders Way, Blackpool,
Lancashire, FY1 6JJ
Main Telephone No: 0871 622 1953
Ticket Office No: 0844 847 1953

Year Ground Opened: 1899
Pitch Size: 112 x 74 yards
Team Nickname: The Seasiders or Tangerines
Home Kit Colours: Tangerine & White
Official website: www.blackpoolfc.co.uk

What's The Ground Like?

The ground has been almost completely redeveloped over the last decade, with three permanent stands being built, along with a temporary stand on the East side. The three permanent sides are of similar design, being single-tiered, of the same height, all seated and covered. The Stanley Matthews (West) Stand on one side of the stadium and the Mortensen Kop (North Stand) at one end, were both opened in February 2002. The North West corner between these stands has also been filled with seating, enclosing this area of the ground. Behind the main seating in the West Stand and the North West corner, is a hospitality balcony with executive boxes at the rear from the south end to the Directors' Box at the halfway line, from which point to the North West corner is the Sir Stanley Matthews Hospitality Suite.

In March 2010 the long awaited South Stand was finally opened, being a mirror image of the North Stand, and extending around and meeting the Stanley Matthews Stand, enclosing the South West corner of the stadium. During the 2011/12 season the South East corner between the South Stand and the temporary East Stand was also filled with an additional 500 seats. The South Stand has

been named the Armfield Stand in tribute to the Blackpool legend, Jimmy Armfield and has a capacity of 3,600 seats. On the East side of the ground the Club have erected a new covered temporary stand. Although temporary it is of a good size housing some 5,000 fans in a single tier of seating. It is also covered, which is a big improvement over the previous smaller structure that was previously in place on this side. The only main drawback is that it has a number of supporting pillars running across the front of it. Situated in one corner of the ground between the East and South stands is a large video screen.

Outside the stadium, behind the North Stand is a statue of the former Blackpool legend Stan Mortensen, while outside the main entrance is a statue of Jimmy Armfield.

What Is It Like For Visiting Supporters?

Away fans are housed on one side of the temporary East Stand, at one side of the pitch, where up to 2,500 supporters can be accommodated. This stand is shared with home fans, with away fans being housed on the northern side. Although the stand is covered, there are a number of supporting pillars running along the front of the stand that may hinder your view. If you find that you are sat towards the middle of the stand, then you will have the 'added comfort' of padded seats. However, the facilities are not that great with portakabin toilets etc.

I did find it amusing though to see notices taped up by the away turnstiles which said; 'Please refrain from bouncing on the floor of this stand.' It didn't exactly give me confidence in its structural integrity!

Where To Drink?

Popular with away fans is the Old Bridge House pub on Lytham Road. It is only short walk away (walk down Bloomfield Road towards the sea front and then turn right into Lytham Road and the pub is down on the right) and has screens showing Sky Sports.

Nigel Richardson, a visiting Hull City fan recommends the 'No 1 Bar, which is a Working Mens Club, that is adjacent to the away supporters entrance to the ground on Bloomfield Road. It was very welcoming and admits away fans for a small fee'. Steve Gardner a visiting Gillingham fan informs me; 'A good family pub close to the ground is the Waterloo in Waterloo Road.'

Steve Lumb adds; 'There is the Wetherspoons pub called the Auctioneer on Lytham Road, near Blackpool South Station. It's about 10 minutes walk to the ground.' Otherwise there are plenty of pubs in Blackpool town centre to choose from. Alcohol is not available to away supporters inside the stadium.

Directions & Car Parking

Leave the M6 at Junction 32. Follow the M55 into the outskirts of Blackpool and continue straight along this road until you see the ground on your right. The ground is roughly located about halfway between the Pleasure Beach and the Tower and is about a quarter of a mile inland from the south shore. A huge pay and display car park is located just across the road from the ground, which stretches all the way from near the Blackpool South station. It costs £3.50 for three hours and £7.50 for up to 12 hours (some of the pay machines also accept credit/debit cards). The car park nearest to the South Station is more expensive to park in (£5 for three hours), but it easier to get out of and back on the road towards the M55 after the game.

Matthew Stimpson informs me; 'Please note that unlike most towns and cities in England the pay and display car parks near to the ground still charge after 6pm. Some visiting fans on my visit assumed that they would be free after 6pm and ended up with a parking ticket'. Otherwise street parking (although there are parking restrictions in the immediate vicinity around the ground).

By Train

The closest railway station to the ground is Blackpool South and is around a 10 minute walk away. However, fewer trains stop at this station with most calling at Blackpool North. Blackpool North station is around two miles away and therefore you may wish to jump in a cab to the ground.

Mark Gillatt adds; 'For anyone arriving by train at Blackpool North a cheaper alternative than a taxi may be the number 11 bus from the bus station across the road. Buses to Lytham St Annes pass the end of Bloomfield Road and run every eight minutes. Fans should alight at the Bridge House pub (okay for a pint) and walk down Lonsdale Road to the stadium'.

Programme

Official Programme: £3

Record & Average Attendance

Record Attendance: 38,098 v Wolverhampton Wanderers, Division One, September 19th, 1955.
Average Attendance: 2011-12: 12,764 (Championship League)

Ground Name: Reebok Stadium
Capacity: 28,723 (all seated)
Address: Burnden Way, Horwich, Bolton, BL6 6JW
Main Telephone No: 0844 871 2932
Ticket Office No: Same as main number

Year Ground Opened: 1997
Pitch Size: 114 x 74 yards
Team Nickname: The Trotters
Home Kit Colours: White & Navy Blue
Official website: www.bwfc.co.uk

What's The Ground Like?

The stadium built by Birse Construction was opened in 1997. From the outside it looks simply stunning and can be seen for miles around. I still think the view of it driving down the slip road from the M61 motorway, is one of the greatest sights to be seen in English football, especially when it is lit up at night. It has a great eye catching design and is unlike anything else in the country.

The inside is functional and tidy, but not unsurprisingly lacks the wow factor of the stadium's external appearance. It is totally enclosed and each stand has a conventional rectangular lower tier, with a semicircular upper tier above. Situated between the two tiers is a row of executive boxes. Above the stands there is a gap between the back of the stands and the roof to allow additional light to reach the pitch. The roofs are then topped with some diamond shaped floodlights that sit above a striking supporting tubular steel supporting structure. There is large video screen in one corner, situated between the South and Nat Lofthouse Stands. One unusual feature of the ground is that the teams emerge from separate tunnels on either side of the halfway line.

What Is It Like For Visiting Supporters?

Away fans are housed in the two-tiered South Stand at one end of the ground, where up to 5,000 supporters can be accommodated, although the normal allocation is nearer 3,000. The lower tier is shared with home supporters, but the upper tier is given entirely to away fans. The leg room and facilities within this stand are good and the atmosphere is boosted in the home end by the presence of a drummer. Alex Smith adds; 'away fans should note that the bottom rows of the lower tier are not covered by the roof and therefore you may get wet if it rains'.

I was particularly impressed with the stadium and for the first time in this country, I felt I could have easily been sitting in a comparable stadium in the United States. The refreshment facilities are good (albeit queuing times can be long on occasion) and I wish that other clubs would copy the way that supporters in the Reebok are served. There are proper queuing barriers and exit lanes. One person takes the order and deals with the money, while another prepares your order at the same time. Simple when you think about it, it is just a pity that other clubs seem to think that supporters enjoy the lottery of being in the scrum that develops around the refreshment kiosk.

The stadium is certainly one of the best in England, although a capacity of under 30,000 means that it is on the small side compared to other stadia. There is 125 room hotel located behind the away end of the ground, 19 of which have views of the pitch. I just wonder if any of the hotel guests occupying these rooms may at some time put on their own half-time show!

Where To Drink?

Alas the favoured away pub of many years the Bromilow Arms has closed down. There is the Barnstormers on Lostock Lane (from the M61, go past the stadium on your left, move into the right-hand filter lane and turn right at the traffic lights into Lostock Lane, the pub is down on the right) which does admit away fans. There is also a mixture of street parking and paid parking (at some industrial units) in this area.

There is also the Beehive Pub near to the ground where you can also park your car. Otherwise alcohol is served within the ground, although for some games such as local derbies, the Club opt not to sell any. In another good move then the Club allow your to pre-order and pay for your half-time drinks, before the game has kicked off, through the purchase of tokens. Thus making it quicker to get your hands on your interval liquid refreshments.

Directions & Car Parking

From The South:

M6 to Junction 21a, take eastbound M62 leaving at Junction 12. Follow signs for M61 (Bolton-/Preston) and leave the M61 motorway at Junction 6. The ground is visible from this junction and is clearly signposted.

From The North:

M6 to Junction 29 and take the M65 towards Blackburn. Leave the M65 at junction two and join the M61 towards Manchester. Leave the M61 at junction six. The ground is visible from this junction and is clearly signposted.

John Walsh adds; 'Because of traffic con-gestion on the M60 (formerly M62), caused by the Trafford Centre, I would recommend that those supporters travelling from the South should take the North directions above. It is about 10 miles further but can save 30 minutes and a lot of frustration!'

There is a car park at the ground, but this costs £6 for cars (£12 for minibuses). Plus on my last visit the cars in the away section of the car park were packed in like sardines, meaning that away fans leaving early (my team had just been stuffed!) couldn't get a quick getaway as there were cars blocking them in. However, a lot of the surrounding industrial estate units offer cheaper parking, usually around the £4-£5 mark. Some of these are located on either side of Lostock Lane. From the M61, go past the stadium on your left, move into the right-hand filter lane and turn right at the traffic lights into Lostock Lane. There is also some street parking available in this area.

By Train

Horwich Parkway railway station serves the stadium, with regular trains from Bolton's main railway station. Horwich Parkway is only a few minutes walk from the stadium.

Programme & Fanzines

Official Programme: £3

White Love Fanzine: £1

Tripes & Trotters Fanzine: £1

Record & Average Attendance

Record Attendance: 28,353 v Leicester City, Premier League, December 28th, 2003.

Average Attendance: 2011-12: 23,670 (Premier League)

Ground Name: Coral Windows Stadium	Year Ground Opened: 1903
Capacity: 25,136 (all seated)	Pitch Size: 113 x 70 yards
Address: Bradford, West Yorkshire, BD8 7DY	Team Nickname: The Bantams
Main Telephone No: 01274 773 355	Home Kit Colours: Claret & Amber, Black Trim
Ticket Office No: 0871 978 8000	Official website: www.bradfordcityfc.co.uk

What's The Ground Like?

The term 'a game of two halves' is often applied to a football game; in the case of the Coral Windows Stadium 'two halves' comes to mind. The ground has now been completely re-built since the mid 80s, but the initial impression is that one half of the ground is twice as big as the other. The Kop End is a relatively modern two-tiered stand that is simply huge and looks quite superb. It once towered over the rest of the ground, but the addition of an another tier to the Main Stand during 2001 has led to it meeting its once larger neighbour. With the corner between these stands also being filled, one has a truly impressive spectacle.

The rest of the ground now looks somehow rather out of place. The Midland Road Stand is a covered single-tiered stand, which has wind-shields to each side. At some other grounds this would look impressive, as it is of a fair size and is free of supporting pillars. However, it is almost lost in the shadow of its larger newer neighbours. At the remaining end is the Bradford End Stand which is an odd looking small 'double decker' type stand. This two-tiered covered stand has the upper tier largely overhanging the lower tier, giving this 'double decker' effect. There is also an electric scoreboard in one corner of the ground.

In the upper tier of the corner of the Main Stand and Kop End, a fan's flag is displayed dedicated to the fans who lost their lives in the Bradford City fire at the ground in May 1985.

What Is It Like For Visiting Supporters?

Away fans are housed on one side of the Midland Road Stand (towards the Bradford End Stand) at one side of the pitch. Around 1,300 supporters can normally be accommodated in this area, for larger followings then another block can be opened, raising the allocation to 1,800. The facilities within the stand are pretty good and there are no supporting pillars to impede your view. Roger Mulrooney, a visiting Barnsley fan adds; 'On my last visit I found the home crowd friendly and non-threatening. The stewards were particularly good natured and helpful. Still a very good away day for a visiting fan'. Make sure though that you wrap up well unless the weather forecast is 80 degrees. This is because Bradford is situated at a bottom of a valley, down which a rather cold wind normally prevails.

Where To Drink?

Chris O'Sullivan, a visiting Bury fan recommends the Bradford Arms on Manningham Lane; 'it is only about two minutes from the ground and was welcoming to away fans. It did basic food and had a large projector showing the early kick-off match that was on'.

There are also a couple of hotels with bars that are about a 10 minute walk away from the stadium. They are the Park & Cartwright hotels. Just continue to walk on the main road by the ground away from the town centre and at the traffic lights where the entrance to the park is, turn right and you will see them in a row on your right. Also about a 10 minute walk away is the Corn Dolly on Bolton Road, which is listed in the CAMRA Good Beer Guide and has a mixture of home and away fans who enjoy their ale. Otherwise alcohol is available to away fans inside the stadium.

Directions & Car Parking

Leave the M62 at Junction 26 and take the M606 for Bradford. At the end of the motorway, keep to the right-hand lane and take the Ring Road East (signposted A6177 City Centre). From this point the stadium is well signposted through the use of a football image. At the next roundabout turn left continuing along the Ring Road East, passing a McDonalds on your left and then an Asda superstore. At the next roundabout turn left onto the A650 (signposted City Centre/Keighley). After crossing a further two roundabouts the road becomes three lanes. Keep in one of the two right-hand lanes (signposted Keighley/Skipton). Continue straight along this road towards Skipton and eventually you will be able to see the stadium in front of you, over on the left. At the Kia Car Dealership on your left, turn immediately left into Station Road. At the top of Station Road turn left along Queens Road, then the second left into Midland Road for the away entrance. For the main offices continue along Queens Road and at the traffic lights turn left into Manningham Road. The ground is quarter a mile away on the left. Mostly street parking around the ground.

By Train

If going by train into Bradford Interchange, it is quite a walk to the ground (20 minutes). Either take a taxi (£6) or alternatively the bus station is located next to the train station (Bus No's 622, 623, 626 or 662). Chris Hawkridge suggests; 'supporters travelling via Leeds should catch the Leeds – Bradford Forster Square service (two trains per hour during the day) rather than those to Bradford Interchange. Forster Square is only 10 minutes walk from the ground'.

Programme & Fanzine

Official Programme: £3

City Gent Fanzine: £2 – The longest established fanzine still running in England.

Record & Average Attendance

Record Attendance: 39,146 v Burnley, FA Cup 4th Round, March 11th, 1911.

Average Attendance: 2011-12: 10,171 (League Two)

Ground Name: Griffin Park
Capacity: 12,763
Address: Braemar Road, Brentford, TW8 0NT
Main Telephone No: 08453 456 442
Ticket Office No: Same as main number

Year Ground Opened: 1904
Pitch Size: 110 x 73 yards
Team Nickname: The Bees
Home Kit Colours: Red, White & Black
Official website: www.brentfordfc.co.uk

What's The Ground Like?

The ground is rather compact and certainly has an individual feel. On one side is the recently christened Bill Axbey Stand (formerly the New Road Stand), which is named after a long time supporter who watched the Bees for an incredible 89 years before passing away in 2007. This stand is a single-tiered, covered all seated stand, which has a number of supporting pillars running across the front of it. The roof of the stand is painted with a large advert, designed to catch the eye of passengers flying into Heathrow Airport. Currently this is an advert for Qatar Airways, but in the past among others, it has been for KLM and easyJet. Opposite is the Bees United (Braemar Road) Stand. Again this stand is single-tiered, all seated and has a number of supporting pillars. It has a very low roof, which makes you wonder what the view would be like from the very back row of the stand.

At one end is the Ealing Road Terrace, which up to 2007, was an open terrace that was given to away supporters. However, the Club have now erected a roof on this end and decided to give it back to the home fans. This should really help boost the atmosphere within the stadium. Opp-

osite is the Brook Road Stand. This stand which was opened in 1986, is a strange affair; a small double decker stand that has seating on the first tier and terracing below. It is known affectionately by the Brentford fans as the 'Wendy House'. The ground is complete with a set of four imposing floodlights. Griffin Park is also used for Chelsea reserve team matches.

What Is It Like For Visiting Supporters?

Away fans are housed in the Brook Road Stand at one end of the ground. This covered two-tiered stand has 600 seats in its upper tier and room for around 1,000 fans below in the terrace. The upper tier has good unhindered views of the playing area, while below in the lower terraced area there are a couple of prominent supporting pillars, which may affect your view. I had an enjoyable visit to the ground and didn't experience any problems.

Tim Porter a visiting Torquay United supporter adds; 'The home fans were the most friendly I've come across for a long time – before kick-off, the stadium announcer asked all the home fans to put their hands together for the Torquay fans who had made such a long journey. I expected indifferent silence or abuse, but there was almost universal clapping!'

Where To Drink?

Brentford is famous for being the only ground in England that has a pub at every corner of the ground. The surrounding land was formerly owned by the Griffin Brewery, hence Griffin Park. If you are feeling thirsty, get there early and have a pint in all four. They are the Royal Oak (a small locals' pub), The Griffin (serves Fullers real ale), The Princess Royal and The New Inn. The New Inn is the favoured pub for away supporters. Derek Hall, a visiting Hartlepool United fan adds; 'Probably the best pub out of the four is the Griffin, with the New Inn a fairly close second, although this was packed on our visit'.

Roger Stamp informs me; 'Probably the best real ale pub in Brentford is the Magpie & Crown which is only five minutes walk away from the ground, on Brentford High Street. The pub has four real ales on tap and welcomes both home and away supporters'.

Directions & Car Parking

Leave the M4 at junction 2 and take the A4, going around the Chiswick Roundabout so that you end up coming back on yourself. Continue along the A4 and at the first roundabout take a left onto the B455 (Ealing Road). The ground is located about half a mile down this road on your right. There is no parking at the ground for supporters. So apart from a small pay and display car park in Layton Road (first right off Ealing Road) which costs £5 for free hours (but is free after 6.30pm), it is street parking.

By Train/Tube

The nearest railway station is Brentford. This is around a five minute walk away from the ground. This station is on the London Waterloo to Reading line, which normally has services running every 15 minutes on Saturday afternoons. To get from the station to the ground, exit onto Station Road. Take the first right into Orchard Road, right again into Windmill Road and then first left into Hamilton Road which leads into New Road and the ground.

Caleb Johnstone-Cowan informs me; 'The nearest Underground Station to the ground is South Ealing, which is on the Piccadilly Line. This tube station is around a 15 minute walk from the ground, down Ealing Road'. Mick Hubbard adds; 'Finding the ground is easy enough though – you simply turn right out of the tube station and just go straight down Ealing Road, then taking your life in your hands to cross the A4 at the bottom! Otherwise as you come out of the station cross over to the other side of Ealing Road and catch a number 65 bus down to the ground'.

Programme & Fanzines

Official Programme: £2.50

Thorne In The Side Fanzine: £1

Hey Jude Fanzine: £1

Beesotted: £2

Record & Average Attendance

Record Attendance: 39,626 v Preston North End, FA Cup 6th Round, March 5th, 1938.

Average Attendance: 2011-12: 5,643 (League One)

Ground Name: American Express Community Stadium
Capacity: 22,500* (all seated)
Address: Village Way, Falmer, East Sussex, BN1 9BL
Main Telephone No: 01273 878288
Ticket Office No: 0844 327 1901

Year Ground Opened: 2011
Pitch Size: 115 x 75 yards
Team Nickname: The Seagulls
Home Kit Colours: Blue & White
Official website: www.seagulls.co.uk

What's The Ground Like?

The Club moved to the new stadium in 2011 after spending 12 years at the Withdean Stadium. At a cost of £93 million the new American Express Community Stadium is a spectacular sight on the Sussex landscape. From afar the semicircular roofs of the stand and the tubular supporting steelwork above them, are at first glance reminiscent of the Galpharm Stadium in Huddersfield. But on closer inspection the similarity ends as this is a far superior ground.

On one side is the impressive looking West Stand. This three-tiered stand, has a large lower tier, a small middle tier and a medium sized upper tier. The seating in the upper tier follows the semicircular design of the stand, giving it an interesting effect. The team dugouts are located on this side, as well as an open press area, which is conveniently situated above the players tunnel on the halfway line. Opposite is the smaller East Stand. Although when first built it was a single-tiered stand, an additional tier is being added in the Summer of 2012. Both ends are small single tiers of seating, and each has an electric scoreboard to the rear. Although the stadium is enclosed the corners are currently unused for spectators, but again the Club has plans to install additional seating at some point.

What Is It Like For Visiting Supporters?

Away fans are housed in the South Stand at one end of the stadium, where up to 2,575 fans can be accommodated. As you would expect from a new stadium, the view of the playing action and leg room are both good. Plus the added bonus of padded seats is a rare 'luxury'. Food available inside the stadium from the wide concourses includes tasty home made style pies that are baked on site, such as Steak & Harveys Ale with mushrooms, Chicken & Ham with leek and Vegetarian butternut squash with spicy tomato. Peter Llewellyn adds; 'The Amex Stadium is an excellent venue, very nicely set in the countryside. The concourse is extraordinarily wide and spacious for such a small stadium. Comfy cushioned seats, excellent view, plenty of leg room, great pitch and the best acoustics of any stadium I've been to. The home fans singing was deafening, all down to the acoustic effect of the stadium design'.

Where To Drink?

There are no pubs near to the stadium that welcome away fans. John Ellis, a visiting Leicester City fan tells me; 'We were directed to the Downs Hotel in Woodingdean, on the Falmer Road (B2123) at the Warren Road junction. The Hotel has a bar and is about two miles away. They offer free parking at the hotel and they do a shuttle run (two minibuses) every 15 minutes between 1.30pm and 2.30pm, the cost is £4 return for adults and £2 for children. We used this with no problems at all and returned after the game by Hotel minibus at 5.15pm'.

If arriving at the Mill Road Park & Ride then a little further on down London Road (A23) on the left is the Black Lion pub which is a Harvester outlet. While just outside the entrance to the Brighton Racecourse Park & Ride there is the 'Fox on the Downs' pub. Otherwise alcohol is served inside the stadium including the locally produced Harveys real ale.

Directions & Car Parking

At the end of the M23, continue onto the A23, heading towards Brighton. At the roundabout which is the junction with the A27, take the A27 towards Lewes. After around four miles you will see the stadium on your right-hand side. Leave at the A27 and take the slip road signposted Falmer (B2123). At the top of the slip road turn right crossing back over the A27 and the entrance to the stadium is down on the right.

There is no parking at the stadium for away fans (although coaches and minibuses will be allowed to park providing that they have been pre-booked with the Club) and there is a large no parking zone in force around the area of the stadium on matchdays.

Park & Ride

The Club are encouraging fans to use the Park & Ride services located at three different locations; Mill Road, Brighton Racecourse and Mithras House at Brighton University.

Probably the easiest for away fans to locate is Mill Road, as it is just off the A23/A27 junction.

However, this is by far the busiest of the three, so if you have time on your hands consider using one of the other alternatives such as Brighton Racecourse. The capacity of Mill Road is 500 cars. The road is located next to a BP garage, which (if coming down from London) you will see over on your right at the top of the slip road off the A23.

The Park & Ride is open from 12 noon on Saturdays (with last departure at 2.30pm) and 5.30pm for evening kick-offs. Although the parking element of the scheme is free, the ride part is not. You have to buy a travel voucher in advance from the Club (you can't pay on the bus). The vouchers cost £1.50 (plus a £1 postage charge), these can be ordered from the Brighton Ticket Office.

By Train

Kevin Bartholomew informs me; 'The quickest and easiest way to get to the stadium though is by train. Falmer station is adjacent to the ground. It is three stops from Brighton central station on the line to Lewes. Alternatively, you can avoid Brighton completely by getting a train to Lewes and changing there for Falmer'.

Brighton Central Railway Station is over four miles away from the stadium. So either get a train, taxi or bus up to the stadium. Brighton & Hove Bus No 25 operates a regular service up to the stadium from Central Brighton.

Programme & Fanzine

Official Programme: £3
Seagull Love Review: £1

Record & Average Attendance

Record Attendance: 21,897 v Liverpool, Carling Cup 3rd Round, September 21st, 2011. (Championship League)
Average Attendance: 2011-12: 20,028

* This is to be increased to 27,500 for the start of the 2012-13 season.

Ground Name: Ashton Gate
Capacity: 21,479 (all seated)
Address: Ashton Road, Bristol, BS3 2EJ
Main Telephone No: 0117 963 0600
Ticket Office No: Same as main number

Year Ground Opened: 1904
Pitch Size: 115 x 75 yards
Team Nickname: The Robins
Home Kit Colours: Red & White
Official website: www.bcfc.co.uk

What's The Ground Like?

The Atyeo stand at one end of the ground is a handsome, covered all seated single-tiered stand. It was opened in 1994, replacing a former open terrace and has made a great difference to the overall look of the ground. It is named after former playing legend John Atyeo. At the other end is the covered Wedlock Stand (also known as the East End), part of which is given to away supporters. This stand which was originally opened in 1928 as a covered terrace was made all seated in the 1990s. It has a row of supporting pillars running across the front of it and has a small electric scoreboard on its roof.

On one side is the Dolman Stand which was opened in 1970. Originally it had an upper tier of seating with an open enclosure in front. But this was later built over with seating too. This area is used as a family area, although it is largely open to the elements. Opposite, the Williams Stand is an older looking single-tiered stand, with several supporting pillars. This stand is the Main Stand at Ashton Gate, with the players tunnel and team dugouts in front. It also has a television gantry suspended below its roof. Unusually for an older ground it is devoid of floodlight pylons, having

instead a row of small lights mounted on the roofs of the Williams and Dolman Stands.

What Is It Like For Visiting Supporters?

Away fans are housed at one end of the ground in part of the Wedlock Stand, which is shared with home supporters. Around 2,800 away supporters can be accommodated in this area. The acoustics of this stand are excellent, so even a small number of away fans can really generate some noise. The close proximity of the home fans also helps boost the atmos phere. The facilities are pretty standard, plus there are a number of supporting pillars running across the front, which could impair your view. The rake of the stand which was a former terrace, is pretty shallow, which means that there is not a great height between rows. Also if you are unfortunate enough to be sitting near to the back, then you may find yourself watching the game through the equivalent of a letter box, as the roof comes down quite low to the front of the stand.

Where To Drink?

Alex Webber recommends the Pumphouse and the Nova Scotia for away supporters by the waterfront, but adds that pubs nearer to the ground such as the Hen & Chicken and the BS3 Bar should be given a wide berth. Chris Gill, a visiting Leeds United fan adds; 'Near Temple Meads station there is the Knights Templar pub, a Wetherspoons outlet that seemed friendly enough. It's a two minute walk straight ahead from the station into the Temple area and off to the left in the square'. Scott Grimwood, a visiting Ipswich Town fan informs me; 'The Cottage in Baltic Wharf, is a nice pub situated on the river front and has good real ale (from the Butcombe Brewery). On my visits both sets of fans mixed pleasantly'.

Matt Greenslade recommends; 'The Orchard pub is about a 10 minute walk from the ground at Hanover Place on Harbourside. Voted Britain's top cider pub in 2009 with a huge sampling of local brews for anyone who wants to try the infamous cloudy stuff'. This pub is listed in the CAMRA Good Beer Guide and apart from having a number of ales on offer, it also has up to 24 different ciders available. The question is though, if you visit this pub before the game, will you still make the kick-off? Please note that alcohol is not available to away fans inside the ground.

Directions & Car Parking
Leave the M5 at Junction 18 and travel along the Portway (A4) following signs for the Bristol Airport/Taunton (A38). As you go over the swing bridge (Brunel Way), branch left into Winterstoke Road, and you will see the ground on your left.

Parking at the ground is for permit holders only. Mitch Ford informs me; 'Parking around Ashton Gate has been severely hindered recently in that many streets now have double yellow lines. There is the Bedminster Cricket club on Clanage Road (A369) that offers parking at a cost of £5 per car. It is then around a 5-10 minute walk to the stadium'. Otherwise it is a case of finding some street parking.

By Train
The nearest railway station is Parson Street which is around a 10 minute walk away from the ground. However, few trains stop at this station so you are more likely to end up at Bristol Temple Meads mainline station instead. This station is at least two miles from the ground and hence too far to walk, so best to jump in a taxi (around £6). Neil Le Milliere, a visiting Exeter City supporter adds 'don't try and walk it from the station unless you really have to and then allow at least three quarters of an hour for the journey'.

Programme & Fanzines
Official Programme: £3
One Team In Bristol Fanzine: £1.20
Cider'ed Fanzine: £1

Record & Average Attendance
Record Attendance: 43,335 v Preston North End, FA Cup 5th Round, 1935.
Average Attendance: 2011-12: 13,846 (Championship League)

BRISTOL ROVERS

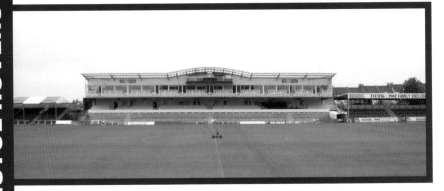

Ground Name: Memorial Stadium
Capacity: 12,011
Address: Filton Avenue, Horfield, Bristol BS7 0BF
Main Telephone No: 0117 909 6648
Ticket Office No: 0117 909 8848

Year Ground Opened: 1921
Pitch Size: 110 x 73 yards
Team Nickname: Pirates
Home Kit Colours: Blue & White Quarters
Official website: www.bristolrovers.co.uk

What's The Ground Like?

The club moved to the stadium in 1996 and two years later bought the ground from the then owners Bristol Rugby Club. Although the Memorial Stadium has seen some changes since the Football Club took up residence, it still has the feel of a rugby ground about it.

On one side is the DAS Stand, which with its pavilion looks more like a cricket stand. It has a row of hospitality boxes across the top, with a few rows of seats in front. Below is an area of terrace. Just under this stand's roof is a television gantry and a small electric scoreboard. The stand runs for about half the length of the pitch and straddles the halfway line. On one side of it, towards the Blackthorn end is a small covered terrace, used as a family area, while the other side has a small covered area of temporary seating, called the South West Stand. Opposite is the Uplands Stand, taller than the DAS Stand, but similar in length. This stand has covered seating to its rear and terracing at the front. It has open terracing to either side, one of which is given to away supporters. The team dug outs are located in front of this stand, although the dressing rooms are located behind the DAS

Stand. This leads to quite a procession of players and officials at half-time and full-time.

At one end is the unusual looking South Stand. This was originally erected as a temporary stand, to fill the previously empty end. It has now been opened for a number of seasons, although it still looks, with its green seats and bright white roof, more suitable for an outdoor show jumping competition than a football ground. The stand only runs for just over half the width of the pitch, has several supporting pillars running across the front and has been nicknamed 'the tent' by Rovers fans. Opposite is the Blackthorn End, which is a covered terrace for home supporters. The ground is shared with Bristol Rugby Club.

What Is It Like For Visiting Supporters?

Away supporters are mostly housed in an open terrace on one side of the Uplands Stand. This area is open to the elements so you might get wet if it rains. The open terrace makes it difficult for away fans to really generate some noise. Up to 1,100 away supporters can be accommodated in this area. If the weather is poor then it may be a better bet to head for one of the seats that are made available to away fans in the South Stand

38

at one end of the ground. I must recommend the huge Cornish pasties that are sold at the ground, huge and tasty, plus they even do a vegetarian alternative. I did not experience any problems on my visits, however, I noted that the Rovers fans seemed to tolerate away fans rather than being over friendly. They can still do a good rendition of their club anthem 'Goodnight Irene', when the occasion stirs.

I found it quite amusing that the Rovers fans are nicknamed gasheads. Nick Wootten of Bristol informed me that this term comes from where the old Eastville stadium in Bristol was sited. Next to a (sometimes smelly) gas works! In fact it was rumoured that if Rovers were losing at half-time, the gas would be turned up, to put off the opposition!

Where To Drink?

There is a bar behind the clubhouse terrace at the ground that allows in away supporters. Pete Stump recommends; 'The Queen Vic pub on the Gloucester Road, which is around a five minute walk from the ground, usually has a comfortable mix of home and away fans, although it does get busy'. Rhys Gwynllyw, a visiting Wrexham supporter recommends the Annexe Inn on Seymour Road. Located half a mile away from the stadium, the pub is listed in the CAMRA Good Beer Guide. It is close to the County Cricket Ground, going further along the A38 towards Bristol. After passing the Old Fox pub, turn left into Nevil Road and then right at the Sportsman Pub into Seymour Road. Please note that alcohol is not made available to away fans inside the stadium.

Directions & Car Parking

Exit M5 at junction 16 (Signposted Filton) and join the A38 (South) towards Bristol City Centre. The ground is about five miles down the A38. You will pass the large British Aerospace works and further on, you will pass on your left the Inn on the Green and the Gloucester pubs. You then pass the Wellington pub on your right and continuing

along the A38 Gloucester Road, turn left into Filton Avenue. The entrance to the Club car park is the second right down this road. There is a fair amount of street parking around the sides and back of the Wellington pub.

By Train

The nearest railway station is Filton Abbey Wood, which as Peter Moody informs me; 'is approximately 1.5 miles or 20-25 minutes walk away from the ground'. More likely though you will end up at Bristol Parkway which is about two miles away from the ground and is really too far to walk from, so you are probably best to jump in a taxi or buses 73/73A/73B run from the station past the stadium.

Programme

Official Programme: £3

Record & Average Attendance

Record Attendance: 12,011 v West Bromwich Albion, FA Cup 6th Round, February 9th, 2008.
Average Attendance: 2011-12: 6,035 (League Two)

BURNLEY

Ground Name: Turf Moor
Capacity: 22,546 (all seated)
Address: Harry Potts Way, Burnley, BB10 4BX
Main Telephone No: 0871 221 1882
Ticket Office No: 0871 221 1914

Year Ground Opened: 1883
Pitch Size: 115 x 73 yards
Team Nickname: The Clarets
Home Kit Colours: Claret & Blue
Official website: www.burnleyfootballclub.com

What's The Ground Like?

Burnley have played continually at Turf Moor since 1883, which is one of the longest continual occupations of ground by any club in the League. Half the ground was redeveloped in the mid 1990s with two smart looking new stands being opened. The first of these the James Hargreaves Stand was opened in early 1996. It has two large tiers, with a row of executive boxes housed between them. This stand replaced the famous Longside Terrace, which was a big steep covered terrace. Later in 1996 the Jimmy McIlroy Stand was opened at one end of the ground. This two-tiered stand is similar in design to the James Hargreaves Stand, which gives half the ground a uniform look.

The other two sides of the ground are much older and look out of place next to their shiny new neighbours. The Bob Lord Stand at one side of the pitch was opened in 1974. It is a small all seated single-tiered stand, with a row of supporting pillars running across its middle and has windshields to either side. The David Fishwick Stand (formerly known as the Cricket Field Stand) at one end of the ground was opened in 1969. Again it is a simple looking single-tiered

stand that has some supporting pillars. There is a Police Control Box situated in one corner of the stadium in between the Bob Lord and Jimmy McIlroy Stands. Unusually the teams emerge from a tunnel at one end of the ground in the David Fishwick Stand. While some rather cramped looking team dugouts are located in front of the Bob Lord Stand.

What Is It Like For Visiting Supporters?

Away fans are housed in the covered David Fishwick Stand at one end of the ground. Approximately 4,125 fans can be accommodated in this area, although the normal allocation is 2,100.

Although I have enjoyed my trips to Burnley, I have always been somewhat surprised at how old the facilities are. From the passing through the antique looking turnstiles, the wooden seating, the rusting roof supports, to the dark and dank concourse, you get the feeling that the stand has seen better days. However, if you can avoid being seated behind a supporting pillar, the view of the playing action is quite good. Also in one open corner at the far end of the ground you also see the Pennine hills rolling into the distance.

Burnley are generally a well supported club

and there is normally a good atmosphere, however, this can sometimes become quite intimidating for the away supporter making your way around the ground, so exercise discretion.

Where To Drink?

Pete Mitton recommends the Cricket Club; 'the clubhouse at the Cricket Club (you can also park there) is open on matchdays and visitors are always made welcome (wearing colours), which is ideal as it is right next door to the ground'. Andrew Woodhall sent in this comment about the Cricket Club bar that he overheard from a visiting Gillingham fan; 'Two pints of Theakstons, a bowl of pie and peas and a cigar...and still change from a fiver!'

Paul Hanson adds 'Another place I could recommend is the Queen Victoria Public House. The away fans are always directed/encouraged to park in one location, by the side of the Burnley fire station; Pass there, away from the football ground and proceed for about 100 yards where you will find the entrance to the Queen Victoria (Brewers Fayre establishment). The ground is no more than 10 minutes walk away. Away fans visit regularly wearing their colours'.

Directions & Car Parking

Leave the M6 at Junction 29 and onto the M65. Leave the M65 at Junction 10 and follow signs for Towneley Hall. This road eventually goes past the ground. There is a car park at the cricket ground by Turf Moor which costs £6. There is also a private car park available on Doris Street, off Belverdere Road (BB11 3DL), which is around 400 yards from the stadium and costs £5. Otherwise, street parking.

By Train

There are two train stations that are in walking distance of Turf Moor, Burnley Manchester Road and Burnley Central.

Central station is around a 20 minute walk away from the ground and is mostly served by local trains. Manchester Road is a 15 minute walk away and is served by the faster express service. Walking directions from both are as follows:

Manchester Road Station

Upon leaving the station cross the main road towards the cinema. The ground should be clearly visible in the distance straight ahead. Turn left and progress down 'Centenary Way' an unmissable dual carriageway (A682) going downhill towards the ground. A few minutes walk down this road will bring you to a roundabout where you should turn right under the canal bridge into Yorkshire Street (A671). Continue down this road and you will reach Turf Moor on your left, with the away stand the first to be reached. Thanks to Rob Quinn for providing the directions.

Central Station

Walk out of the station and across the road down towards a small retail area including Fads and Halfords Cycles. You will reach the inner ring road (A679), where you turn left and after about 200 yards you will reach a set of traffic lights. Turn right at the lights into Church Street (A682). Continue down Church Street until you reach a large roundabout at which you turn left under the canal bridge into Yorkshire Street (A671). Continue down this road and you will reach Turf Moor on your left, with the away stand the first to be reached. Thanks to Paul Hanson for providing the directions.

Programme & Fanzine

Official Programme: £3
When The Ball Moves Fanzine: £1

Record & Average Attendance

Record Attendance: 54,775 v Huddersfield Town, FA Cup 3rd Round, February 23rd, 1924.
Average Attendance: 2011-12: 14,048 (Championship League)

Ground Name: Pirelli Stadium
Capacity: 6,912 (2,034 Seated)
Address: Pirelli Stadium, Burton Upon Trent,
Staffs, DE13 0AR
Main Telephone No: 01283 565 938
Ticket Office No: Same as main number

Year Ground Opened: 2005
Pitch Size: 110 x 72 yards
Team Nickname: The Brewers
Home Kit Colours: Yellow & Black
Official website: www.burtonalbionfc.co.uk

What's The Ground Like?

In 2005 the Club left their Eton Park ground, which had been their home since 1958 and moved to a new £6.5 million purpose built stadium nearby (well almost across the road to be exact!). On one side is the attractive looking Main Stand, which is covered and all seated. The Club's administration offices and corporate facilities are located in this stand and so at the back of the seated area is a row of windows running across it. Above this glassed area is white panelling, which gives the stand an interesting look. The other three sides are small, steep covered terraces. They are a little ugly looking as they each have a large visible back wall. Each of these terraced stands has solid windshields to either side, apart from one side of the South Stand where there is a Police Control Box present. The stadium is completed with a set of four tall looking floodlights.

What Is It Like For Visiting Supporters?

Away fans are predominantly housed in the Coors East Stand Terrace at one end of the ground, where just over 1,400 fans can be accomm-

odated. In addition 400 seats are also made available to visiting supporters in the Main Stand. As you would expect from a modern stadium, the view of the playing action (there are no supporting pillars) and facilities are good. The atmosphere is not bad too (although there is a bit of a monotonous drummer in the home end), the grub available includes among other fayre, the legendary Faggots & Mushy peas. There is also a bar for away fans in which you can sit inside, There are TV screens showing Sky Sports News and then live coverage of the match itself. The bar is open until 15 minutes after the second half has started.

Also look out for the cumbersome looking 'Billy Brewer Mascot', who is a bit of a character. On one visit the announcer reminded younger supporters that they shouldn't forget to obtain Billy Brewer's autograph! On the whole Burton is one of the better days out in the League, with excellent pubs, a good stadium with good facilities, atmosphere and virtually hassle free.

Where To Drink?

The nearest pub is probably the The Beech Inn which is around a 10 minute walk, up the A5121 Derby Road (going in the opposite direction to Burton town centre) on the left. Otherwise there is the Great Northern pub, which serves Burton Bridge Beers, along with a guest ale. This pub is located on Wetmore Road, which leads off the roundabout near to the stadium entrance, go up and over the railway bridge and the pub is on the left.

Near to the railway station are the Roebuck, Devonshire and Cooper's Tavern which are all recommended. If you walk from the station to the ground, you will pass the Albert on your left which serves well kept Burton Bridge Beers as well as the Derby Inn that also offers real ale and has SKY television. Otherwise alcohol is also available within the stadium.

Directions & Car Parking

The ground is situated in North Burton, near to the Pirelli factory just off the A5121 (Derby Road). This is about a mile from the A38 which runs across the Midlands.

From the North (M1)

Leave the M1 at junction 28 and join the A38 towards Derby. Continue on the A38 through Derby towards Burton. Leave the A38 at the Burton North exit and follow the A5121 towards Burton. Go straight across a roundabout and you will then pass a McDonalds on your right. Just before the next roundabout you will see the stadium on your right. Turn right at the roundabout into Princess Way. A short distance along Princess Way on the right, is the entrance to the Club car park.

From the South (M1)

Leave the M1 at junction 22 and join the A511 towards Coalville/Burton. Turn right at the junction of the A5121, towards Burton North. As you come into the outskirts of Burton you will pass a McDonalds on your right. Just before the next roundabout you will see the stadium on your right. Turn right at the roundabout into Princess

Way. A short distance along Princess Way on the right is the entrance to the Club car park.

There is a large car park at the ground which costs £2. Alternative car parking is available at the Ryknild Trading Estate, by the roundabout leading to Princess Way. Otherwise street parking.

By Train

Burton train station is around a mile and a half from the ground. As you come out of the station turn left and go down the hill. Turn right into Derby Road and from there it is a straight road up to the stadium. It should take about 25 minutes to walk. Otherwise there is a taxi rank at the station and the cost up to the ground is around £5.

Programme & Fanzine

Official Programme: £3

Clough The Magic Dragon Fanzine: £1

Record & Average Attendance

Record Attendance: 6,192 v Oxford United, Blue Square Premier League, April 17th, 2009.

Average Attendance: 2011-12: 2,809 (League Two)

Ground Name: Gigg Lane
Capacity: 11,669 (all seated)
Address: Gigg Lane, Bury, Lancashire, BL9 9HR
Main Telephone No: 08445 790009
Ticket Office No: Same as main number

Year Ground Opened: 1885
Pitch Size: 112 x 73 yards
Team Nickname: The Shakers
Home Kit Colours: White & Royal Blue
Official website: www.buryfc.co.uk

What's The Ground Like?

The ground was completely rebuilt in the 1990s with the Cemetery End being the last stand to be completed in 1999. The new stands which are all covered, have vastly improved the overall look of the ground, while at the same time making it an all seated one. The only real disappointment is three of the stands contain a number of supporting pillars. On one side is the Main Stand. This all seated stand has its spectators area raised up above pitch level meaning that supporters have to climb a small set of steps to enter it. Part of the front has a small box like structure, with a number of windows running along the front. It particularly caught my eye, as with the windows being almost at pitch level, I wondered just how many broken windows they get each season? Oddly the players tunnel and team dugouts are set to one side of the halfway line, suggesting that at some point the pitch has been moved from its original position.

Opposite is the Les Hart Stand, a single-tiered affair which extends around to meet the Cemetery End, enclosing that corner of the stadium. In this corner there is a small Police control box suspended beneath the roof. The Les Hart Stand also has a small TV gantry, plus there are a number of supporting pillars running across the stand that may impede your view.

The Manchester Road Stand at one end is of a fair size. However, it does not run the full width of the pitch, with one side ending with the edge of the penalty box. There is also an electric scoreboard at this end. The stadium is completed with a set of modern looking floodlights. Jeff Johnson informs me; 'Le Stade de Gigg as the locals call it, is also shared with FC United of Manchester'.

What Is It Like For Visiting Supporters?

Away fans are housed in the Manchester Road End where just over 2,000 away supporters can be accommodated. Normally fans enjoy a good view of the action. However, there is a row of supporting pillars about a third of the way up the stand, which could cause problems if your team has a large following. The stand is also situated quite well back from the pitch and is slightly below pitch level. My only grumble was the archaic looking toilets in this relatively modern stand. On the whole, however, it was a relaxed and normally good day out, although sometimes lacking in atmosphere.

Where To Drink?

There are a few pubs around the ground and along Manchester Road in particular. There is also a supporters club at the ground, which sometimes allows in small numbers of away fans, for a small fee (£1). My pick of the pubs on Manchester Road, is the Swan & Cemetery, around a 10 minute walk from the ground. This Thwaites pub, is quite comfortable, serves good hand pulled beer and has a separate restaurant area. Nearer to the ground is the Staff Of Life pub, which is a basic pub serving hand pulled Lee's. Also recommended on Manchester Road, is the Waterloo, nearer to the town centre.

Neil Le Milliere, a visiting Exeter City supporter recommends the Rose & Crown on Manchester Old Road. 'It's not the biggest pub but it was very friendly; served a variety of real ales and is only a 10 minute walk away from the ground.'

Directions & Car Parking

Leave the M66 at Junction 3. Take the left-hand exit at the junction and follow this road until you come to the junction with the A56 Manchester Road. At this T-junction which has traffic lights, turn right towards Bury. You will pass the Swan & Cemetery pub on your left and then some playing fields. At the end of the playing fields just before the traffic lights and a couple of pubs, turn right into Gigg Lane for the ground. However, please note that Gigg Lane is normally closed on matchdays and the ground itself is not easily seen from the A56. Street parking, although beware of a residents only parking scheme in operation in the nearby streets, which operates on both matchdays end evenings, with wardens patrolling the area.

By Train/Metro

There is no railway station in Bury itself, so most fans travelling by train are likely to end up at one of the Manchester stations. Bury Metrolink is served by trams from Manchester Victoria & Piccadilly railway stations. Bury Metrolink Station is about a 15 minute walk from the ground. Turn left out of the station along a pedestrian walkway going underneath the dual carriageway. On the other side of the dual carriageway turn right towards the Town Hall. Just before the Town Hall, turn left into Knowsley Street and at the bottom, turn left again onto the main A56 Manchester Road. It is then a case of going straight along Manchester Road for about half a mile and you will reach Gigg Lane on your left. Thanks to Andy Grainger for supplying the directions.

Jon Hall adds; 'Alternatively bus numbers; 90, 92, 135 and 137 run every 10 minutes down Manchester Road past the end of Gigg Lane'.

Programme

Official Programme: £2.50

Record & Average Attendance

Record Attendance: 35,000 v Bolton Wanderers, FA Cup 3rd Round, January 9th, 1960.

Average Attendance: 2011-12: 3,552 (League One)

CARDIFF CITY

Ground Name: Cardiff City Stadium
Capacity: 26,828 (all seated)
Address: Leckwith Road, Cardiff, CF11 8AZ
Main Telephone No: 0845 365 1115
Ticket Office No: 0845 345 1400

Year Ground Opened: 2009
Pitch Size: 110 x 75 yards
Team Nickname: The Bluebirds
Home Kit Colours: All Blue With White Trim
Official website: www.cardiffcityfc.co.uk

What's The Ground Like?

After 99 years the club have left Ninian Park and moved to a new stadium, which is situated only around a quarter of a mile away (for those that were familiar with Ninian Park, the new stadium is more or less located behind the large open car park, that was situated behind the Main Stand). The stadium which cost £48 million to build has a capacity of 26,828. Inside it is a lovely looking stadium and has some great facilities, but like a number of other new stadiums that have been built over the last 10 years, it is functional, but lacking in that 'wow' factor.

All four stands are of the same height and the stadium is completely enclosed with all four corners having spectator seating. Three sides of the stadium are identical, all being single-tiered, all seater affairs. The roofs above these stands are situated quite high above the seating areas, with a large back wall, part of which contains Perspex panels to provide more light to the playing surface. The Grandstand is a little different, having a second tier of seating that overlaps the back of the lower tier. In this area at the rear of the lower section there is a row of executive boxes. While at the back of the second tier there is visible a glassed frontage to an area used for corporate entertainment. The team dug outs are located at the front of this stand. There is a medium sized video screen in corner of the stadium between the Ninian & Grange Stands (above the away fans section), which doesn't quite look big enough for a stadium of this size. Above each end is a small digital clock displaying how many minutes have elapsed in each half of the game. The stadium is shared with Cardiff Blues Rugby Union team.

What Is It Like For Visiting Supporters?

Away fans are located in one corner of the stadium, between the Ninian & Grange stands. Up to 1,800 fans can be accommodated in this area. The Club operate automatic turnstiles, where you have to put your ticket (which has a bar code on it) into a slot reader, which then allows the turnstiles to admit you. As you would expect from a new stadium the view of the playing action and facilities are good. The acoustics are also good, with the stadium having a loud PA system. The concourses are spacious, have televisions to keep you entertained and serve the usual fayre of food. Inside the stadium away fans are kept separate from home fans, by an area of 'no mans land' to each side. While outside there is a fenced in compound, which is also used to accommodate the away coaches, but again keeps fans separated after the game has finished which should avoid most problems. The move to the new stadium, marks a new era for Cardiff City and there was no doubt on my visit to the ground, that things seem more relaxed than before at Ninian Park.

Where To Drink?

There are no bars in the close vicinity to the stadium that I could see. As the stadium is close the old Ninian Park supporters will tend to use the pubs they did previously, most of which can be quite intimidating for away supporters and are not recommended.

One suggestion that I have received is the Gol Centre on Lawrenny Avenue (off Leckwith Road, See Google Map below) which has among other facilities a bar. Gwilym Boore informs me; 'We are a five-a-side centre located about an eight minute walk from Cardiff City Stadium. We charge £4 to park at the centre but this is returned to customers in the form of a bar voucher which can be used against purchases of hot dogs, alcoholic and soft drinks, tea and coffee and confectionery. We also encourage FREE use of our pitches by visiting children'. Plus further along Lawrenny Avenue is the Canton Rugby Football Club, which has a bar, large screen television showing Sky Sports and also offers free parking.

Otherwise it is probably best to drink in the city centre and then go on up to the stadium. Alcohol is also available inside the ground.

Directions & Car Parking

To avoid driving through the centre of Cardiff, leave the M4 at junction 33 and take the A4232 towards Cardiff/Barry. Keep on the A4232 towards Cardiff and then leave the dual carriageway at the B4267 exit. At the end of the slip road, turn left at the roundabout, signposted 'Cardiff International Athletics Stadium'. The stadium is situated a short distance down this road on the right. If you continue past the stadium on your right and turn right at the next traffic lights and right again at the HSS Hire shop then this leads you down to the away fans coach and car park. It is £5 for cars to park there, although this is limited. Please note that parking in the nearby retail park is limited to 90 minutes as this is being enforced. Also be sure also to park your car properly, as I have been informed that traffic wardens are out in force on matchdays.

By Train

The nearest train station is Ninian Park Halt, which is only a five minute walk from the stadium. This station is on a local line (city line-direction Radyr) which is served by trains from Cardiff Central, which run every 30 minutes on Saturday afternoons. On leaving Ninian Park Halt station proceed along Leckwith Road and you will see the new stadium over on your left. Alternatively if you are an away fan turn left into Sloper Road and then turn right into the protected compound at HSS Plant Hire, which leads to the away turnstiles.

Programme & Fanzines

Official Programme: £3
The Thin Blue Line Fanzine: £1
Ramzine Fanzine: £1

Record & Average Attendance

Record Attendance: 26,058 v Queens Park Rangers, Championship League, April 23rd, 2011.
Average Attendance: 2011-12: 22,100 (Championship League)

Ground Name: Brunton Park
Capacity: 18,202
Address: Warwick Road, Carlisle, CA1 1LL
Main Telephone No: 01228 526 237
Ticket Office No: 0844 371 1921

Year Ground Opened: 1909
Pitch Size: 112 x 74 yards
Team Nickname: The Cumbrians
Home Kit Colours: Blue & White
Official website: www.carlisleunited.co.uk

What's The Ground Like?

The East Stand on one side of the pitch, is a covered all seated stand, which looks quite smart. This stand was opened in 1996. The other side is an old partly covered (to the rear) Main Stand, which has seating at the back and a terraced paddock to the front. The central part of this stand was built in 1954 and the wings added at a later stage. The Warwick Road End is a covered terrace that has a peculiar looking roof, which consists of three triangular sections. The other end, the Petterill End (aka The Waterworks End), is largely a small open terrace, which oddly contains a small section of seating on one side. This end is only used for the bigger games. On one side of this end is a Security Control Box, which also has a small electric scoreboard mounted below it. There is also a video screen situated at the back. The ground also has some strange looking floodlights that don't have the normal bank of lighting on top of the pylon, but instead have the lights mounted up the side. Outside the ground entrance is a statue of former Carlisle favourite Hughie McIlmoyle, who over three separate spells at the club, scored 91 goals in 189 appearances.

Another unusual aspect of the ground is that the central point of the East Stand is located just off the halfway line. This means that one side of the stand extends past the one goal line, while the other side falls short of this. This was due to the fact that the Club were intending to rebuild the whole ground and move the pitch a few yards further north, but alas the development funds ran dry…

What Is It Like For Visiting Supporters?

Away fans are housed on one side of the Story Homes (East) Stand (towards the Petterill End) where around 2,000 fans can be accommodated. This all seated, covered stand is located at one side of the pitch. It is fairly modern and the facilities within, plus the view of the playing area are good. For larger games then the Petterill End terrace can also be allocated which houses around 1,700 supporters. Please note though that this end is open to the elements. I personally found the Carlisle fans to be friendly and helpful. The atmosphere was also particularly lively and I had an enjoyable afternoon there.

Where To Drink?

The Carlisle Rugby Club next to Brunton Park on the Warwick Road, has a club bar which allows in away supporters and is family friendly. Also near to the ground on Warwick Road is the Beehive, which serves a good pint of Theakstons. The pub does employ doormen on matchdays and for certain games away fans may not be allowed entrance. Barrie Mossop recommends another Theakstons House, called the Howard Arms, which is on Lowther Street. This is just off Warwick Road, towards the Town Centre, down from the White House. Simon Tunstall adds; 'At the back of the main car park there is the Stoneyholme Golf Club, which has a bar, serves food and welcomes fans on matchdays'. Paul Sawyers adds; 'I would recommend the Lakeland Gate for a drink on match days, which is a family friendly pub'. Also if you leave the M6 at Junction 43 and take the A69 towards Carlisle, then you will pass a recently opened Toby pub/carvery, which is not that far from the ground.

Directions & Car Parking

The ground is easy to find. Leave the M6 at junction 43 and take the A69 towards Carlisle. After a mile the ground is on your right (look out for the statue of a footballer on the corner). The club car park (cost £2) can be found by taking the first right immediately after Brunton Park into Victoria Place and then turn first right onto St Aidans Road. Otherwise street parking.

By Train

James Prentice informs me; 'Brunton Park is situated about a mile from Carlisle Citadel station, but is relatively easy to get to. Upon exiting the station's main entrance, walk the short distance around the Crescent until reaching Warwick Road. You will be able to see the old Main Stand and the strangely-shaped roofs of the Warwick Road end after walking for about 20 minutes. There are directions to the away supporters' turnstiles above the Carlisle United club shop'.

Programme

Official Programme: £3

Record & Average Attendance

Record Attendance: 27,500 v Birmingham City, FA Cup 3rd Round, January 5th, 1957 and equalled 27,500 v Middlesbrough, FA Cup 5th Round, February 7th, 1970.

Average Attendance: 2011-12: 5,247 (League One)

CARLISLE UNITED

Ground Name: The Valley
Capacity: 27,111 (all seated)
Address: Floyd Road, Charlton, SE7 8BL
Main Telephone No: 020 8333 4000
Ticket Office No: 0871 226 1905

Year Ground Opened: 1919
Pitch Size: 112 x 73 yards
Team Nickname: The Addicks
Home Kit Colours: Red & White
Official website: www.cafc.co.uk

What's The Ground Like?

The opening of the North Stand in 2002, completely transformed the look of the ground. What was a single-tiered separate stand, is now a large two-tiered affair, extending and completely enclosing the North East & North West corners. In total it houses 9,000 fans. Both sides were also redeveloped in the mid 1990s and anyone who saw the derelict Valley some years back, now wouldn't believe their eyes. The West Stand on one side is a good sized two-tiered stand, while opposite is the smaller single-tiered East Stand, where the vast open terrace, reputedly the country's biggest, was located until demolished in the 1990s. There is a row of executive boxes that run across the back of this stand and it has a television gantry suspended beneath its roof. The older South Stand, behind the goal, is given to away supporters and now looks out of place in its smart surroundings. On one side of this is a police control box. The stadium doesn't have any floodlight pylons as such, but has rows of small floodlights running across the tops of the stands. The stadium is overlooked by a block of flats beyond the South Stand and it is not uncommon to see fans out on their balconies watching most of the game for nothing and others hanging flags from their balconies in support of other teams. In one corner of the stadium between the Jimmy (South) Seed and East Stands is a large video screen. Outside the ground there is a statue of Charlton's legendary former goalkeeper Sam Bartram.

What Is It Like For Visiting Supporters?

Away fans are housed in the Jimmy Seed (South) Stand at one end of the ground, which is slightly raised above pitch level, making for a generally good view. Up to 3,000 away fans can be accommodated in this end. However, if the visiting team are unlikely to sell their full allocation of 3,000 tickets, then this end may be shared with home fans. Peter Inwood, a visiting Leeds fan adds; 'There is one solitary supporting column in the entire ground and guess where it is? Right in the middle behind the goal, in the away supporters end. Very annoying it is as well. However, I would commend the stewards, who took a relaxed attitude to the away supporters who stood throughout the match, although expect to be searched on the way in'. Otherwise the height between rows is good and the stand quite steep, keeping you fairly close to the playing action. It is worth noting that if your team is allocated the whole stand, that there are refreshment areas on either side of the stand.

As to be expected those located by the entrance turnstiles, tend to be busiest, while those on the other side of the stand are normally less congested. There is also a betting kiosk inside the ground. Adam Hodson a visiting Stockport County fan adds; 'There is a decent fish and chip shop at the top of Floyd Road, which you pass on the way to the away fans entrance.'

I was quite impressed with the atmosphere at the Valley and I can see why many away fans see it as one of their favourite away days to the capital. The Charlton fans are clearly passionate about their team, but in a non-intimidating way. I had pleasant day out and would go again. I was particularly impressed with the loud PA system that played some great music before the game commenced which rocked around the stadium. It is worth noting that you can only gain entrance to the ground by ticket, which you have to buy from a ticket booth beforehand.

Where To Drink?

Simon Phillips informs me that 'The Antigallican, a big pub near Charlton station, seems to be the favourite haunt of away supporters'. While Colin Gilham recommends the Rose of Denmark on Woolwich Road. The pub not only allows in away supporters but absolutely welcomes them. They have a photo display on the wall of fans from visiting clubs that have frequented the pub this season and it also has SKY television'. Alternatively alcohol is available in the away end.

Directions & Car Parking

Leave the M25 at Junction 2 and follow the A2 towards London. After around 12 miles the road splits with the A2 going off to the left and the right hand lanes becoming the A102. Proceed on the A102 towards the Blackwall Tunnel. Leave the A102 at the next slip road (signposted Woolwich & Ferry A206). At the bottom of the slip road turn right at the traffic lights towards Woolwich/Charlton. Proceed along the A206 passing the The Antigallican pub on your right (the ground and away entrance are diagonally behind this pub). For the main club entrance and car park go straight over the next roundabout, passing a retail park on the left. At the next roundabout, go right around it turning back on yourself along the A206. Then take the first left into Charlton Road (beware that there is a seven feet width restriction along this road). Cross over the railway and after passing the Royal Oak pub on the right, turn right into Harvey Gardens. The ground is down on the left.

Parking at the ground is for permit holders only. There is street parking, but due to a local residents parking scheme, not in close vicinity to the ground or Charlton railway station. However, as you come off the A2 onto the A206, there is some street parking to be had on your right, in a couple of streets, before you reach the Rose of Denmark pub. Colin Gilham informs me; 'There is some street parking to be had around the industrial estates in the area, in Westmoor Street, Eastmoor Street (the very road where the club was apparently formed 100 years ago!), Warspite Road and Ruston Road. If you are coming up the Woolwich Road from the the Blackwall Tunnel, then as you go past the ground, the industrial estates are on the left-hand side.

By Train

The ground is a short walk from Charlton railway station, which is served by Charing Cross, London Bridge and Waterloo East stations. On Saturdays there are also services from Cannon Street station.

Programme

Official Programme: £3

Record & Average Attendance

Record Attendance: 75,031 v Aston Villa, FA Cup 5th Round, February 12th, 1938.
Average Attendance: 2011-12: 17,402 (League One)

Ground Name: Stamford Bridge
Capacity: 41,837 (all seated)
Address: Fulham Road, London, SW6 1HS
Main Telephone No: 0871 984 1955
Ticket Office No: 0871 984 1905

Year Ground Opened: 1905
Pitch Size: 113 x 74 yards
Team Nickname: The Blues
Home Kit Colours: Royal Blue, White Trim
Official website: www.chelseafc.com

What's The Ground Like?

The ground is quite impressive looking, having had three new stands built since the mid-1990s. The developers have taken advantage of the fact that the 'old' Stamford Bridge was oval shaped and have stretched the new stands right around the ground 'filling in' the corners, so that the stadium is totally enclosed. The latest addition to the stadium is the attractive looking West Stand, which was opened in 2001. Located on one side of the pitch, it is a superb three-tiered affair having a row of executive boxes running across its middle, the type of which you are able to sit outside. Its roof is virtually transparent, allowing more light to reach the pitch and gives it a unique look. Opposite is the older East Stand. Opened in 1973 this towering stand is also three-tiered and has the team dugouts situated at its front.

Both ends are smaller being two-tiered. One of these is the Matthew Harding Stand, named in memory of the man who did so much to transform the club. Opposite is the Shed End which has a Police Control Box suspended below its roof. There are two large video screens located in opposite corners of the stadium.

Outside the ground, behind the West Stand is a statue of former playing legend, Peter Osgood.

What Is It Like For Visiting Supporters?

Away fans are located on one side of the Shed End lower tier (towards the East Stand side), where the normal allocation for League games is 3,000 tickets. For cup games the whole of the Shed End can be allocated. The view from this area of the ground is pretty good and the refreshment areas are modern. There are also televisions on the concourses to keep you entertained.

On the whole I found Stamford Bridge a pleasurable day out. There was a good atmosphere within the ground and even though there wasn't a lot of space between the home and away fan sections, it didn't feel intimidating. The stewards were also pretty laid back. I was seated in the Shed End and I did find it a little difficult to go up and down the steps of the stand, due to the stand itself being quite steep and the steps between rows quite small. The only 'real hassle' I had was trying to get through the lines of stewards situated outside the stadium at the entrance to the away section. They seemed to assume that I was a Chelsea fan and kept ushering me towards the home end. Only after showing my ticket for the visiting section for a third time did I finally make it inside!

Where To Drink?

The pubs near the ground can be quite partisan, so I would recommend getting a drink somewhere on the journey there. Alcohol is normally available inside the stadium, however, for certain fixtures the Club opt not to sell any to away supporters, so don't bank on it!

Directions & Car Parking

Leave the M25 at Junction 15 and take the M4 towards London, which then becomes the A4 up to Hammersmith. Carry on over the Hammersmith flyover and after a further one and a half miles, take the turning Earls Court. Continue past Earls Court station and down the one way system until you reach the junction with Fulham Road. At this junction, turn right at the traffic lights and after about half a mile, you will see the ground on your right.

A number of local resident schemes are in operation around the stadium, so you may well end up having to park some way from the ground itself.

By Train/Tube

The nearest tube station is Fulham Broadway which is on the District Line. Take a tube to Earls Court and if necessary, change for a Wimbledon bound tube. The nearest over ground train station is West Brompton, which is served by trains from Clapham Junction (which is in turn served by trains from London Waterloo and Victoria stations). It is around a 15 minute walk to the ground from West Brompton station. As you come out of the station turn right and proceed along Old Brompton Road, passing the Tournament Pub on your left. You will soon see the Brompton Cemetery immediately on your right and further along set back from the road is its impressive looking entrance. Turn right through the entrance into the cemetery (there are

normally a number of other supporters doing the same) and as you walk on through the cemetery you will soon see the tops of the stands of Stamford Bridge. If it is a night game then do not go into the cemetery, but take the next right after the cemetery into Finborough Road. After a half-mile, turn right onto the Fulham Road and the stadium is located down on the right.

Programme & Fanzines

Official Programme: £3

Chelsea Independent Fanzine: £1.50

CFCUK Fanzine: £1

Record & Average Attendance

Record Attendance: 82,905 v Arsenal, Division One, October 12th, 1935.

Average Attendance: 2011-12: 41,478 (Premier League)

Ground Name: Abbey Business Stadium
Capacity: 7,066 (3,912 seated)
Address: Whaddon Road, Cheltenham, GL52 5NA
Main Telephone No: 01242 573 558
Ticket Office No: Same as main number

Year Ground Opened: 1932
Pitch Size: 111 x 72 yards
Team Nickname: The Robins
Home Kit Colours: Red & White
Official website: www.ctfc.com

What's The Ground Like?

At one end of the ground is the newest addition to the stadium. The Hazlewoods Stand which was built by Barr Construction, was opened in December 2005 and has a capacity of 1,100 fans. It is particularly steep in its design, has a perspex windshield to one side and perspex panels incorporated into its roof, to allow more light to reach the pitch. The stand is unusual in the respect that it has a couple of more rows of seats on one side of it. There is also a small electric scoreboard on its roof. On one side of the ground is another relatively new stand. The In2Print Stand was opened in November 2001 and was built by Barr Construction. This stand sits proudly at one side of the pitch and houses 2,034 supporters. It is a covered, all seated, single-tiered stand, part of which is given to away supporters. The ground is now enclosed in one corner where the two new stands meet, although it is not used for spectators. On the other side of the pitch is the Main Stand, which was opened in 1963. It has seating to the rear and terracing at the front. Straddling the halfway line, it does not extend the full length of the pitch, having open spaces to either side. At one end is the small covered terrace, called the Speedy Skips Stand, which is the home end of the ground.

What Is It Like For Visiting Supporters?

Away supporters are housed in the Hazlewoods Stand at one end of the ground, where just over 1,100 supporters can be accommodated. The view of the playing area from the Hazlewoods Stand and the facilities inside are good, plus it has good leg room. If demand requires it, then part of the In2Print Stand at one side of the pitch can also be allocated to away fans.

I found Cheltenham itself to be quite pleasant and the supporters friendly. The picturesque Cotswold Hills around Cheltenham can easily be seen from inside the ground. The atmosphere is also pretty good and there is a drummer in the home end. I did find the PA to be a bit deafening though.

Where To Drink?

There is a club bar at the ground called the Robins Nest which allows in small numbers of away fans for a small admittance fee. The 'Sudeley Arms' or 'The Conservatory' are both popular with away fans. There is even a handy fish & chip shop situated in between the two. To find these pubs, turn right out of the club car park, and then turn left at the end of the road. Go straight over the roundabout, and The Sudeley Arms is on your left and the Conservatory is further up on your right. It is no more than a 10 minute walk from the ground.

Otherwise there is the Parklands Social Club. Simply go down Whaddon Road, passing the ground and the bowling club on your left. Take the first left-hand turn and the entrance to the social club car park is a short distance down on the left. Robert Middleston, a visiting Nottingham Forest fan adds; 'The Club had a friendly welcome, and the locals we met were all happy to chat football. The club has a number of TV screens including a very big screen, on which the Sky Premier plus game was broadcast.'

Directions & Car Parking

From The North

Leave the M5 at junction 10 and take the A4019 towards Cheltenham. Keep straight on through the traffic lights, until you come to a large roundabout (there is a McDonalds on the left), at which you turn left. Continue up this road going over a double mini-roundabout. Keep going for about 300 yards and then turn right into Swindon Lane. Go over the level crossing and straight over the next roundabout (signposted Prestbury) passing the race course on your left. Turn right into Albert Road (signposted Gloucestershire University) and at the bottom at the roundabout turn left into Prestbury Road, (the ground is signposted from here) and then further down Prestbury Road, turn right into Whaddon Road. The ground is down on the left.

From The South

Leave the M5 at Junction 11 turning right towards Cheltenham. Go across first roundabout – GCHQ is on your left. Turn left at the next roundabout, into Princess Elizabeth Way. Go straight over the next roundabout, (the exit is over at about '1 o'clock'). Keep on up this road, and you will come to a big roundabout, where you will see a

McDonalds on the corner. Go straight across this roundabout and continue up this road going over a double mini-roundabout.
Then as North.

There are a limited number of spaces available in the Club car park at the ground which cost £5. The Parklands Social Club does allow some parking at £4 per car. There is little in the way of nearby street parking close to the stadium.

Otherwise there is a free 'Park & Ride' service to the ground operating from Cheltenham Racecourse, which is well signposted around the town.

By Train

Cheltenham Station is over two miles from the ground, so best to jump in a taxi. If you are going to embark on the 35-40 minute walk then thank Dave Lucas for the following directions; 'Turn right out of station car park and follow Queens Road for around half a mile. At the end of Queens Road turn left into Lansdown Road. At the next (Montpellier) roundabout, turn left into Montpellier Walk (which later becomes the Promenade). At the end of the Promenade, turn right into the High Street. Go along the High Street for around 100 yards and then turn left into Winchcombe Street (by a branch of the Cheltenham & Gloucester Building Society). Continue straight along Winchcombe Street and into Prestbury Road. Straight across the next roundabout and then first right into Whaddon Road'.

Programme

Official Programme: £3

Record & Average Attendance

Record Attendance: 8,326 v Reading, FA Cup 1st Round, November 17th, 1956.

Average Attendance: 2011-12: 3,425 (League Two)

Ground Name: b2net Stadium
Capacity: 10,400 (all seated)
Address: 1866 Sheffield Road, Whittington Moor,
Chesterfield, S41 8NZ
Main Telephone No: 01246 209 765
Ticket Office No: 01246 556 799

Year Ground Opened: 2010
Pitch Size: 111 x 71 yards
Team Nickname: Spireites
Home Kit Colours: Blue & White
Official website: www.chesterfield-fc.co.uk

What's The Ground Like?

Built at a cost of £13 million, Chesterfield's new 10,400 capacity all seater stadium is located around one and a half miles north of the town centre. On one side is the Main HTM Products Stand. This stand has a capacity of 2,902 seats on a single tier, with a glass fronted executive lounge at the rear. The players emerge from the tunnel at the centre of the stand, while the centre seating of the stand is taken up by the Directors Box, Sponsors and Legends seating areas, with the press seating situated towards the North end wing section. The stand has a graceful curved roof with white steelwork and a glazed windshield at the north end, with a ground floor and top level viewing area for disabled supporters and their helpers in the South wing section. At one side of the stand, towards the Karen Child Kop is an unusual looking stadium control tower which extends beyond the touchline.

Opposite is the Midlands Co-operative Community Stand which is similar in appearance, having a curved roof line and a capacity of 3,144 seats with glazed windshields on either side, but

with no executive facilities at the rear. The television camera gantry is situated in this stand below the roof steelwork. Both ends are similar affairs, both being single tiered, covered and housing just over 2,000 supporters. Unlike the other stands the roofs on these ends are not curved, but again glass windshields are in place on both sides. The only real difference is that the Karen Child Stand has two ground floor level disabled viewing areas as opposed to one in the Printability Stand. The ground is complimented at present by four modern slim corner floodlight pylons which each have 14 lights on four rows.

The stadium has a pleasing balanced feel with no single stand dominating the whole ground. The only minor downsides are that the stadium has no scoreboard or clock and one corner is overlooked by a Tesco's store and car park, which detracts from the overall look.

What Is It Like For Visiting Supporters?

Away supporters are mostly housed in the Printability Stand at the North end of the stadium, where up to 2,112 supporters can be seated. If demand requires it then additional seating can also be made available in the Midlands Co-operative Community Stand. Unlike most new stadiums the fans are housed pretty close to the pitch, ensuring good views of the playing action. The leg room is good too. The concourses are built to a high standard, with large flat screen televisions (showing Sky Sports, plus the game going on inside with commentary) to keep the fans entertained. Food on offer from the concourse includes the locally produced Jacksons Pies. Pleasingly, the refreshment areas stay open throughout the match (although no alcohol is allowed to be served after 9pm for evening games).

The roof of the away end is quite low, which ensures that a relatively small number of away supporters can really make some noise. I noted that the stewards allowed standing at the back of the stand but not at the front. In effort to further boost the atmosphere there is a drummer in the home end and on my visit a drum was also allowed into the away stand. If Chesterfield score then the tune 'Tom Hark' echoes around the stadium.

Please note that cash is not accepted at the turnstiles, entrance is by ticket only. Away fans can purchase their tickets from the small portakabin located outside the Printability (Away) Stand.

Where To Drink?

Nearest to the away end of the ground, along Sheffield Road (a five minute walk, passing a Chinese/Fish & Chip shop on the way) is the Derby Tup. This pub is featured in the CAMRA Good Beer Guide and normally has 10 ales available. Although the pub does not sell food, the landlord allows customers to bring in food from outside. Further on up Sheffield Road on the right is the tiny Beer Parlour shop, which is primarily a real ale and cider off licence, but also allows ales to be bought and consumed inside. A little further on, on the same side of the road is the handily located North Sea Fish and Chip shop. While up on the left is the Red Lion pub, which is serves beers from the Old Mill Brewery and shows Sky Sports. Otherwise alcohol is served inside the ground

Directions & Car Parking

Leave the M1 at Junction 29 and take the A617 towards Chesterfield. At the end of the dual carriageway at the edge of the town centre, turn right onto the A61 towards Sheffield. At the first roundabout turn left and the stadium is down on the right. For the main entrance turn right into Sheffield Road and then right again into the Club car park. However, the Club car park is for permit holders only. There is nearby street parking available on side roads off the Sheffield road, if you arrive early enough. Don't think about parking in the nearby Tesco store, as the car park is patrolled on matchdays and you may end up having your car towed away.

By Train

Chesterfield railway station is walkable from the stadium, although it will take you between 20 and 30 minutes to walk to do so. Alternatively, there is a taxi rank outside the station though as traffic is likely to be slow along Sheffield Road on a matchday this could end up costing you more time and money than you thought.

The Club also have a shuttle bus which operates on matchdays (every 10 minutes 13.30–14.40 Saturdays and 18.20–19.30 weekdays). It departs from Rose Hill by the Town Hall. The bus is also in operation after the game (last bus on Saturdays is 17.45, weekdays 22.25). The fare is £1 each way.

Programme
Official Programme: £2.50

Record & Average Attendance
Record Attendance: 10,089 v Rotherham United, League Two, March 18th, 2011.

Average Attendance: 2011-12: 6,530 (League One)

Ground Name: Weston Homes Community Stadium

Capacity: 10,105 (all seated)

Address: United Way, Colchester, CO4 5UP

Main Telephone No: 01206 755 100

Ticket Office No: 0845 437 9089

Year Ground Opened: 2008

Pitch Size: 110 x 70 yards

Team Nickname: The U's

Home Kit Colours: Blue & White

Official website: www.cu-fc.com

What's The Ground Like?

In 2008 the Club left their Layer Road ground, their home for 71 years, and moved to a new stadium on the edge of town. The new Weston Homes Community Stadium as it has been named in a corporate sponsorship deal was built by Barr Construction at a cost of around £14 million. The cost was largely met by Colchester Borough Council, who own the stadium, with the football club as tenants.

The stadium is functional and well presented, but as with a number of new stadiums built in recent years, it lacks character and is nothing 'out of the ordinary'. The ground is comprised of four separate stands. The Main (West) Stand on one side of the pitch is a little taller than the other three stands, which are the same height. All the stands are covered single-tiered, all seated stands. The Main Stand has a row of executive boxes /corporate hospitality areas running across the top of it, while the others are simply seating areas. The Weston Homes Stand though, at the South end of the stadium, does have a Police Control Box incorporated into it, on one side beneath the roof. All the stands have translucent panels built into their roofs as well as a perspex strip just below them, which allows more light and facilitates pitch growth.

What Is It Like For Visiting Supporters?

Away fans are normally housed at the North end of the stadium in the ACJ Stand, where up to 2,000 supporters can be accommodated. For Clubs with a small travelling support then part of the JobServe Stand (towards the North End) is allocated instead. As you would expect from a new stadium the facilities and view of the playing action are good. The stands are particularly steep, meaning that fans are kept close to the pitch and resulting in good sight lines. Entrance to the stadium is via electronic turnstiles and tickets need to be purchased as no cash is accepted at the turnstiles.

John Hill, a visiting Huddersfield Town fan adds; 'One pleasing feature was that at 6'2", I was still okay for leg room, which is not always the case at some other grounds. We caught the shuttle bus from the station and it worked surprisingly well. We got to the ground easily, and afterwards they let the buses out of the car park before cars, which led to a fairly swift return to the station and an easy getaway'.

Where To Drink?

With the stadium situated on the very outskirts of Colchester, then there is little choice of nearby pubs. There is the Dog & Pheasant on Nayland Road which is around three quarters of a mile away. Away fans are admitted as long as team colours are not being worn. To find the pub, go down to the end of United Way, then at the end turn left into Boxted Road and at the mini-roundabout go straight over into Nayland Road. The Dog & Pheasant is on the right next to a fish and chip shop.

The Club allow access to the bar and toilets located on the concourse area of the Weston Homes Stand, before each home game (from 12.15pm for a 3pm kick-off). Drinks can be taken back outside the stadium to enjoy the pre-match entertainment such as live bands which are often playing under the marquee. This bar is available to both home and away supporters. Alcohol is also made available to away fans inside the stadium.

Directions & Car Parking

From The North & M11:
Leave the A14 and then join the M11. Come off the M11 at J8 (Stansted Airport/A120) and follow the A120 towards Braintree & Colchester. The A120 then joins the A12 and after passing the stadium on your right, leave the A12 at Junction 28. Turn left at the first roundabout, then turn right into United Way from the second roundabout.

From the South:
Leave the A12 at Junction 28. Turn right at the first roundabout. Go across the bridge and then go straight over the second roundabout, before turning right into United Way from the third roundabout.

Car Parking:
There are 700 car parking spaces at the stadium which cost £6. There is also an overspill car park located on the nearby industrial estate (about a 10 minute walk away from the stadium) which costs £8. There is also an extensive residents only parking scheme in operation around the stadium, so you may need to journey to over a mile away, before you can find a legitimate parking space. Mick Hubbard adds; There are a number of local businesses in the area also offering parking for around £5'.

By Train

The nearest station to the ground is Colchester North which is just under two miles away from the stadium. Located near to the station at Bruff Close is a free shuttle bus service that will take you to the ground. It takes around 10 minutes to reach the stadium. I have heard of some fans paying to park at Colchester North Station, where there is a fair sized car park (which costs £2.10) and then taking the shuttle bus.

Apparently there is some street parking to be had on Mile End Road near to the Bricklayers pub.

Shuttle Bus to the Stadium:
A shuttle bus operates from Bruff Close, which is close to Colchester North station (at the end of the station approach turn left and take the second exit at the roundabout, the buses park behind the "Big Yellow" storage facility that you can see from the station). For 3pm kick-offs it runs from 1pm, with the last bus returning from the stadium at 6pm. For 7.45pm kick-offs, the service commences at 6pm with the last bus returning from the stadium at 10.15pm. The cost of the bus is £1.50 return, but it is free for OAPs, who can show a senior citizen bus pass. The journey time to the stadium is around 10 minutes.

Programme

Official Programme: £3

Record & Average Attendance

Record Attendance: 10,064 v Norwich City, League One, January 16th, 2010.

Average Attendance: 2011-12: 3,865 (League One)

Ground Name: Ricoh Arena
Capacity: 32,500 (all seated)
Address: Phoenix Way, Foleshill, Coventry, CV6 6GE
Main Telephone No: 0844 873 1883
Ticket Office No: Same as main number

Year Ground Opened: 2005
Pitch Size: 115 yards x 74 yards
Team Nickname: The Sky Blues
Home Kit Colours: Sky Blue & White
Official website: www.ccfc.co.uk

What's The Ground Like?

Like many grounds built in this country in recent years, the new Coventry stadium is functional and fairly conservative in its design. Three sides of the stadium, which are large single-tiered stands are fairly bland affairs. Happily, the complex has an exhibition centre attached to its West side, resulting in a unique looking stand that gives more of a continental feel. Known as the Lloyds-pharmacy Stand, it has a small tier of seats overhanging the larger lower tier, with a row of corporate hospitality boxes, running along the back of the lower section. Along the top of the stand is a large area of white panelling (adorned with the logo of the stadium sponsors) that runs along the length of the stand and around the corners of either side of it. In one of these corners is located a Police Control box. Below the white panelling is a large windowed corporate hosp-itality area.

The stadium is fully enclosed with all corners of the stadium being filled with spectator seating and all the stands are of the same height, giving it a symmetrical look. There are a number of clear perspex panels located in the roof at the South end of the stadium, plus a large strip of perspex

that runs around the stadium just below the roof at the back of three sides. These measures allow more natural light to enter the stadium which helps the growth of the grass pitch. There is also a large video screen type scoreboard located in one corner of the stadium between the South and Tesco East Stands. Outside the stadium in front of the club shop is a statue of former manager and chairman Jimmy Hill.

What Is It Like For Visiting Supporters?

Away supporters are mostly accommodated to one side of the South Stand (Blocks 6 & 7) towards the corner with the Lloydspharmacy Stand. Around 3,000 supporters can be seated in this area. The angle of the stand is quite steep, meaning a fair bit of effort to climb to the top. Normally a steep stand means that fans are close to the playing action, but not here. Not only is there a sizeable red coloured track surrounding the playing area, but the stand itself is further set back from the pitch. This does lead to some viewing problems, especially when the action is taking place at the other end. The leg room is adequate for most and the stadium does have good acoustics, which helps boost the atmosphere.

Entrance to the stadium is through automatic turnstiles, where you have to put your ticket (which has a bar code on it) into a slot reader, which then allows the turnstiles admit you. Behind the stands there are spacious concourses and a number of food and drink outlets. The concourses also have a number of televisions which show the game being played inside.

Where To Drink?

On one corner of the stadium, near to the Club Shop is the Grosvenor Casino, which has a bar, has Sky Sports television and admits both home and away fans on matchdays.

Robert Nunn, a visiting Reading fan informs me; 'We found the JK English Pub on Longford Road to be most welcoming. This Indian/Pub had a pub feel (pool table, jukebox, etc) but was also an Indian restaurant. Also on Longford Road, but heading away from the City Centre are the Longford Engine and Coach & Horses pubs which both welcome away fans. There is also a handily placed fish & chip shop located across the road from the Longford Engine.

Jamie Greenway adds; 'The Black Horse Pub, in between Longford and Exhall has been attracting a fair amount of away supporters for most games. If you go to the top of Longford Road and around the roundabout towards Exhall, it's on the right and normally has a burger van outside'. Also in this area is a Novotel that has a bar. Alternatively alcohol is also available inside the stadium.

Directions & Car Parking

Leave the M6 at Junction 3. Take the A444 towards the city centre and after one mile you will reach the stadium on your left.

Parking at the stadium is mostly for permit holders, although the Club do sell on the day spaces in Car Park C at £10 per car, however, it is best to book a space in advance. In addition there are also a number of unofficial car parks in the area also costing around £5. These tend to be in and around the Foleshill Road area (From Junction 3 of the M6 take the B4113 towards

Bedworth and at the first roundabout take the 2nd exit into Foleshill Road). Please note that an extensive 'residents only' parking scheme has been put in place for all residential streets within a least a mile of the ground.

By Train

Coventry train station is about three and half miles away from the stadium and really is too far to walk. Either take a bus from the Pool Meadow Bus Station or jump in a taxi.

Lori Kilpatrick adds; 'There is a bus stop directly outside the train station, from which most passing buses go to the Pool Meadow Bus Station. On checking that the bus indeed goes to the Bus Station ask for a "match day ticket" which will cost you £4 and will cover all journeys on that day in Coventry (note no change is given on Coventry buses so have the exact cash ready). Get off at the Bus Station and look for the Bus Stand letter 'U' from which the Football Special Shuttle Service operates from. The service number is 101 and runs every 10 minutes from two hours prior to kick-off and then returns every five minutes, for one hour after the game has ended'.

Programme & Fanzines

Official Programme: £3
Twist & Shout Fanzine: £1
The West Terrace Fanzine: £1

Record & Average Attendance

Record Attendance: 31,407 v Chelsea, FA Cup 6th Round, March 7th, 2009.
Average Attendance: 2011-12: 15,119 (Championship League)

Ground Name: Broadfield Stadium
Capacity: 5,500 (3,295 Seated)
Address: Winfield Way, Crawley,
West Sussex, RH11 9RX
Main Telephone No: 01293 410 000
Ticket Office No: Same as main number

Year Ground Opened: 1997
Pitch Size: 110 x 72 yards
Team Nickname: The Red Devils
Home Kit Colours: Red & White
Official website:
www.crawleytownfc.net

What's The Ground Like?

This relatively new stadium was opened in 1997, the Club moving there from their old Town Mead ground. The stadium looks to be a quality one in terms of standard of build. It is dominated by the good sized West Stand on one side. This smart looking stand, is covered, all seated and runs for about two thirds the length of the pitch. It is raised above pitch level meaning that fans have to climb a small flight of stairs at the front to enter the seated area. The stand also has windshields to either side, plus three unusual looking floodlight pylons on its roof. It has a capacity of 1,150 seats. Opposite is the new East Stand which was opened in April 2012. This semi-permanent all seated stand, accommodates 2,145 spectators in 12 rows of seating. The stand does though have a fair few supporting pillars running across the front of it that could impede your view. A new pair of floodlight pylons have also been erected to either side of the stand. Both ends are virtually identical, being small covered terraces that extend around both corners of the ground towards the West Stand, enclosing the stadium at those points. The stadium perimeter is surrounded on two sides by a number of trees, giving a rural look.

What Is It Like For Visiting Supporters?

Away fans are primarily housed in the KR-L Stand at one end of the ground. This mostly covered terrace can accommodate up to 1,600 fans. A small number of seats are also available to away supporters in the West Stand. The segregation of the terrace can be adjusted depending on the size of the away following. For example clubs with a small following will be given only the North West corner up to the corner flag, while the largest will be allocated that corner plus the whole of that end. The facilities at the stadium are pretty good and it is normally a relaxed and enjoyable day out.

Where To Drink?

There is a bar at the stadium at the back of the Bruce Winfield Stand called the Redz Bar, which allows in away fans. Entrance to this bar is gained from outside the stadium. Peter Bellamy informs me, 'The closest pub to the stadium is the Half Moon on Brighton Road (A2219). This is about a five minute walk away going towards the town centre. Another pub close by is The Downsman, which is on Wakehurst Drive, just off Southgate Avenue'.

To find these pubs, come out of the stadium car park entrance and turn right and go back up to the main roundabout. Cross the dual carriageway using the underpass and go straight on into Southgate Avenue (A2004). For the Half Moon take the first left off Southgate Avenue into Brighton Road (A2219) and the pub is further up the road on the right. For the Downsman also go to Brighton Road, then take the first right in to Wakehurst Drive. Continue along Wakehurst Drive to find the pub on the left.

Directions & Car Parking

From the M25 take the M23 Southbound towards Gatwick Airport and Brighton. At the end of the M23 (before it becomes the A23) leave the motorway at the last exit, Junction 11 (sign posted A264 Horsham, Pease Pottage Services). At the roundabout at the end of the motorway slip road turn right onto the A23 going towards Crawley. The ground is down on the left just before the next roundabout. It is a little obscured by trees, so look for the large red and white football on the roundabout itself and you will see the stadium entrance. Turn left at the roundabout and then left again for the stadium car park, which costs £2. Peter Bellamy adds; 'There is an overflow car park in the offices at Broadfield Park, accessible from the A23 as you come down the hill from the motorway'. Otherwise street parking.

Please note that after the end of the game it can take quite a while to exit the stadium car park. So if you are looking for a quick getaway after the game, then it may be an idea to street park instead.

By Train

Crawley station is just over a mile away from the stadium. You can either take a taxi (about £6), or from the bus station across the road, you can take a Fastway number 10 bus to the ground (this runs every 10 minutes). Otherwise it is about a 20 minute walk.

As you come out of the station turn left and walk down to the T-junction. At the junction turn left into Brighton Road. Keep walking straight down Brighton Road for just under a mile and at its end turn right. You should now be able to see the stadium in the distance behind the traffic island. Use the underpass to cross the A23 to the ground.

Programme

Official Programme: £3

Record & Average Attendance

Record Attendance: 4,723 v Crewe Alexandra, League Two, April 6th, 2012.

Average Attendance: 2011-12: 3,256 (League Two)

Ground Name: Alexandra Stadium
Capacity: 10,066 (all seated)
Address: Gresty Road, Crewe, Cheshire, CW2 6EB
Main Telephone No: 01270 213 014
Ticket Office No: 01270 252 610

Year Ground Opened: 1898
Pitch Size: 100 x 66 yards
Team Nickname: The Railwaymen
Home Kit Colours: Red, White & Blue
Official website: www.crewealex.net

What's The Ground Like?

The opening of the £6 million Air Products Stand (formerly known as the Railtrack Stand) in 1999 changed forever the look and feel of the ground. Before, it had always been small and homely, but the addition of the Air Products Stand has drastically changed the overall scene. The stand, which sits proudly along one side of the pitch, is a single tier cantilever holding just under 7,000 people. It looks huge compared to the other stands and is probably three times the size of the old Main Stand. It is simply designed, sits well back from the pitch and has windshields to either side. Considering that the overall capacity of the ground is just over 10,000, one can understand how the Air Products Stand dominates Gresty Road, accounting for 70% of the available seating.

The other three stands are roughly of the same height, covered and all seated, but are rather small when compared to the Air Products Stand. So much so that balls are regularly kicked out of the ground during a game. The newest of these smaller stands is the Mark Price Stand (also known as the Gresty Road End), which is the home end of the ground. This replaced a former open terrace and seats around 900.

Opposite is the Wulvern Homes Stand, which was previously known as the Railway End. This has some executive boxes at the rear, but the seating area is only opened for the bigger games. The Blue Bell BMW Stand at one side of the ground, has an unusual television/press gantry on its roof. It almost looks as if part of a portakabin was at some point bolted onto the roof and it looks a bit precarious. In the corner between the Blue Bell BMW and Wulvern Homes Stands is a large clock, while on the other side of the Blue Bell BMW Stand is a Police Control Box, keeping a close eye on the away contingent. The ground is completed with a set of modern looking floodlights.

What Is It Like For Visiting Supporters?

Away fans are housed in the Blue Bell BMW Stand at one side of the ground. The whole of this stand is given to away supporters and houses 1,680 fans, though if required the Wulvern Homes Stand can also be allocated to away fans. Entrance to the away stand is by ticket only, (no cash is accepted at ironically some of the oldest turnstiles I have ever seen at a League Ground). Tickets need to be purchased from the ticket booth next to the supporters club at the entrance to this stand. Please also note that alcohol is not available in this stand.

I found Crewe to be relaxed and friendly, making for a good day out. There was a large away support on my last visit which boosted the atmosphere of the ground, however, I have heard reports that it can be a bit flat at certain games, even with the efforts of a drummer in the home end. There are a couple of supporting pillars in the Blue Bell BMW Stand which if you are unlucky could affect your view of the playing action. There is a popular fish and chip shop just outside of the stadium, the smell of which, early in the game, wafts across the ground.

Where To Drink?

If you get there reasonably early before the game, the supporters club at the ground allows small numbers of away fans in. There are also a number of pubs within walking distance of the ground. The pick of these, is probably the Royal Hotel on Nantwich Road. As Barry Cutts, a visiting Coventry City supporter adds; 'I found the Royal Hotel to be a warm and welcoming drinking house. Turn left out of the railway station & the pub is 50 yards down this road on the right-hand side. There is also a fantastic chippie opposite'. Although the pub does not look that welcoming, with a number of bouncers on the door, once inside you will find it okay. There are separate bars for home and away supporters. The away supporters bar is called Clancys and is decked out in an Irish theme. On my last visit it had a large screen showing Sky Sports.

If you park on the industrial estate just off Weston Road, then on your way to the ground you will pass the Brocklebank Pub, a Brewers Fayre outlet, which is very popular with away fans. It is also has a large screen showing Sky Sports. You can also park in their own car park which costs £1 for three hours. The cost of parking is refundable off your bill if you use their restaurant.

Directions & Car Parking

Leave the M6 at Junction 16 and take the A5020 towards Crewe. Follow this road right into Crewe. At the roundabout junction with the A534, Nantwich Road, turn left. Gresty Road is down past the Railway Station on the left. Just before you reach this island on Weston Road, you will see a sign pointing to the right, which displays; 'Away Supporters On Street Parking'. This directs you to an industrial estate on the right of the road (you will also see the Volkswagen dealership, L C Charles on the front of it). It takes about 15 minutes to walk to the ground from here. Otherwise at the ground behind the Air Products Stand is a pay and display car park which costs £2.50 for the day. Obviously this fills up quite quickly on matchdays.

By Train

The ground is only a few minutes walk from the train station. As you come out of the Railway Station turn left and Gresty Road is down the road on your left.

Programme

Official Programme: £2.50

Record & Average Attendance

Record Attendance: 20,000 v Tottenham Hotspur, FA Cup 4th Round, January 6th, 1960.

Average Attendance: 2011-12: 4,124 (League Two)

CREWE ALEXANDRA

Ground Name: Selhurst Park
Capacity: 26,309 (all seated)
Address: Selhurst Park, London, SE25 6PU
Main Telephone No: 0208 768 6000
Ticket Office No: 0871 2000 071

Year Ground Opened: 1924
Pitch Size: 110 x 74 yards
Team Nickname: The Eagles
Home Kit Colours: Red & Blue
Official website: www.cpfc.co.uk

What's The Ground Like?

The ground is a mixture of the modern and the old, with two old side stands and two more modern looking end stands. The newest edition is the two-tiered Holmesdale Road Stand at one end, which was opened in 1995. This stand has a large lower tier, with a smaller upper tier that overhangs it. The stand looks impressive and has a large curved roof, as well as windshields on either side of the upper tier. This is where the bulk of home supporters congregate.

Opposite is the Whitehorse Lane Stand. This was originally a large open terrace but was reduced in capacity in the early 1980s when land was sold for a Sainsbury's supermarket which is still present outside the ground. During the early 1990s the terrace was made all seated and a double row of executive boxes was constructed above it, giving it an unusual look. Later a roof was added and then a large video screen installed upon it. This stand has now been renamed the 'Croydon Advertiser Family Stand'.

One side is the large, covered, single -tiered Arthur Wait stand, which was built in 1969, while on the other side the Main Stand, which dates back to when the ground opened in 1924, is also single-tiered. Both stands are now beginning to show their age; for example both have some wooden seating, as well as a number of supporting pillars. The Arthur Wait Stand has a TV gantry suspended beneath its roof, while the Main Stand has a number of ancient looking floodlights on its roof. Michael Clement adds; 'To add a bit of razzmatazz to the beginning of games, the club play a programme of loud music, as the teams emerge onto the pitch'. This includes playing 'Glad All Over' by the Dave Clarke Five, which is enthusiastically joined in to by the Palace fans.

What Is It Like For Visiting Supporters?

Away fans are still housed on one side of the Arthur Wait Stand, however, they have been relocated to the opposite side near the 'Croydon Advertiser Family Stand'. Just over 2,000 away supporters can be accommodated. Nikita, a visiting Gillingham fan informs me; 'If you are seated towards the rear of the stand then you will find that you are sitting on old wooden seats and there is very little leg room'. Plus the views of the playing action are not particularly great from the back of the stand, due to the overhang of the roof. And if that is not enough then there is the odd supporting pillar to contend with too!

On my last visit there was a particularly good atmosphere within the ground, especially from the home fans in the Holmesdale Road End. I was impressed with the Palace fans, who clearly were passionate about their Club, but in a non-intimidatory manner, towards away fans. In fact there was plenty of good banter going on between the two sets of supporters. There are plenty of refreshments available, however, if there is a sizeable away support, then getting food and drink could be a problem because there is only one small refreshment area to cater for the whole away support. Plus as there is no formal queuing system, then joining the scrum that inevitably ensues at the counter, is not for the faint hearted so you may consider getting something outside of the ground before the game starts. Also if you do happen to visit the Gents, watch out for the small downward flight of steps to the toilets. I almost went flying!

On the whole Crystal Palace is a fairly relaxed ground to visit and you are unlikely to encounter any problems, except perhaps getting stuck in the traffic on the way to the game!

Where To Drink?

Opposite Thornton Heath Railway Station there is a Wetherspoon pub, called the The Flora Sandes which is popular with both home and away supporters. Also close by is The Railway Telegraph on Brigstock (as you come out of Thornton Heath station turn right and the pub is further down on the left). Near Norwood Junction Railway Station on the High Street is another Wetherspoon outlet called The William Stanley (from the Station turn right at the Clock Tower into the High Street and it is down on the left). Generally beer and lager are served inside the ground. Please note though that for certain high profile games, the Club choose not to serve alcohol to away supporters.

Directions & Car Parking

Leave the M25 at Junction 7 and follow the signs for the A23 to Croydon. At Purley bear left onto the A23 at its junction with the A235 (to Croydon). You will pass roundabouts and junctions with the A232 and A236 as you pass Croydon, after which the A23 bears left at Thornton Heath (at the Horseshoe pub roundabout). Here you must go straight over, into Brigstock Road (B266), passing Thornton Heath Station on your left and bearing right on - roundabout, (Whitehorse Road/Grange Road) go left into Whitehorse Lane. The ground is on your right.

Most streets around the ground are either designated residents only parking on matchdays or are pay and display with a four hour limit. So please take note of any street signs advising of parking restrictions, or else you will run the risk of being towed away. Please note that the traffic can be pretty bad on Saturdays even without football traffic, so make sure you allow yourself some extra time to make the journey.

By Train

The nearest railway stations are Selhurst or Thornton Heath which are served by London Victoria main line station, Clapham Junction, London Bridge (every 30 mins) and East Croydon (every 15 mins). You can also use Norwood Junction station which is also served by Victoria, but is a little further away. It is then a 10-15 minute walk to the ground. Please note that Crystal Palace station is nowhere near the ground.

Programme

Official Programme: £3.

Record & Average Attendance

Record Attendance: 51,482 v Burnley, Division Two, May 11th, 1979.

Average Attendance: 2011-12: 15,219 (Championship League)

Ground Name: London Borough of Barking and
Dagenham Stadium
(But still known to many fans as Victoria Road)
Capacity: 6,000 (2,200 Seats)
Address: Dagenham, Essex RM10 7XL
Main Telephone No: 0208 592 1549

Ticket Office No: Same as main number
Year Ground Opened: 1917
Pitch Size: 112 x 72 yards
Team Nickname: Daggers
Home Kit Colours: Red & Blue
Official website: www.daggers.co.uk

What's The Ground Like?

The stadium has been improved recently with the construction of the Traditional Builders Stand (aka Pondfield End) at one end of the ground, which replaced a small open terrace. This new all seated stand which was opened during the 2009/10 season, is a sizeable affair, housing 1,200 spectators. The stand is covered, raised above pitch level and has windshields to either side. Although only eleven rows high, it is free from supporting pillars and is quite steep, meaning that fans are kept close to the playing action.

On one side is the relatively modern Main Stand, which was opened in 2001. Sponsored by Carling, this 800 capacity stand, is covered and all seated, with the team dugouts situated at the front of it. The stand comprises of six rows of seating and has a small executive area at the back of it. The stand, which is free of supporting pillars, is elevated above pitch level which means that supporters have to climb small sets of steps at the front of it, to gain access. The stand though, only runs for three quarters of the length of the pitch and at one end towards the Traditional Builders Stand, another separate stand exists. This stand which is called the Barking College Family Stand,

is a small covered, seated stand. It is smaller in height than the Main Stand and contains around 200 seats, with some supporting pillars running along the front of it. Again it is raised above pitch level and is accessed via a small staircase.

The rest of the ground is terracing, with a small open terrace behind one goal and a covered terrace along one side. The home end, the Bury Road End (aka the Clock End), has a small basic electric scoreboard situated above it. This area also contains the club shop and Police control box. The North Terrace, which runs along one side of the pitch, is known affectionately by the Dagenham fans as 'The Sieve' as apparently at one time it was famed for its leaking roof. This old fashioned looking terrace is partly covered to the rear and has a number of supporting pillars. It also has a television gantry perched upon its roof.

What Is It Like For Visiting Supporters?

Away fans are housed in the new Traditional Builders Stand at one end of the stadium. Up to 1,200 fans can be accommodated in this area. As you would expect from a new stand the views of the playing action and facilities are both good. I experienced no problems, apart from outside the ground, it was not obvious (unless I missed the signs) showing where the entrance to the away section was.

The stand itself is easily the best stand at the stadium, so it is intriguing that it is given over to away supporters. It is raised above pitch level, meaning that you have to climb a small set of steps to enter it. One drawback is that the team's tunnel is located in this stand and awning is pulled out to the playing area before kick-off. This means that at this time fans can't easily access the other side of the stand along the front of it, as they are effectively 'cut off' until the awning is withdrawn again. On the plus side away fans are treated to their own indoor bar area.

Where To Drink?

There is a fair sized Social Club at the ground, which apart from a few high profile games, welcomes away supporters and costs 50p to enter. It is fairly basic, but comfortable and shows SKY Sports television. It is also contains a local betting outlet and a programme booth. The beer is reasonably priced with hand pulled Youngs Bitter available. Inside the ground alcohol is available to away supporters in the Traditional Builders Stand.

If it is a pub that you prefer, then going further along Rainham Road and going past Golds Gym is the Eastbrook pub. Otherwise, to be honest, there is not much of interest in the area, so there is not much point in wandering off too far.

Directions & Car Parking

From The North:

Leave the M25 at Junction 27 and take the M11 towards London. At the end of the M11 continue onto the A406 towards Docklands (A13) and London City Airport. At the intersection with the A13, turn onto this road in the direction of the Dartford Crossing. At the junction with the A1306, leave the A13 and join the A1306 towards Dagenham. At the third set of traffic lights turn left just before the McDonalds into Ballards Road. At the end of this road you will come to a large roundabout, (known as the Bull roundabout, after the public house of the same name) at which you turn left, into Rainham Road. Proceed up Rainham Road passing Dagenham East tube station on the left and Victoria Road is a quarter of a mile further on, on the same side of the road.

There is no parking available at the ground itself. However, there is plenty of street parking, some of which is available on the main Rainham road.

By Train/Tube

Take the District Line to Dagenham East (and not Dagenham Heathway). Turn left as you come out of the station and the ground is clearly signposted and only five minutes walk away. Please note that the journey by tube from Central London can take around 45 minutes. Neil Le Milliere adds; 'The tube journey out there can be a bit of a nightmare and it's probably better to get a train from Fenchurch Street to Barking Station and then a tube to Dagenham from there'.

Programme

Official Programme: £3

Record & Average Attendance

Record Attendance: 5,949 v Ipswich Town, FA Cup 3rd Round, January 5th, 2002

Average Attendance: 2011-12: 2,091 (League Two)

Ground Name: Pride Park Stadium
Capacity: 33,597 (all seated)
Address: Pride Park Stadium, Derby, DE24 8XL
Main Telephone No: 0871 472 1884
Ticket Office No: Same as main number

Year Ground Opened: 1997
Pitch Size: 115 x 74 metres
Team Nickname: The Rams
Home Kit Colours: White & Black
Official website: www.dcfc.co.uk

What's The Ground Like?

The Club moved to Pride Park in 1997 after spending 102 years at their former Baseball Ground home. Pride Park which was opened by Her Majesty the Queen, is totally enclosed with all corners being filled. One corner is filled with executive boxes, giving the stadium a continental touch. The large Toyota West Stand which runs down one side of the pitch is two tiered, complete with a row of executive boxes. The rest of the ground is smaller in size than the West Stand, as the roof drops a tier to the other sides, making it look unbalanced. It is a pity that the West Stand could not be replicated throughout the rest of the stadium as this would have made it truly magnificent. Outside the stadium on one corner is a statue of Brian Clough and Peter Taylor.

What Is It Like For Visiting Supporters?

Away fans are located at one end of the stadium in the Winfield Construction (South) Stand, where the allocation is 3,100, although this can be increased to 5,600, for cup games. The facilities within the stadium and view of the playing action are both very good. This coupled with normally a great atmosphere and a deafening PA system,

make for a memorable experience. I have visited Pride Park a number of times now and have found the Derby supporters to be friendly and have not experienced any problems.

Available on the concourse are a selection of Hollands Pies and Pasties, as well as Cheese-burgers, Burgers and 'Beechwood smoked' hot dogs. There is also a betting outlet too. There are televisions on the concourses showing the game going on inside, with commentary, so that you don't have to miss anything while waiting for your half-time cuppa.

Please note that you have to buy a match ticket before entering the stadium from the lottery office adjacent to the away turnstiles. I have received reports of away fans not being allowed entry into the stadium for being 'too drunk' in the opinion of the stewards, so be on your best behaviour. The teams emerge to 'White Riot' by the Clash.

Where To Drink?

Pete Stump informs me; 'On a recent visit, the police directed us to a Harvester about five minutes walk away from the stadium. It was full of away fans, however, we were told that they don't always admit visiting supporters'. The Navigation Inn on London Road, is also popular with away supporters.

There are a couple of pubs opposite the station, such as the Merry Widows, that tend to be the favourite haunts of away supporters. However, unless you are going to arrive mob handed, then it is probably best to turn right out of the station and make your way down to The Brunswick or Alexandra Hotel. Both these pubs have a railway theme, serving a great range of real ale. Although they both have bouncers on the doors away fans are normally let in as long as there is no singing. Alcohol is also made available to away fans inside the stadium.

Directions & Car Parking

From the M1, exit at Junction 25 and take the A52 towards Derby. The ground is signposted off the A52 after about seven miles. There is not a great deal of parking available around the stadium so it may an idea to park in the centre of town and then walk out to the ground. Kenny Lyon suggests; 'perhaps a better place to park for all fans is the cattle market car park. This costs £3 and is about 15-20 minute walk from the ground and is just off the A52. To get there, go past the normal turning for the stadium and go up to the 'pentagon roundabout'; take the first turning off there and then take the next left – you then drive about 300 yards back on yourself, passing it on your left as you drive along the A52'. Also around this area are a number of private businesses offering parking at around £5-£6 per car.

Steve Cocker informs me; 'There is free street parking available on Downing Road on the West Meadow Industrial Estate (DE21 6HA), which is off the A52. It is then about a 10-15 minute walk to the stadium. Make sure though that you get there in plenty of time before the kick-off, as the road fills up quickly'.

By Train

The ground is about a 10 minute walk away from Derby railway station and is signposted. A new exit has been opened at the station which leads directly onto the retail park, as Dave Plunkett adds; 'When you go up the stairs from the platform, turn right and walk to the end of the bridge. Go down the stairs, exit and turn right down Roundhouse Road. Bear left at the roundabout, go straight down Riverside Road or turn right and go down Pride Parkway where there are couple of places to eat and drink, including Old Orleans. You will reach the ground in front of you'.

If you want the pubs by the station, then turn left at the top of the stairs from the platform and on exiting the station entrance turn right. Further down on the right just past the Brunswick cross over the road and then descend some steps use the underpass, and follow the fans. The stadium is about a 20 minute walk in total from the station using this route.

Programme

Official Programme: £3

Record & Average Attendance

Record Attendance: 33,597 England v Mexico, Friendly, May 25th, 2001

For a Derby game at Pride Park: 33,475 v Glasgow Rangers, Friendly, May 1st, 2006

Average Attendance: 2011-12: 26,020 (Championship League)

Ground Name: Keepmoat Stadium

Capacity: 15,231 (All seated)

Address: Stadium Way, Lakeside, Doncaster, DN4 5JW

Main Telephone No: 01302 764 664

Ticket Office No: 01302 762 576

Year Ground Opened: 2007

Pitch Size: 109 x 76 yards

Team Nickname: Rovers

Home Kit Colours: Red & White

Official website: www.doncasterroversfc.co.uk

What's The Ground Like?

After 84 years of playing football at their old Belle Vue ground, the Club moved to the Keepmoat stadium, which was opened on January 1st 2007. The Keepmoat stadium cost £21 million to build and is also home to Doncaster Lakers Rugby League team as well as ladies football team Doncaster Belles. The stadium complex was built by and is owned by Doncaster Council.

To be honest the Keepmoat Stadium, in common with a number of new stadiums, looks far more interesting from the outside that it does on the inside. The stadium is situated next to a lake (which I believe makes Doncaster the only League ground to do so) and looks smart with four interesting looking floodlights, protruding at an angle from the stadium roof. However, on the inside the stadium is rather nondescript. Yes it looks tidy, the stadium is completely enclosed and all the covered stands are of the same height. But it lacks character and it is rather similar to other new stadiums that have been built, except that it is on a smaller scale.

On one side is the West Stand, which is the Main Stand, containing the teams' dressing rooms and having the players tunnel and team dugouts at its front. The primary television gantry is also housed on this side, along with press facilities. Opposite is the Doncaster Success Stand which contains a row of 16 executive boxes, outside which patrons can sit. These run across the back of the stand. Both ends are identical, with the North End of the ground being allocated to away fans.

Unusually the stadium has large access points in three corners of the ground, which can be used if need be, by emergency services. There are two small electric scoreboards situated in the North East & South West corners of the stadium. The stadium is completed with a set of four floodlights which are mounted on the roof in each corner.

What Is It Like For Visiting Supporters?

Away fans are located in the North Stand at one end of the stadium, where around 3,344 fans can be accommodated. Clubs with a smaller following will be allocated around a third to two thirds of that number meaning that on those occasions the end is shared with home supporters. The view of the playing action, leg room, and facilities in this stand are all good, although fans are set well back from the pitch as there is a substantial track which surrounds it. The concourses are a good size and there are a number of televisions on view to keep supporters entertained.

I found the stadium to be more atmospheric than the Belle Vue ground which was largely open to the elements. This is a bit unusual as most clubs that move to new grounds usually complain that the atmosphere suffers in the new arena, however, at the Keepmoat this is not the case. The stewarding was relaxed on my visit and no problems were experienced. The pitch also looked in top condition, although you could still see the lines of a previous rugby league game. Please note that cash is not accepted at the turnstiles, they are ticket only. Tickets can be purchased from the South Stand ticket office.

Where To Drink?

As the stadium is on the outskirts of town, then there is not much choice in the way of pubs. There is though the Lakeside, a Beefeater outlet near Stadium Way (you should catch sight of it, if you drive towards the stadium from Junction 3 of the M18). Chris Parkes, a visiting Nottingham Forest supporter informs me; 'I had no problems with getting a drink in the Lakeside Beefeater, in fact there were more Forest fans in there than home fans before the game'. Alcohol is also available inside the stadium.

Directions & Car Parking

From the A1(M) join the M18 Eastbound at Junction 35 (signposted Hull) or from the M1, join the M18 Eastbound at Junction 32.

Once on the M18, leave at Junction 3 and take the A6182 towards Doncaster (the stadium is well signposted from Junction 3 and is about one and a half miles away). You will pass a retail park on your left and then at the next island (which has the Lakeside Pub visible behind it) turn left onto White Rose Way. The Lakeside Shopping Centre is now on your right (the stadium is located directly behind the shopping centre). At the next island turn right onto the industrial estate and after passing the Tesco distribution centre on your right, turn right at the bottom of the road and the stadium is further down on your left.

There are just 1,000 car parking spaces at the stadium which cost £5. Alan Wilson adds; 'Having parked at the stadium it took me nearly an hour to get out of the car park and back onto the main road after the game had ended'. Alternatively, a number of firms on the nearby industrial park, offer matchday parking at around £3-£4 per vehicle. If you happen to arrive early then there is also some free street parking to be had in this area.

By Train

Doncaster Station is just under two miles away so you are probably best taking a taxi to the ground. If you do have time on your hands and you fancy the long walk (around 25-30 minutes) then as you come out of the station turn right and then keep straight on this road (the A6182 Trafford Way) and you will eventually reach the stadium complex on your left.

Colin Barrett informs me; 'There is a dedicated shuttle service from Doncaster Interchange bus station, which is adjacent the train, which commences two hours before kick-off. This is Route 75X and runs every 10 minutes direct to the Stadium. It leaves Stand C6 and the journey takes less than 10 minutes depending on traffic. Cost is £1.10 each way'.

Programme
Official Programme: £3

Record & Average Attendance
Record Attendance: 15,001 v Leeds United, League One, April 1st, 2008
Average Attendance: 2011-12: 9,341 (Championship League)

EVERTON

Ground Name: Goodison Park
Capacity: 40,569 (all seated)
Address: Goodison Road, Liverpool, L4 4EL
Main Telephone No: 0871 663 1878
Ticket Office No: 0871 663 1878

Year Ground Opened: 1892
Pitch Size: 112 x 78 yards
Team Nickname: The Toffees
Home Kit Colours: Royal Blue & White
Official website: www.evertonfc.com

What's The Ground Like?

Looking from the outside, Goodison, with its tall stands seems huge. The crowds filling the narrow streets around the ground on matchday, make you feel that you are going back in time, to when the outside of every football ground appeared like this. However, that's Goodison's problem. Apart from the modern Park Stand (which has an electric scoreboard on its roof and was opened in 1994), the rest of the ground looks tired. Yes the ground is still large, but it needs modernising. For example there are lots of supporting pillars and the ground just looks as if it has seen better days. Nevertheless unlike some new grounds, Goodison oozes character and the three-tiered Main Stand, which was opened in 1971, is still an impressive sight. There are two large video screens at opposite corners of the ground. If you are a home/neutral fan who is not scared of heights then try and get a ticket for the top balcony of the Main Stand. Not only do you get a 'birds eye' view of the game, but also views across Stanley Park, with Anfield in the distance. Now thinking about it if you were an Everton fan you probably wouldn't want to see Anfield during the game, so this advice is for neutrals!

A unique feature of the stadium is a church called St Lukes which sits just beyond one corner of the ground (selling teas & snacks at reasonable prices on matchdays). If you have time before the game look out for the statue behind the Park Stand; a tribute to the legend that was Dixie Dean. After all these years, the Everton team still come out to the theme tune of the old police series, Z-cars.

What Is It Like For Visiting Supporters?

Away fans are located in one corner of the two-tiered, Bullens Road Stand, which is at the side of the pitch, where just over 3,000 away fans can be accommodated. If a small following is expected, then only the lower tier is allocated, which holds 1,700. For larger followings the upper tier is also made available. If you can, try to avoid getting tickets for the rear sections of both the upper and lower tiers, as the view can be quite poor. For example, in the rear of the lower tier there are a number of supporting pillars that can hinder your view, the seating is of the old wooden type and the gap between rows is tight. The front of the lower tier is a lot better having newer seats and no supporting pillars to contend with.

The facilities within the stand are basic and it

is really showing its age (it was first opened in 1926). The concourse area is particularly small and can get quite cramped, especially at half-time. However, on the whole I have enjoyed a number of good days out at Goodison, especially as away supporters can really make some noise from the away section contributing to a great atmosphere. Outside the ground it was relaxed and friendly, with both sets of fans mixing freely before the game. Neil Thompson, a visiting Preston supporter adds; 'The stewards inside the ground were superb and the best I have seen at any ground. They just ran things with a sensible head and communicated with people, first class. There are lot of grounds that can learn from the Everton stewarding'.

Where To Drink?

About a 15 minute walk away from the visiting supporters' entrance, is the Thomas Frost pub on Walton Road. This Wetherspoon outlet, is a fair sized pub, that had a good mixture of home and away supporters, when I last visited. Rob Elmour adds; 'We found the Thomas Frost on Walton Road packed out, so we tried the Bradleys Wine Bar, which is just further down and across the road. It was very good. not a wine bar at all but a proper family run local with a good selection of beers including some real ales. Good mix of fans all very friendly. Alcohol is served in the away section of the ground, including beer from the Club's sponsors Chang.

Directions & Car Parking

Follow the M62 until you reach the end of the motorway (beware of a 50mph speed camera about a quarter of a mile from the end of the motorway). Then follow the A5058 towards Liverpool. After three miles turn left at the traffic lights into Utting Avenue (there is a McDonalds on the corner of this junction). Proceed for one mile and then turn right at the corner of Stanley Park into Priory Road. Goodison is at the end of this road.

If you arrive early (around 1pm) then there is street parking to be found around Walton Lane.

Otherwise park over towards Anfield or in Stanley Park itself (the entrance to the car park which costs £8, is in Priory Road).

By Train

Kirkdale station is the closest to the ground (just under a mile away). However, it may be more advisable to go to Sandhills Station as this has the benefit of a bus service to the ground, which runs for a couple of hours before the game and around 50 minutes after the final whistle. The bus which costs £1.50 return, drops you off within easy walking distance of Goodison.

Programme & Fanzine

Official Programme: £3

When Skies Are Grey Fanzine: £2

Record & Average Attendance

Record Attendance: 78,299 v Liverpool, Division One, September 18th, 1948.

Average Attendance: 2011-12: 33,228 (Premier League)

Ground Name: St James' Park
Capacity: 8,830 (3,800 Seated)
Address: Stadium Way, Exeter, Devon, EX4 6PX
Main Telephone No: 01392 411 243
Ticket Office No: Same as main number

Year Ground Opened: 1904
Pitch Size: 114 x 73 yards
Team Nickname: The Grecians
Home Kit Colours: Red & White Stripes
Official website: www.exetercityfc.co.uk

What's The Ground Like?

The ground is a mixture of the old and the modern. On one side is the old Grandstand that was originally opened in 1926. It is all seated, covered and has windshields to either side. However, it is in size about half the length of the pitch and although part of it straddles the halfway line, it mostly sits to one side towards the St James' Terrace End. This means that the area to the other side of stand is open and apart from a row of floodlight pylons is unused for spectators. Although not readily apparent from inside the ground, this is due to the very close proximity of a railway line, running behind this side of the ground. The Grandstand also has an unusual set of small floodlights aligned along the front of its roof that protrude at an awkward angle.

Opposite is the Flybe Stand which is the newest addition to the ground and was opened in 2001. This smart looking all seater stand, is single-tiered, with some executive boxes located in the middle to the rear. It has the players tunnel and team dug outs situated at its front. At one end is the 'Big Bank' covered terrace, which was opened in February 2000 and replaced a former open terrace. This stand is quite impressive

looking and with a capacity of just under 4,000, means it is now the largest terrace left in the Football League. Unusually both the Flybe & Big Bank Stands, have an open gap between the roof and back of the stands. The other end is a very small open terrace, called the St James' Road terrace. This terrace which is given to away supporters extends around one corner towards the Grandstand. It is that small, you can clearly see a row of houses that sit beyond it, from which the residents get a great view of the game!

What Is It Like For Visiting Supporters?

Away fans are mostly housed in the St James' Road terrace at one end of the ground, where just over 1,000 fans can be accommodated. In addition the Club make 150 seats available to visiting supporters in the Grandstand. The facilities in both these areas are basic. The views from the St James' Road terrace are not great as due to its limited size fans are situated quite low down and close to the pitch. It is also does not have a cover and is open to the elements. Although the Grandstand is covered, it does have some supporting pillars running across its front which may affect your view. I personally have enjoyed my visits to St James' Park, with no problems experienced.

Where To Drink?

There is a Social Club at the ground itself, which allows in away supporters. Close to the stadium is the Wells Tavern on Well Street, which is popular with away fans.

Otherwise, the ground is walkable from the city centre where there are plenty of pubs. Mike Faulkner from Somerset, recommends the Duke Of York and the Amber Rooms in Sidwell Street. Tony Fort recommends 'The Victoria' on Victoria Road (follow Victoria Street from the back of the Grandstand). As Tony says 'You can park here (for free) but it is a good 10-15 minutes walk from the ground and steep! The pub is great, very "studenty", but full of friendly Exeter supporters. Both the food and ale were excellent both from a quality and value perspective'. While Mick Hubbard adds; 'We walked on from the city centre towards the ground and, instead of following Old Tiverton Road which leads to the ground, we forked right, up Blackboy Road and stopped at the Bowling Green pub, which is about a quarter of a mile from the ground. We enjoyed this pub very much – good beer (i.e. proper ale), comfortable and quite airy, very friendly (locals were hospitable and fans of both clubs mixed amicably) and a separate pool table for those so inclined. A definite recommendation'.

Directions & Car Parking

Leave the M5 at Junction 30 and follow signs for Exeter city centre along Sidmouth Road (A379) and then onto Rydon Lane (A3015). Take the Sidmouth Road turn off (B3183) towards the city centre. Keep going towards the town centre as the road becomes Heavitree Road. On nearing the city centre take the fourth exit at the large roundabout onto Western Way. At the next roundabout take the second exit onto Old Tiverton Road, then turn left into St James Road for the ground. There is street parking, but quite a way from the ground as there is a local residents scheme in operation.

By Train

The nearest railway station is St James Park, which is adjacent to the ground and only a short walk away, However, this station is on a local line and most fans will arrive first into the mainline stations of Exeter St Davids or Exeter Central, from which you can then get a local train to St James Park.

Exeter Central is the closer of the two mainline stations and is just under a mile away from the ground and should take around 20 minutes to walk. As you come out of the main station entrance, turn left and proceed along Queen Street. As the road bends around to the right, continue straight on along the pedestrianised area. At the end of this area (where it meets the High Street) turn left and then continue along Sidwell Street. After the roundabout turn left into St James' Road for the ground.

Programme

Official Programme: £3

Record & Average Attendance

Record Attendance: 21,014 v Sunderland, FA Cup 6th Round Replay, March 4th, 1931.

Average Attendance: 2011-12: 4,474 (League One)

FLEETWOOD TOWN

Ground Name: Highbury Stadium
Capacity: 5,094 (Seats 2,550)
Address: Park Avenue, Fleetwood,
Lancashire FY7 6TX
Main Telephone No: 01253 770702
Ticket Office No: Same as main number

Year Ground Opened: 1939
Pitch Size: 112 x 74 yards
Team Nickname: Cod Army
Home Kit Colours: Red and White
Official website: www.fleetwoodtownfc.com

What's The Ground Like?

The stadium is modern having been completely rebuilt over the last five years, matching the team's meteoric rise up the leagues with five promotions in seven seasons. The latest addition to the ground is the very impressive looking Parkside Stand which was first opened to spectators in March 2011. This 2,000 capacity all seated stand was built at a cost of around £4 million. It has a single tier of seating, while above are offices and a top row of executive boxes and hospitality area, all of which have a small tier of seating outside. These are covered by a semicircular roof, with large glassed areas to either side which allow light to get to the pitch. At the front of this stand are the team dugouts.

Opposite is the Highbury Stand, which is a small all-seated covered stand, which was opened in 2008. It is only six rows high, has a capacity of 550 and runs for only half the length of the pitch, meaning that there is a large open area next to it, although this area does feature some buildings. On the roof of the Highbury Stand is a small television gantry. For the 'eagle eyed' then directly behind it you can see a small roof which is the roof

of the old Main Stand which is still in existence having had the new stand built in front of it. It just shows how much the stadium has come on, when you consider that at one time there was this stand and not much else at the ground.

Both ends are covered terraces, which are similar in size in terms of height. The Percy Ronson Terrace which is given to away supporters, runs for around two thirds of the width of the pitch. While the home end, the Memorial Stand (named in memory of the service and trawlermen who have previously lost their lives from the port of Fleetwood) is larger, extending the full width of the pitch and housing just under 1,500 supporters. In one corner of the stadium between the Parkside and Memorial Stands is a large video screen. The stadium is completed with a set of modern floodlights.

What Is It Like For Visiting Supporters?

Away fans are mostly housed in the Percy Ronson terrace at one end of the stadium, where 831 fans can be accommodated. This terrace which was opened in 2007, is covered, free from supporting pillars and affords a good view of the playing action. The terrace capacity also includes an open flat standing area on the Highbury Stand side.

Visiting supporters are also allocated 300 seats in the Parkside Stand and this can be increased if required. The facilities in this stand are far better than the terrace with alcoholic drinks available to purchase and there are large screens on the concourse showing Sky Sports. For teams with a smaller following then only the Parkside seats will be made available and not the Percy Ronson Terrace.

If you are feeling hungry then apart from the catering inside, there is a handy fish and chip shop, located across the road from the ground in Highbury Avenue.

Where To Drink?

There is Jim's Sports Bar at the ground, which admits away fans. The facilities in this bar are excellent, but get there early as it is bound to be very popular on matchdays. It is located at the back of the Memorial Stand and can be accessed from the park pathway that runs along that side of the ground. The Highbury Club which is located adjacent to the away turnstiles does not allow in visiting supporters. Martin Crimp a visiting Southport fan informs me; 'We were directed to the Queens Hotel, on Poulton Road, about a 15 minute walk away. It has Sky Sports on multi screens along with a decent pint of Thwaites. Go up Highbury Avenue then left at the St Nicholas church into Poulton Road. The Queens is about 300 yards along this road on the left.'

Otherwise it is probably best to take the 10-15 minute stroll into Fleetwood itself (on leaving the stadium entrance go up to the main road and turn left) where there are plenty of pubs to be found. My choice would be the Wetherspoon outlet the Thomas Drummond on London Street (off Lord Street) which is listed in the CAMRA Good Beer Guide. About the same distance away is the Strawberry Gardens pub on Poulton Road. This is owned by the local Fuzzy Duck brewery and features beers from that brewery as well as guest ales. Alcohol is also available inside the stadium

but only to away fans who have seating tickets in the Parkside Stand.

Directions & Car Parking

Leave the M6 at Junction 32 and take the M55 towards Blackpool. Then leave the M55 at Junction 3 and take the A585 towards Fleetwood. On the outskirts of Fleetwood you will come to a roundabout with Blackpool and Fylde college on your left. Continue straight on towards Fleetwood but after the roundabout take the first left into Copse Road. After about a mile and as you pass Fleetwood Fire station on your left then branch left and turn left onto to Radcliffe Road (going back on yourself but in parallel with Copse Road).Then take the next right into Stanley Road and the stadium is at the bottom of this road on your left. There is no parking for away supporters at the stadium itself but there is plenty of street parking available in the area.

By Train

There is no railway station in Fleetwood itself. The closest is at Poulton-le-Fylde, which is just over five miles away. However, it is more likely that fans will head to Blackpool North station which is around seven miles away. A taxi from the station to Fleetwood will cost you the best part of £20, which may okay if there is a group of you. For smaller groups it may be better to catch a bus to Fleetwood, Service numbers 1 and 14, run from Blackpool to Fleetwood.

Programme

Official Programme: £3

Record & Average Attendance

Record Attendance: 5,092 v Blackpool, FA Cup 3rd Round, January 7th, 2012.

Average Attendance: 2011-12: 2,265 (Blue Square Premier)

FLEETWOOD TOWN

Ground Name: Craven Cottage
Capacity: 25,678 (all seated)
Address: Stevenage Road, London, SW6 6HH
Main Telephone No: 0843 208 1222
Ticket Office No: 0843 208 1234

Year Ground Opened: 1896
Pitch Size: 109 x 71 yards
Team Nickname: The Cottagers or The Whites
Home Kit Colours: White With Black Trim
Official website: www.fulhamfc.com

What's The Ground Like?

On one side of the ground is the Stevenage Road Stand, which has been renamed the Johnny Haynes Stand after the former Fulham great. It previously had terracing at the front, but this has now been made all seated. The stand was originally was opened in 1905. Considering its age, it can be forgiven for having a number of supporting pillars and old wooden seating in its upper tier. It does though have a fine classic looking gable on its roof; labelled Fulham Football Club.

Opposite is the aptly named Riverside Stand which sits on the banks of the River Thames. This all seated, covered stand was opened in 1972. It has a row of executive boxes running across the back of it and also houses a television gantry. Overlooking the ground from one corner, between the Johnny Haynes Stand and Putney End, is the unique Pavilion building, which many fans refer to as 'the Cottage' (although this is technically incorrect as the original cottage after which the ground is named, was demolished many years ago). This looks somewhat misplaced being more reminiscent of a small cricket pavilion, rather than something found at a football ground, but it does add to the overall character.

Both ends which were previously terraced have now been replaced by two new large all seated, covered stands, that look fairly similar in design. They both though have some supporting pillars which is disappointing. Attached to these stands in three corners of the ground are some three storey structures that are used to house corporate executive boxes. An unusual feature is that the teams enter the field from one corner of the ground, by the Cottage and then make their way up onto the pitch as it is raised. Outside the stadium alongside Stevenage Road is the Johnny Haynes Statue, while outside the Hammersmith End overlooking the River Thames is a statue of Michael Jackson, which was paid for by the owner of the Club, Mohamed Al Fayed.

What Is It Like For Visiting Supporters?

Away fans are housed to one side of the Putney End Stand, on the river side of the ground. The stand is shared with home and neutral supporters, with away fans being allocated around 3,000 seats. There are a couple of supporting pillars that could impede your view, but this only applies to certain seats in Row DD and above. The leg room is ample and as the rows of the stand seem to have been constructed from metal and plywood, rather than concrete, fans can't resist making some noise, by stamping up and down on it.

Food and drink are served from a number of outlets and stalls situated behind the stands. These areas although mostly covered are not enclosed, which is great in the Summer but can be rather cold in Winter. However, if you go to the outlets around to the left of the stand then you can enjoy some nice views of the Thames, while having your beer.

Where To Drink?

Near to the tube station is the Eight Bells which is popular with away fans. While the Crabtree on Rainville Road, normally has a pleasant mix of both home and away supporters.

Directions & Car Parking

From the North M1

At the end of the M1, turn right (west) onto the A406 (North Circular) and follow it towards Harrow for nearly four and a half miles. Turn left (east) onto the A40 heading into London (passing close to Loftus Road and after a little over four miles turn right (west) onto the A402 for just about 350 yards. Here you turn left (south) along the A219 for a little over half a mile. This brings you into Hammersmith where you turn right onto the A315 and then after just 130 yards or so turn left (south) back onto the A219. Follow this road for a little over a mile, and the ground is down the side streets off to your right.

From The North M40 & West M25

Leave the M25 at Junction 15 and take the M4, which then becomes the A4, towards Central London. After around two miles branch off left into Hammersmith Broadway (before the flyover). Go around the ring road around central Hammersmith, keeping to the right. Then take the A219 Fulham Palace Road. Keep straight on this road, passing Charing Cross Hospital on your left. After about another half a mile turn right into Crabtree Lane for the ground.

Parking close to the ground can be quite difficult as Jim Huegett informs me; 'please note that parking on the streets near to the ground is restricted to one hour 'pay & display' on match-days. This isn't obvious from the parking meters and signage and the wardens are out in force on match day'. To compound matters these restrictions are also in place for Bank Holidays, Sundays and evenings up to 9.30pm, so it will be a case of finding some parking further away from the stadium.

By Tube

The nearest London Underground station is Putney Bridge, which is on the District Line. The ground is about a 15 minute walk away. Turn left out of the station and then immediately turn right into a street called Ranelagh Gardens. As the road bends around to the right you will see the Eight Bells pub on your right. Turn left after the pub to take you up to the main road by Putney Bridge. Cross over to the other side of the main road and proceed up to the bridge and then on reaching the bridge turn right to enter into Bishops Park alongside the Thames. Just proceed through the park (keeping the Thames on your left) and you will reach the ground ahead.

Programme & Fanzine

Official Programme: £3
One F In Fulham Fanzine: £2

Record & Average Attendance

Record Attendance: 49,335 v Millwall, Division Two, October 8th, 1938.
Average Attendance: 2011-12: 25,293 (Premier League)

Ground Name: MEMS Priestfield Stadium
Capacity: 11,582 (all seated)
Address: Redfern Ave, Gillingham, Kent, ME7 4DD
Main Telephone No: 01634 300 000
Ticket Office No: Same as main number

Year Ground Opened: 1893
Pitch Size: 114 x 75 yards
Team Nickname: The Gills
Home Kit Colours: Blue With White Trim
Official website: www.gillinghamfootballclub.com

What's The Ground Like?

Priestfield Stadium has been virtually rebuilt since the current Chairman Paul Scally took over in 1995. On one side of the ground is the impressive looking Medway Stand. Opened in 2000, it is two-tiered, with a large lower tier and a small upper tier. In between these tiers are a row of executive boxes, which also have seating outside. Opposite is the Gordon Road Stand. Opened in 1997, this is a much smaller single-tiered stand, which is partly covered (to the rear). It contains a number of supporting pillars running across the back of it, plus it also has an unusual looking TV gantry perched on its roof. The Rainham End was opened in 1999. It is a single tier cantilevered stand, which replaced a former terrace. Opposite is the Brian Moore Stand. This is in fact a temporary seated stand that has been situated on top of an existing terrace. When I say temporary (considering that it has been there since 2003) I mean that the stand can be easily dismantled and reassembled. This is the only open area at the stadium. This stand is named in memory of the legendary commentator and lifelong Gills fan, Brian Moore.

What Is It Like For Visiting Supporters?

Away fans are housed in the Brian Moore Stand where around 3,400 supporters can be accommodated. Like last season the stand is of the temporary variety i.e. the type that you would see around the 18th hole at the British Open Golf Championship, although it is of a good size and height (you can get some great views of the surrounding area at the very top of it), plus the views of the playing action are fine. Unlike most temporary stands though the facilities are surprisingly good, being of a permanent nature behind the structure. However, it is uncovered, so although the Club hand out free rain macs if it rains, still be prepared to get wet! The absence of a roof also dampens the atmosphere somewhat, although fans do try to make some noise by stamping on the metal rows of the stand. One unusual aspect of visiting Priestfield Stadium is that away supporters have to walk down a very narrow terraced street to reach the away entrance, or if coming from adjacent streets down very tight alleyways. However, there are never normally any problems with this although after the game the Police sometimes close of some of the surrounding streets to keep fans apart.

Where To Drink?

The ground is walkable from the town centre, where there are a fair few pubs to be found. Paul Kelly, a visiting Preston fan adds; 'we have used the Will Adams in the town centre. The pub is in the good beer guide and does good cheap food. Plus a very friendly crowd of football locals happy to indulge in friendly banter – the landlord is a Gill fan too!' Robert Donaldson recommends the Southern Belle opposite the railway station, which also has a cafe located next door.

Michelle Dixon, the landlady of the Livingstone Arms on Gillingham Road informs me; 'Our pub is known as an "Away Supporters" pub and is situated approximately 100 yards from the away turnstiles. The atmosphere within the pub is both warm and friendly'. This pub which also has a beer garden, is popular with both away and home supporters and as you would expect it gets rather busy on matchdays. There is a handy fish & chip shop, situated across the road from the pub.

Directions & Car Parking

Leave the M2 at Junction 4 and take the A278 towards Gillingham, going straight across two roundabouts. At the third roundabout turn left onto the A2 towards Gillingham town centre. At the traffic light junction with the A231, turn right into Nelson Road and passing the small bus station take a right turn into Gillingham Road, the ground is down on your right.

Alternatively Roger Blackman provides an alternative route from the M2; 'At the start of the M2 keep left and follow the A289 towards Gillingham. Continue towards Gillingham and go through the Medway Tunnel (Priestfield Stadium is signposted from here). Continue on the A289 ignoring the turn off for Gillingham town centre, until you reach the Strand roundabout after about a mile. Turn right at this roundabout and up the hill and over the level crossing. Take the second left past the level crossing into Linden Road and the ground is along this road on the right'.

There is a residents only parking scheme in operation around the ground, so if you want to street park, this will mean driving a bit further away to do so. Chris Bell, a visiting Northampton Town fan adds; 'There is a cheap pay and display car park (£1.40 for four hours) on Railway Street near Gillingham station, which is less than 10 mins walk from the ground'.

By Train

The ground is about a 10 minute walk away from Gillingham railway station, which is served by trains from London Victoria (every 15 mins), Charing Cross (every 30 mins), St Pancras and Stratford International (both located on the same line, every 30 mins). It is worth noting that the quickest trains leave from St Pancras (journey time around 45 mins) and Stratford International (journey time 37 mins).

Robert Donaldson provides the following directions; 'Turn left out of the station and follow the road until you come to a crossroads. Go straight on into Priestfield Road. The visitors turnstiles are at the far end of Priestfield Road. Allow 10 minutes to get from the station and into the ground'.

Programme

Official Programme: £3

Record & Average Attendance

Record Attendance: 23,002 v Queens Park Rangers, FA Cup 3rd Round, January 10th, 1948.

Average Attendance: 2011-12: 5,146 (League Two)

Ground Name: Victoria Park
Capacity: 7,787 (Seats 4,180)
Address: Clarence Road, Hartlepool, TS24 8BZ
Main Telephone No: 01429 272 584
Ticket Office No: As main number

Year Ground Opened: 1908
Pitch Size: 113 x 77 yards
Team Nickname: The Pool
Home Kit Colours: Blue & White Stripes
Official website: www.hartlepoolunited.co.uk

What's The Ground Like?

Victoria Park is a traditional compact ground that was greatly improved in the mid 1990s, with the construction of two new stands at one end and at one side. One of these the Cyril Knowles Stand (named after a former manager) was opened in 1995. It is a small single tier covered all seated stand, raised above the ground level. The other modern stand is the Town End which opened shortly afterwards. It is a covered terrace that is the home end. Opposite is the Rink End Stand which is a small covered all seated stand which houses away supporters. On the remaining side is the Niramax Stand that has covered seating to the rear and open terrace to the front. This stand does not run the full length of the pitch and has an odd mix of orange and green seating, that clashes with the club colours. It was opened in 1968. The ground has a set of four tall traditional floodlight pylons.

What Is It Like For Visiting Supporters?

Ben Fuggles advised me to 'bring a jumper even in August!'. He was right. The wind whipping the North Sea goes right through you, so wrap up well unless there is a heat wave. Away fans are in the Rink End Stand at one end of the ground, where up to 967 can be seated. Unfortunately there are a few supporting pillars in this stand, which may hinder your view, especially if there is a large away following. However, acoustics are good even for small numbers.

If you wonder why Hartlepool are referred to as the 'Monkey Hangers' then it is because the residents of Hartlepool are famously said to have hanged a monkey that was washed up from a ship that had sunk during the Napoleonic wars, because they thought the monkey was a French spy. The Club take this to good heart and of course who else would they have as their club mascot? H'Angus the monkey of course!

Where To Drink?

The Victoria Suite near the entrance to the away end is for members only. At the same end but at the opposite corner, is the 'Corner Flag Supporters Bar' that welcomes away fans. The entrance fee is 50p, but this basic bar has a good friendly pre match atmosphere and SKY TV, however, it does not serve any food. Popular with away fans is the Jackson's Wharf Pub near the ground. It has good food and real ale on tap. This pub is over the road from the ASDA store, to the left of the old sailing ship. Otherwise the ground is not far from the town centre where there are plenty of pubs to be found.

Ronnie Chambers adds; 'The Engineers Social Club five minutes from the ground opposite the police station, just off the town centre is okay, as is the Raglan Club just behind the visitors end. Usual club rules apply regarding entry for these'.

Directions & Car Parking

From the A19 take the A689 towards Hartlepool. Stay on this road following the Town Centre signs for 2.8 miles, over two roundabouts. Go straight over the next two sets of traffic lights, passing Hartlepool College on your right. The next left takes you to the stadium. If you miss the turning (as I did), go past ASDA on your left, left at the next roundabout and then turn left at the next set of traffic lights for the ground. There is a fair sized car park at the ground. Otherwise there is some street parking albeit a bit of a distance away, as a residents only parking scheme is in operation on matchdays around the ground.

By Train

Hartlepool railway station is a 10 minute walk from the ground. Leave the station and go straight up a short approach road. At the end of the approach, turn right and head up Church Street towards the large church. At the end of this road is a bridge and junction with the A689. Go straight across the junction and the ground is in front of you on the left-hand side of the road. Thanks to Richard Brackstone for providing the directions.

Programme & Fanzine

Official Programme: £2.50
Monkey Business Fanzine: £1

Record & Average Attendance

Record Attendance: 17,426 v Manchester United, FA Cup 3rd Round, January 5th, 1957.
Average Attendance: 2011-12: 4,961 (League One)

Ground Name: Galpharm Stadium
Capacity: 24,500 (all seated)
Address: Galpharm Stadium, Huddersfield, HD1 6PX
Main Telephone No: 0870 444 4677
Ticket Office No: 01484 484123

Year Ground Opened: 1994
Pitch Size: 115 x 76 yards
Team Nickname: The Terriers
Home Kit Colours: Blue And White Stripes
Official website: www.htafc.com

What's The Ground Like?

The club moved the short distance to the then called Alfred McAlpine Stadium in 1994 after leaving their former Leeds Road ground, their home for 86 years. When the stadium originally opened it had just three sides with the North Stand being opened later in 1997. In 2004 it was renamed the Galpharm Stadium in a new sponsorship deal with Galpharm Healthcare. Most new stadiums in this country are rather boring affairs with little character, but the Galpharm does not fall into this category. Each stand is semicircular rather than rectangular, and is further enhanced with large white steel tubing above the contours. In fact from the car park I first thought it looked like a new ride at Alton Towers! It is good to see something different from the architects for a change. The ground has won many design awards and is well worth a visit. The only disappointment is that the corners of the ground are open. The FNorth Stand at one end and the Direct Golf UK (Riverside) Stand at one side are both two-tiered stands, each with a row of executive boxes running across the middle. The other two sides of the ground are large single-tiered affairs. One of these the Britannia Rescue Stand, at one side of the pitch, can accommodate 7,000 supporters. There is an electric scoreboard at the back of the away end. The stadium is completed with a striking set of four floodlights. The stadium is shared with Huddersfield Giants Rugby League Club.

What Is It Like For Visiting Supporters?

Away fans are located at one end of the ground in the South Stand, where up to 4,000 supporters can be accommodated. The facilities in this stand and the view of the playing action are both good. There is also a betting outlet and a bar serving alcoholic drinks at the back of the stand, which if you can't bear to watch your team during the game, you can always escape to, as the bar remains open during the first half and half-time. I have enjoyed my visits to the Glapharm Stadium. I have been thoroughly impressed with the stadium and the general set-up.

Where To Drink?

Robert Smith recommends the Bradley Mills Working Mens Club and Rickys Bar, both of which are located on Leeds Road, about five-ten minutes walk from the Stadium. There is also a cinema and entertainment complex behind the North Stand, where there is the Rope Walk pub. However, on my last visit all of the above bars were not allowing in away fans, although I did manage to get into the Rope Walk Pub (I was not wearing colours), where I enjoyed an excellent pint. Dougie Hames recommends the Gas Club on Gasworks Street; 'all fans and families are welcome. Bass beers, food available and you can also park in the patrolled club car park at a cost of £2. The club is easy to find as it is right by the large gas holder'. While Tim Oscroft informs me; 'The Head of Steam pub at the railway station is pretty good and serves food too'. Alcohol is also available inside the stadium.

Directions & Car Parking
The stadium is just off the A62 Leeds Road. It can be easiest reached from Junction 25 of the M62, simply follow the signs for Huddersfield (A62) and you will come to the stadium on your left. Alternatively, if approaching from the South, then leave the M1 at Junction 38 and take the A637 towards and then the A642 into Huddersfield. As you approach the town centre try to keep to the right-hand lane as you will turn right at the roundabout and onto the A62 Leeds Road. The stadium is a short distance down this road on the right. For the car parks turn right at the traffic lights, where the Market Pub is on the corner. The stadium is generally well signposted around Huddersfield town centre. There is a fair sized car park located at the ground (£5) and a number of unofficial car parks nearby (expect to pay around £3-£4).

By Train
The ground is walkable from Huddersfield train station, it should take no more than 15 minutes at a comfortable pace. After coming out of the Railway Station, turn down past the front of The George Hotel. Go straight over the crossroads into Northumberland Street and walk down across the Ring Road straight on into Leeds Road. Turn right down Gasworks Street. Straight over the cross-roads to the ground.

Programme
Official Programme: £3.

Record & Average Attendance
Record Attendance: 23,678 v Liverpool, FA Cup 3rd Round, December 12th, 1999.

Average Attendance: 2011-12: 14,145 (League One)

Ground Name: KC Stadium
Capacity: 25,404 (all seated)
Address: The Circle, Walton Street, Hull, HU3 6HU
Main Telephone No: 01482 504 600
Ticket Office No: 01482 505 600

Year Ground Opened: 2002
Pitch Size: 114 x 78 yards
Team Nickname: The Tigers
Home Kit Colours: Amber & Black
Official website: www.hullcityafc.net

What's The Ground Like?

The Club moved to the KC Stadium in December 2002 after leaving their former Boothferry Park home where they had been resident for 56 years. It cost almost £44 million to build, by Birse Construction and is home to both Hull Football & Rugby League Clubs. I'm not a fan of most of the bland new grounds, but the KC Stadium is an exception to this rule. Built in a parkland setting, the stadium can be seen for some distance around and has won a number of awards for its impressive design.

The stadium is totally enclosed, with the West Stand being around twice the size of the other three sides. The roof rises up and curves around the West Stand, giving the stadium an interesting look. Inside the curves continue as each of the stands slightly bow around the playing area, drawing the eye to sweep panoramically around them. Apart from the West Stand, each of the other three stands is single-tiered. The West Stand also benefits from having a row of executive boxes running across its middle. There is a large video screen at the North End of the stadium, where the Police Control Box is also situated. The PA system within the stadium is also excellent.

What Is It Like For Visiting Supporters?

Away fans are located in the North Stand End of the ground, where up to 4,000 supporters can be housed, although the normal allocation is half that number. The facilities available are good, plus there is not a bad view of the playing action to be found anywhere (although you are a little set back from the pitch). On the concourse alcohol is available, plus burgers, Hollands pies etc. I found the atmosphere to be good within the stadium, but unfortunately there is an element of Hull support that feel the need to berate away supporters throughout the game, which was somewhat unsavoury.

Dave Winsor, a visiting Nottingham Forest fan adds; 'Our seats were roomy and comfortable with a raised behind the goal view. Plenty of leg room and helpful stewards along with a nice fat matchday programme and a really good selection of food and drink from the concourse all contributed to the favourable impression. An interesting ground with much more to it than the usual depressing flat pack stadium of some other designs'. Phil, a visiting West Ham United fan tells me; 'The stadium is great with good facilities on the concourse. I was located right at the back of the away section and the view was very good with no obstructions'.

Please note that the stadium has been designated a no standing area, which on the face of it seems a little ridiculous. This has led to some unpleasant confrontations between away fans and stewards, so you have been warned.

Where To Drink?

Tim Jones, a visiting Aston Villa supporter informs me; 'The Brickmakers pub virtually opposite the stadium car park entrance allows in away fans. It has a good atmosphere and the Hull fans there were friendly. It also has a big screen showing Sky Sports and a burger van outside'. While fellow Villa fan Neil Tate adds; 'There is also the nearby Walton Street Social Club that also admits away supporters. Although it costs £1 to go in, it has good cheap beer, is of a good size and offers a separate area for sale of food such as burgers and chips etc. There were plenty of fellow Villa fans in there during our recent visit. Turn right out of the main car park entrance and it is down the road on the left-hand side'.

Otherwise alcohol is available within the stadium. However, for some high profile matches, the club do not provide alcohol to away supporters.

Directions & Car Parking
From The West:

At the end of the M62, continue onto the A63 towards Hull. Stay on the A63 and the stadium is clearly signposted (KC Stadium and a football symbol) as you approach Hull. About one mile from the centre of Hull leave the A63 (just after you pass B&Q on the opposite side of the carriageway and is signposted Local Infirmary) and take the 2nd exit at the roundabout. Turn left at the lights and then over the flyover, right at the next lights and the ground is down on the right.

From The North:

Leave the A164 at the Humber Bridge Roundabout and take the first exit into Boothferry Road. The stadium is three miles down this road on the left.

Jo Johnson informs me; 'The stadium has its own massive car park right next to the stadium, with access from Walton Street. It is floodlit, with a covered surface and open to home and away supporters alike. The cost of parking at the stadium is £5. However, there is one drawback, namely, getting away again at the end of the game. It can take up to half an hour or more, if you park a long way from the exits'.

Alternatively there is a Park & Ride facility signposted off the A63 (shared with home supporters). Many fans opt to park in one of the many town centre car parks and then walk out to the stadium.

By Train

The Stadium is around a 20 minute walk away from Hull Paragon station. Turn left at the end of the railway station platform and then left into the bus station (without going outside the station). Exit the bus station at the far end. Walk past Tesco on your right, cross over Park Street at the traffic lights. Following blue pedestrian signs to the KC Stadium, go along Londisborough Street (where there is a handy fish and chip shop). Cross Argyle Street and onto the pedestrian walkway and bridges over railway lines to the stadium. For the away end turn right at the bottom of steps. Thanks to Brian Scott a visiting Ipswich Town supporter for the directions.

Programme
Official Programme: £3

Record & Average Attendance
Record Attendance: 25,030 v Liverpool, Premier League, May 10th, 2010.
Average Attendance: 2011-12: 18,790 (Championship League)

Ground Name: Portman Road
Capacity: 30,300 (all seated)
Address: Portman Road, Ipswich, IP1 2DA
Main Telephone No: 01473 400 500
Ticket Office No: 0844 8011 555

Year Ground Opened: 1888
Pitch Size: 112 x 70 yards
Team Nickname: Blues or Tractor Boys
Home Kit Colours: Blue & White
Official website: www.itfc.co.uk

What's The Ground Like?

The overall look of the ground has greatly improved, with the redevelopment of both ends. Both these ends, the South Stand and the Sir Bobby Robson Stand, are similar in appearance and size, and dwarf the smaller older stands, located on each side of the ground. Unusually, both ends have a larger upper tier which over-hangs slightly the smaller lower tier. Both have windshields to either side of the upper tier and they are completed, with some spectacular floodlights perched on their roofs. They were both fully opened a year apart in 2001 and 2002. The South Stand was originally called the Churchmans Stand in reference to the Churchmans Cigarette factory which used to be located behind that end of the stadium.

Both sides are much older stands and now look quite tired in comparison. On one side, the fair sized Britannia Stand is a three-tiered covered stand, with a row of executive boxes running across its middle. This stand was originally opened in 1957 and was then known as the West Stand. In 1984 an additional tier was added along with a new roof. Opposite is the smaller Cobbold Stand. Again it is two-tiered and has a row of executive

boxes. However, it is only partly covered, with the small lower tier of seating being open to the elements. This stand which was first opened in 1971 and was originally called the Portman Stand. It was later renamed the Cobbold Stand in respect of the Cobbold family who were former owners of the club and old Suffolk brewers Tolly-Cobbold. Unusually the teams emerge onto the field from one corner of the ground between the South and Britannia Stands. Outside are two statues of two former Ipswich and England managers. One is of World Cup winner Sir Alf Ramsey and is located on the corner between the Cobbold and Sir Bobby Robson Stand, while Sir Bobby Robson's statue is placed behind the Cobbold stand in Portman Road.

What Is It Like For Visiting Supporters?

Away fans are placed on one side of the upper tier of the Cobbold Stand at one side of the pitch, where up to 1,900 away supporters can be accommodated. Although the views from this area are generally not too bad (unless you are at the very back of the stand where there are some supporting pillars), the leg room is rather cramped and as with the rest of the stand the facilities are beginning to show their age. On the plus side, away fans can really make some noise from this area, contributing to a good atmosphere. Stewarding was fairly strict, with fans at the front of the upper tier being asked to keep seated (while those at the back were allowed to stand) and on my last visit a few fans were ejected for smoking (okay they should known better, but a warning first would have been more fair in my book). The concourses offer among the normal range of Pies & Pasties, the tasty Portman Steak & Ale Pie. The stand also has one of the poshest gents toilets that I have visited at a football ground (this was one of the two toilet blocks on the upper concourse). They wouldn't have looked out of place at a hotel. Normally a friendly day out.

Where To Drink?

The main away supporters pub is the Station Hotel, which as the name suggests is located close to the railway station which is only a five minute walk away from Portman Road. Otherwise the Punch & Judy pub on Cardinal Park, which is close to the ground has also been recommended to me as a pub which is family orientated and where both sets of fans can enjoy a drink. If you arrive in good time then you can take the walk into the town centre where there are plenty of pubs to be found. Otherwise alcohol is on sale inside the ground including Adnams Bitter, Carlsberg Lager and Aspall Suffolk Cyder. Please note that alcohol is not available to away fans at half -time.

Directions & Car Parking

Follow the A14 around Ipswich from which the ground is well signposted. The official route takes you from the A14 onto the A1214 into Ipswich. I though prefer to leave at the next junction and take the A137. Stay straight on this road straight into Ipswich and as you cross the bridge over the river, stay in the left-hand lane (marked town centre). Once over the river turn left at the roundabout (signposted Colchester/Bury St Edmunds) passing the Punch & Judy pub on your right. Continue along this road as it bends to the left into Commercial Road, you should be able to

see the Portman Road floodlights over to your right. Move into the right-hand filter lane (marked town centre) and continue to follow the road around to the right. As you reach Fitness First move over to the left-hand lane and at the traffic lights turn left into Princes Road. Take the next left into Portman Road itself for the ground.

As the ground is near to the town centre there is very little free street parking. Along Portman Road there are three Pay & Display car parks which cost £4.60 for a Saturday afternoon. For evening games it is less as the car parks are free after 8pm, just pay for the relevant number of hours up to then. There are a number of other car parks located in the town centre which are signposted, plus there is a NCP multi storey car park located next to the railway station, which costs £2.30 on both Saturday afternoons and weekday evenings.

By Train

The ground is only a quarter of a mile away from Ipswich train station and is only a five minute walk away. You will see the Portman Road floodlights in the distance as your train comes into the station. Ipswich is served by trains from London Liverpool Street and Peterborough.

Programme

Official Programme: £3.

Record & Average Attendance

Record Attendance: 38,010 v Leeds United, FA Cup 6th Round, March 8th, 1975.
Average Attendance: 2011-12: 18,267 (Championship League)

Ground Name: Elland Road
Capacity: 37,900 (all seated)
Address: Elland Road, Leeds, LS11 0ES
Main Telephone No: 0871 334 1919
Ticket Office No: 0871 334 1992

Year Ground Opened: 1919
Pitch Size: 117 x 76 yards
Team Nickname: United
Home Kit Colours: White, Blue & Yellow Trim
Official website: www.leedsunited.com

What's The Ground Like?

The ground is dominated by the East Stand on one side of the stadium. This huge stand which holds 17,000 supporters was opened in the 1992-93 season, and is at least twice the size of the other three stands at Elland Road. The East Stand is a two tier stand which has a large lower tier of seating with a smaller tier above. In between the two tiers is a row of executive boxes. The stand is completed by a large imposing roof. The good thing about the rest of the stadium is that it is totally enclosed, with the corners of the ground being filled with seating. The downside is that compared to the East Stand the other stands are looking rather tired and old in comparison. All the remaining stands have a number of supporting pillars and at the back of the West Stand (which was renamed in March 2004, the 'John Charles Stand' in honour of their former great player), there are a number of old wooden seats, which look as if they have been there since the stand was first opened in 1957. This stand also houses the team dugouts and television gantry. There is an electric scoreboard in one corner of the ground between the South & John Charles Stands. Outside the stadium there are statues of former playing great Billy Bremner and former manager Don Revie.

What Is It Like For Visiting Supporters?

Away fans are now housed on one side of the John Charles Stand (towards the South Stand), in the upper tier where up to 3,000 supporters can be housed. The seating is a mixture of old wooden and plastic seating, the leg room sparse, plus there are a number of supporting pillars running along the front of the upper tier which could impede your view. However, the facilities within the stand are very good. Food on offer on the concourse includes; Cheeseburgers (£3.80), Burgers (£3.50), Peppered Steak Pies (£2.90), Chicken Balti Pies (£2.70) Potato and Meat Pies (£2.70) and Cheese, Onion and Potato Pies (£2.70). On previous visits, I have seen a number of away fans being ejected (without warning) for swearing. So be on your best behaviour.

Although on my visits I have not had any problems around the stadium, I have received reports of others who have. So I would exercise caution and keep colours covered outside the ground and in the city centre, especially if your own club has had shall we say 'previous history'.

Where To Drink?

There is the Drysalters pub which is about a 10 minute walk away from the ground. On my last visit it had a good mix of home and away supporters, real ale and large screen SKY TV. To find this pub; with the Old Peacock pub behind you, turn left and follow the road down to the very end. Pass the entrances to a number of car parks and go under a railway bridge. At the end of the road, turn left along the dual carriageway and the pub is a short way down 'tucked in' on the left. Otherwise alcohol is served within the ground in the form of draught Becks Vier, Boddingtons Bitter and Blackthorn Cider (all £3.50 a pint), plus small bottles of red and white wine (£4).

Directions & Car Parking

Elland Road is well signposted around the Leeds area and is situated right by the M621.

From The North:

Follow the A58 or A61 into Leeds city centre, then follow signs for the M621. Join the M621 and after one and a half miles leave the motorway at the junction with the A643. Follow the A643 into Elland Road for the ground. Go down Elland Road past the ground on your right and the Old Peacock pub on your left, you will come to entrances to a couple of very large car parks (£5).

From The South:

Follow the Motorway M1 and then onto the M621. You will pass the ground on your left and then you need to take the next exit from the motorway and turn left onto the A6110 ring road. Take the next left onto Elland Road for the ground. Just as you go under a railway bridge there are entrances on either side to a couple of very large car parks (£5).

Surprisingly (considering the number of vehicles) the traffic leaving the car parks seemed to disperse quite well after the end of the game. Richard Drake informs me; 'a good tip for Elland Road is to park in Car Park A. They normally put away fans coaches here. From here we were back on the M621 within 10 minutes of coming out of the ground'.

By Train

Leeds train station is around a 35 minute walk from the station. Probably best to either take a taxi or one of the shuttle buses, that run from just outside the station to the ground. Tom Whatling adds; 'The shuttle buses cost £2.50 return. As you come out of the station main entrance, cross the road and take the stairs down to the street below. Turn right and cross the road and you will see the double-decker buses lined up. The first bus in the queue also sells the tickets for all the other buses. The buses drop off and pick up at the corner of the North and East stands. It's best to get a return ticket as then you don't have to queue up after the match to get a ticket back to the station, you just walk straight onto the bus'.

Programme & Fanzine

Official Programme: £4
The Square Ball Fanzine: £1.50

Record & Average Attendance

Record Attendance: 57,892 v Sunderland, FA Cup 5th Round Replay, March 15th, 1967.
Average Attendance: 2011-12: 23,283 (Championship League)

Ground Name: King Power Stadium
Capacity: 32,500 (all seated)
Address: Filbert Way, Leicester, LE2 7FL
Main Telephone No: 0844 815 6000
Ticket Office No: 0844 815 5000

Year Ground Opened: 2002
Pitch Size: 110 x 76 yards
Team Nickname: The Foxes
Home Kit Colours: Blue & White
Official website: www.lcfc.co.uk

What's The Ground Like?

In August 2002 the club moved into its new home, only a stone's throw away from their old Filbert Street ground. Then called the Walkers Stadium, it was renamed the King Power Stadium in 2011, under a sponsorship deal. The stadium is completely enclosed with all corners being filled with seating. The sides are of a good size, built in the same style and height. The West Stand though on one side of the pitch does contain a row of executive boxes. The team dug outs are also located at the front of this stand. Running around three sides of the stadium, just below the roof, is a transparent perspex strip, which allows more light and facilitates pitch growth. There are also two large video screens located in opposite corners of the stadium.

Like most new stadiums, the King Power Stadium is functional but lacks character. I don't know whether I'm starting to suffer from 'new stadium fatigue' having visited so many in the last few years, but to me it seemed somewhat bland looking both inside and out. Unusually the public address system is also broadcast on the speakers around the outside of the stadium. The King Power Stadium does have one redeeming feature –

atmosphere. The acoustics are very good and both sets of supporters can really make some noise, making for an enjoyable visit.

What Is It Like For Visiting Supporters?

Away supporters are housed in the North East corner of the stadium, where just over 3,000 fans can be accommodated. The view of the playing action is good (although you are set well back from the pitch) as well as the facilities available. The concourse is comfortable and there is your normal range of hot dogs, burgers and pies available. There are also television screens on the concourse showing the game going on within the stadium. My only slight grumble was that the gents toilets are poorly designed. They have a narrow 'zig zag corridor' of an entrance which hindered people coming in or out and didn't help the major traffic flow at half-time! On the positive side though, the atmosphere within the stadium was good, with the home fans singing on both sides of the away section. The atmosphere is further boosted by a huge bare chested drummer, who is located at the back of the home section, immediately to the left of the away fans. The stewarding was also pretty relaxed. The teams come out to the Post Horn Gallop tune, reminiscent of fox hunting! (Leicester are nicknamed the Foxes).

Where To Drink?

Andy Jobson, a visiting Southampton fan informs me; 'Probably the best bet for away fans is the Counting House pub on Freemens Common Road. It has a good mix of both sets of supporters, with all the normal facilities on offer'. Beaumont Fox adds; 'This pub is located just off the Aylestone Road, behind the Local Hero pub (home fans only) and next to Morrisons Supermarket. It does though exclude away supporters when the game is deemed to be a 'high profile' one. I have also been informed that the nearby Holiday Inn Express on Filbert Way, also has a bar which away fans have been using'. David Moore adds; 'If away fans fancy a quiet drink in a CAMRA Good Beer Guide listed pub then the Swan & Rushes (on Infirmary Square, near the Royal Infirmary) always has excellent guest ales on'.

For those arriving by train, then as you come out of the main entrance turn left and cross to the other side and there you will find The Hind which serves a selection of real ales. If you turn right out of the station and cross the road and turn left into Granby Street, then down on the left is a Wetherspoons called the Last Plantagenet.

Otherwise alcohol is available inside the stadium, however, this can be a bit of a 'hit and miss affair' depending on which team you support, as the Club opt not to sell any to away fans when the fixture has been deemed to be 'high profile'.

Directions & Car Parking

Leave the M1 at Junction 21, or if coming from the Midlands, follow the M69 until the end of the motorway (which meets the M1 at Junction 21). Take the A5460 towards Leicester city centre. Continue on this road, until you go under a railway bridge. Carry on for another 200 yards and turn right at the traffic lights into Upperton Road (sign posted Royal Infirmary) and then right again into Filbert Street for the stadium.

Allow yourself a little extra time to get to the ground as traffic does tend to get quite congested near the stadium. Plenty of street parking to be found (especially around the Upperton Road area and on streets running off the A5460 by the railway bridge. It is then around a 15 minute walk to the stadium), although as Greg Barclay warns; 'don't double park as the traffic wardens tend to have a field day at every match'. Alternatively you can park at Leicester Rugby Club (£3) which is a 10 minute walk away from the stadium.

By Train

The train station in the city centre, is situated just under 1.5 miles away and is walkable from the ground. A walking route to the stadium is signposted from across the road from the station. This should take you around 20-25 minutes. Please note that there is normally a heavy Police presence around the station itself.

Programme & Fanzine

Official Programme: £3
The Fox Fanzine: £2.50

Record & Average Attendance

Record Attendance: 47,298 v Tottenham Hotspur, FA Cup 5th Round, February 18th, 1928.
Average Attendance: 2011-12: 23,037 (Championship League)

Ground Name: Matchroom Stadium
Capacity: 9,271 (all seated)
Address: Brisbane Road, Leyton, London, E10 5NF
Main Telephone No: 0871 310 1881
Ticket Office No: 0871 310 1883

Year Ground Opened: 1937
Pitch Size: 115 x 80 yards
Team Nickname: The O's
Home Kit Colours: Red and Black
Official website: www.leytonorient.com

What's The Ground Like?

The ground has seen a lot of redevelopment in recent years, with the construction of three new stands. At one end is the single-tiered, Tommy Johnston (South) Stand (capacity 1,336 seats), that was opened in 1999. This stand replaced a former open terrace and is named after the club's leading all time goal scorer. An interesting feature of this covered area is that it is raised above pitch level, meaning that you have to climb a small set of steps at the front to reach the seating area. The old Main (East) Stand, which was originally opened in 1956, has been reduced in length, but is still a fair size. This partly covered stand is now all seated after having seating installed on the former front terrace. Unfortunately, it has several supporting pillars and the roof doesn't quite cover all of the front seating. It does though have an interesting gable on its roof which has 'Leyton Orient' proudly emblazoned across it and gives a nice link to the Club's history.

Opposite is the new West Stand which was opened for the 2005-06 season. This all seated stand which has a capacity of 2,872, has an unusual look about it, as above the seating area is a tall vertical structure that houses the Club

offices. In fact to be honest it looks more like an office block that has some seats installed on a large viewing gallery, rather than a football stand. It also has some corporate hospitality areas, which look a little precarious, as the outside seating area of these, overhang the lower tier. At the very top of the stand is a fair sized viewing gallery for television cameras and press and the roof of the stand contains a lot of perspex panels to allow more light to reach the pitch.

At the North End of the ground is the most recent addition to the stadium. The North Stand was opened at the beginning of the 2007/08 season and replaced a former open terrace. This simple looking covered all seated stand, has space for 1,351 spectators and looks similar to the Tommy Johnston Stand. The ground also has a set of four modern looking floodlight pylons.

What Is It Like For Visiting Supporters?

Away supporters are housed in one side (towards the South End) of the Main Stand. The facilities inside this stand are fairly basic and where there are a couple of supporting pillars that may impede your view. Around 1,000 fans can be accommodated in this area. I have been to Orient a number of times and have always been impressed by the state of the pitch. Even in January it is immaculate and at the start of the season you could almost play snooker on it!

Where To Drink?

There is a supporters club at the ground that does admit visiting supporters at a cost of £1. The supporters club which is located in the West Stand is listed in the CAMRA Good Beer Guide. However, it can get uncomfortably full of people. Otherwise the nearest pub to the ground is the Coach & Horses. To get there take a right out of Leyton station and walk down for about half a mile. It is on your left, within sight of the floodlights. John Baumber adds; 'There is also the Northcote on Grove Green Road. They have Sky television and it is only a 10 minute brisk walk from the ground. To find the pub turn right out of the tube station and then right again into Grove Green Road, at the bottom of the hill by the first main junction of traffic lights'.

Stephen Harris informs me; 'the best pub near to the ground is the Birkbeck Tavern in Langthorne Road, behind the tube station'.

Directions & Car Parking

Leave the M25 at Junction 27 and take the M11 towards London. At the end of the motorway keep in the right-hand lane and follow the signs for the North Circular A406 (W). At the bottom of the flyover where the roads merge, move into the left-hand lane for the A104. At the roundabout turn left onto the A104 towards Leytonstone. After about one mile at the next roundabout take the second exit continuing on the A104 towards Walthamstow & Leyton. Half a mile further on, turn left at the traffic lights into Leyton Green Road (signposted to Leyton Leisure Lagoon & Lea Valley Sports). Continue along this road and as you reach a large elevated block of flats on your right turn left into a short slip road that runs past the bus garage and then left into Leyton High Road (you'll see the Leyton Leisure Lagoon in front of you as you wait to make the turn). Continue along Leyton High Road passing the Leyton Midland Road overground station. After passing a Jet Garage and as the High Road bears around to the left then the ground is beyond the High Road to the right. So take the most suitable right-hand turn (as some have vehicle restrictions) and they will take you down towards the stadium. Street parking.

By Tube

The nearest London Underground Station is Leyton (about a quarter of a mile away) which is on the Central Line. Come out of the station and turn right down Leyton High Road. Cross over the road to the other side and continue down it. You will come to Coronation Gardens on your left and the floodlights of the ground can be clearly seen behind them. Take the next left past the gardens into Buckingham Road for the ground.

Programme

Official Programme: £3

Record & Average Attendance

Record Attendance: 34,345 v West Ham United, FA Cup 4th Round, January 25th, 1964.

Average Attendance: 2011-12: 4,298 (League One)

Ground Name: Anfield
Capacity: 45,362 (all seated)
Address: Anfield Road, Liverpool, L4 0TH
Main Telephone No: 0151 260 1433
Ticket Office No: 0151 260 8680

Year Ground Opened: 1884
Pitch Size: 110 x 75 yards
Team Nickname: The Reds
Home Kit Colours: All Red
Official website: www.liverpoolfc.tv

What's The Ground Like?

Walking up to the ground alongside Stanley Park, I have to say, that from a distance, Anfield is not particularly impressive. Inside though, the ground is a different proposition. Although showing its age in parts it is a unique venue and one where the stands almost feel that they are imposing upon the pitch.

The famous Kop Terrace at one end of the ground was replaced in 1994, by a huge stand designed to emulate the shape of the old Kop, hence its kind of semicircular look and large single tier. The other end, the Anfield Road Stand, part of which is given to away supporters, is the most recent addition to the ground, having been opened in 1998. It has boosted not only the overall capacity of the stadium, but has given Anfield a more balanced and enclosed feel as all corners are now filled. On one side of the stadium is the large, two tiered, Centenary Stand, where the front tier leg room is one of the tightest I have ever known. The Centenary Stand was originally called the Kemlyn Road Stand, part of which was built in 1963 with an additional tier and row of executive boxes being added in 1992. Opposite is the Main Stand. Opened in 1973 it is looking its age with a number of

supporting pillars. This stand has a TV gantry suspended beneath its roof. In the corner between the Kop & Centenary stands is an electric scoreboard, which surprise, surprise, shows the match score in bright red letters.

Around the outside of the ground, there are the Bill Shankly Gates on Anfield Road. These wrought iron gates have the legendary Liverpool phrase 'You'll Never Walk Alone' displayed above them. There is also a statue of the great man, Bill Shankly near the Club shop. Also along Anfield Road, there is the moving memorial to the victims of the Hillsborough disaster, which always has flowers adorning it.

What Is It Like For Visiting Supporters?

Away fans are located in the Anfield Road Stand at one end of the ground, where just under 2,000 seats are available, although this can be increased for cup games. This stand is also shared with home supporters, some of whom will be sitting in the small seated tier above the away fans. Malcolm Dawson a travelling Sunderland supporter adds; 'Try to avoid getting tickets sold as restricted view, for the rear rows of the Anfield Road Stand as it can be difficult to see the goals with people standing up in front of you'.

Kimberly Hill adds; 'Restricted view doesn't even begin to describe what it was like. The Wolves fans insisted on standing so it was like trying to watch the game through a letterbox!' The facilities within the stand are not bad. There is a betting outlet and the refreshment kiosks sell a wide variety of burgers, hot dogs and pies, including a 'Scouse Pie'.

I have always found it to be a good day out at Anfield, getting the feeling that you are visiting one of the legendary venues in world football. This is enhanced with the teams coming out to 'You'll Never Walk Alone' reverberating around the ground, with the red and white scarves and flags of the fans displayed across the Kop, at the beginning of the match. The atmosphere is normally great, so sit back and enjoy the experience.

Where To Drink?

The Arkles pub near to the ground, is known as the pub for away fans, but as can be expected it can get extremely crowded. Alcohol is also available inside the stadium.

Directions & Car Parking

Follow the M62 until you reach the end of the motorway (beware of a 50mph speed camera about a quarter of a mile from the end of the motorway). Then follow the A5058 towards Liverpool. After three miles turn left at the traffic lights into Utting Avenue (there is a McDonalds on the corner of this junction). Proceed for one mile and then turn right at the Arkles pub for the ground. If you arrive early (around 1pm) then there is street parking to be found. However, recently a residents only parking scheme has been introduced in some streets around the ground, so check any signs first. Otherwise it as an idea to park in the streets around Goodison and walk across Stanley Park to Anfield, or you can park in a secure parking area at Goodison itself which costs £10.

By Train

Kirkdale station is the closest to the ground (just under a mile away). However, it may be more advisable to go to Sandhills Station as this has the benefit of a bus service to the ground, which runs for a couple of hours before and a couple of hours after a game and drops you within easy walking distance of the ground. The bus costs £2 return if you pay on the bus. Or when buying your train ticket, if you ask for a return to Anfield (even though you are getting off at Sandhills) then the cost of the bus is included in the price of the ticket and is £1 less. Both Sandhills & Kirkdale stations can be reached by first getting a train from Liverpool Lime Street to Liverpool Central and then changing there.

The main railway station in Liverpool is Lime Street which is located just over two miles away from the ground and so is quite a walk (although it is mostly downhill on the way back to the station), so either head for Sandhills or Kirkdale stations or jump in a taxi.

Programme & Fanzines
Official Programme: £3
The Liverpool Way Fanzine: £2
Red All Over The Land Fanzine: £2

Record & Average Attendance
Record Attendance: 61,905 v Wolverhampton Wanderers, FA Cup 4th Round, February 2nd, 1952.
Average Attendance: 2011-12: 44,253 (Premier League)

Ground Name: Etihad Stadium
Capacity: 48,000 (all seated)
Address: Sportcity, Rowsley Street,
Manchester M11 3FF
Main Telephone No: 0161 444 1894
Ticket Office No: 0161 444 1894

Year Ground Opened: 2002*
Pitch Size: 116 x 77 yards
Team Nickname: The Blues or Citizens
Home Kit Colours: Sky Blue & White
Official website: www.mcfc.co.uk

What's The Ground Like?

After playing at Maine Road for 80 years, the Club moved to the then called City Of Manchester Stadium in August 2003. The stadium was originally built for the Commonwealth Games, held in 2002 and cost in the region of £90 million to construct. After that event it was agreed Manchester City would become the new tenants, thus incurring the envy of clubs who would also relish the chance to gain such a wonderful stadium. The club spent £20 million in refitting costs, including the removal of the running track and extending the stands further downwards (adding a further 10,000 seats to the capacity) so that the spectator areas are closer to the playing action. A roof was also added to one end of the stadium.

The stadium has a bowl design and is totally enclosed. Both stands on either side of the pitch are virtually identical, being semicircular in shape, three-tiered, with a row of executive boxes running across the stands between the second and third tiers. The ends are smaller in size, being two tiers high, again with a row of executive boxes, but this time running across the back just below the roof. Both these ends are of the more traditional rectangular design. The second tier around the stadium slightly overhangs the lower. The roof runs continuously around the stadium stretching up over the stands and down to the ends, creating a spectacular effect. There is a perspex strip just below the roof and the spectator areas, allowing light to reach the pitch. The upper tiers are steeper than the lower, ensuring that spectators are kept close to the playing action. The stadium also has two large video screens in opposite corners of the ground. Outside the ground near the main club entrance is a memorial garden, which includes a tribute to former city player Marc-Vivien Foe. Also of interest is that the playing surface is the largest in the League.

Man City get my vote for the weirdest looking mascots in the League. While most clubs have elected to recreate some furry creature, Man City have as their mascots a pair of aliens called 'Moonchester' and 'Moonbeam'.

What Is It Like For Visiting Supporters?

Away fans are located in one side of the South Stand at one end of the ground, in both the upper and lower tiers, where up to 3,000 fans can be accommodated (4,500 for cup games). Entrance to the stadium is gained by placing your ticket into an electronic reader and I noted on my last visit that fans were being searched by stewards outside the turnstile entrance. Inside the facilities are pretty good with spacious concourses with large plasma flat television screens showing the game and a good selection of food on offer. The view of the action is also pretty impressive although the atmosphere within the stadium is a bit 'hit and miss' at times. I did hear though on my last visit one very good rendition of the Man City fans anthem 'Blue Moon'. My only real complaint was the lack of distance between the home and away supporters. Only a few seats and a row of stewards stood in between the two sets of fans, which led to a lot of unpleasant baiting between the two.

Where To Drink?

There are not a great deal of pubs around the stadium, and the few available are predominantly for home support. However, The Stanley (aka Sports Bar) pub does let in away fans in small numbers. It is about a 10 minute walk away from the stadium, just set back from the main A6010 (Pottery Lane), going towards Ashburys train station. Otherwise alcohol is available inside the stadium.

Directions & Car Parking
From the South M6

Leave the M6 at Junction 19 and follow the A556 towards Stockport and then join the M56 going towards Stockport. Continue onto the M60 passing Stockport and heading on towards Ashton-under-Lyne. Leave the M60 at Junction 23 and take the A635 towards Manchester. Branch off onto the A662 (Ashton New Road) towards Droylsden and Manchester. Stay on the A662 for around three miles and you reach the Stadium on your right.

From The M62

Leave the M62 at Junction 18 and then join the M60 Ashton-under-Lyne. Leave the M60 at Junction 23 and take the A635 towards Manchester. Branch off onto the A662 (Ashton New Road) towards Droylsden/Manchester. Stay on the A662 for around three miles and you will reach the Stadium on your right.

Car Parking

There is some parking available at the stadium itself which costs £10 per car. The East Car Park is nearest to the away entrance. Please be aware that there is a residents only parking scheme in place in the streets near to the ground, which extends about a mile out from the stadium. So if you want to street park, it means parking further away and then walking to the stadium. There are also quite a number of unofficial car parks on both sides of Pottery Lane, costing around £5 per car.

By Train

The closest train station is Ashburys which is a short five minute train ride away from Manchester Piccadilly Station. The stadium is about a 15 minute walk away from Ashburys station. As you come out of the station turn left and after proceeding up the road you will come to the stadium on your left.

Programme & Fanzine:
Official Programme: £3
King Of The Kippax Fanzine: £2.50

Record & Average Attendance
Record Attendance: 47,726 Zenit St Petersburg v Glasgow Rangers UEFA Cup Final, May 14th, 2008.
For a Manchester City game at the stadium: 47,435 v Queens Park Rangers, Premier League, May 13th, 2012.
Average Attendance: 2011-12: 47,045 (Premier League)

*Originally built for the 2002 Commonwealth Games, Manchester City took up residence a year later.

Ground Name: Old Trafford
Capacity: 76,100 (all seated)
Address: Sir Matt Busby Way,
Manchester, M16 0RA
Main Telephone No: No: 0161 868 8000
Ticket Office No: 0161 868 8000

Year Ground Opened: 1910
Pitch Size: 116 x 76 yards
Team Nickname: The Red Devils
Home Kit Colours: Red, White & Black
Official website: www.manutd.com

What's The Ground Like?

Old Trafford has always been a special place as it was one of the few grounds where the stands envelop the corners. Although more stadiums are now also totally enclosed, Old Trafford's sheer size still makes it a bewildering sight. It has been steadily expanded over the last couple of decades raising its capacity to a staggering 76,100, making it the largest Club ground in Britain. Both ends, which look almost identical, are large two-tiered stands, which were originally built in the early 1990s and had an additional tier added at the turn of the millennium. Each are quite steep, with a large lower tier and smaller upper tier. The three-tiered Sir Alex Ferguson Stand, opened in 1996, at one side of the ground, is the largest capacity stand of any League Ground in England. The corners to each side of this stand are also filled with seating and extend around to meet both ends. These redeveloped stands dwarf the older Main (South) Stand opposite. This stand (part of which dates back to 1910) is single-tiered, with a television gantry suspended below its roof. All the stands have a row of executive boxes at the back of the lower tier.

Unusual aspects of the ground include the raised pitch, and that the teams enter the field from the corner of the Main Stand. Outside the ground is the Sir Matt Busby Statue fronting the impressive green glassed East Stand façade.

There is also a clock and plaque in remembrance of the Munich disaster. Across Sir Matt Busby Way is the recently erected United Trinity Statue of three of the 1968 European Cup winning team; George Best, Denis Law and Bobby Charlton (now Sir).

What Is It Like For Visiting Supporters?

Away supporters are normally located in one corner of the ground, taking up part of the East and South stands. The view from the away sections are excellent and up to 3,000 away supporters can be accommodated. Entrance into the stadium is gained by first being searched by a steward and then placing your ticket into an electronic bar code reader. It is then up a few flights of rather steep stairs to the concourse. Although the concourse looks a little cramped, it is adequate and there seems to be enough food and drinks outlets that the queues never seem to get too long. At the far end of the concourse is a large flat screen television showing Sky Sports.

The away fans section is set back from the pitch as there is a disabled area to its front. The leg room between rows is a little tight, as well as the space between the seats themselves. This results in most away fans standing throughout the game. The good thing though, is that the away fans can really make some noise from this part of the stadium.

Where To Drink?

The pubs nearest the ground generally won't let you in if you are wearing away colours. The best bet is probably to drink in the city centre or along one of the stops on the Metrolink, such as Altrincham or Sale. On my last couple of visits I have drank at the Quadrant pub which had a mixture of home and away fans and a couple of handy Chinese/Chippies nearby. The pub is about a 10-15 minute walk away from Old Trafford, in the direction of the Cricket Ground. Luke Burns, a visiting Birmingham City fan adds; 'There is also the Lime Bar in nearby Salford Quays. Good beer, quick service and good mix of home and away supporters'. Alternatively alcohol is normally served within the ground, although for some high profile games the Club opt not to sell any.

Directions & Car Parking

From the South:

Leave the M6 at Junction 19 and follow the A556 towards Altrincham. This will lead you onto the A56 towards Manchester. Keep on the A56 for six miles and then you will come to see Sir Matt Busby Way on your left. The ground is half a mile down this road on your left, although on matchdays this road may well be closed to traffic.

From the North:

Leave the M6 at Junction 30 and take the M61 towards Bolton. At the end of the M61, join the M60. Leave the M60 at Junction 9 and follow the A5081 towards Manchester. After about two miles you will reach Sir Matt Busby Way on your right for the ground.

From The West:

Follow M56 until its end and then take the M60 (W&N) as for Trafford Centre. At Junction 7 leave M60 and take the A56 towards Stretford. Stay on the A56 for 2 miles then you will come to see Sir Matt Busby Way on your left. The ground is half a mile down this road on your left, although on matchdays this road may be closed to traffic.

Car Parking

You can park at the nearby Old Trafford Cricket Ground, which costs £10 per car. Try to arrive early (before 1pm) as if you arrive later, it takes ages leaving the car park after the game. Gareth Hawker adds; 'I parked at the Salford Quays Lowry Mall, a 10 minute walk away from the stadium, the cost of which was £3.50'.

By Train & Metrolink

Probably the best way to get to the stadium is by Metrolink or train from Manchester Piccadilly mainline station, as Old Trafford has both its own railway station next to the ground and a Metrolink station which is located next to Lancashire County Cricket Club on Warwick Road, which leads up to Sir Matt Busby Way. Normally the railway station is less busy than the Metrolink.

Programme & Fanzines

Official Programme: £3
Red Issue Fanzine: £2.50
United We Stand Fanzine: £2.50
Red News Fanzine: £2.50

Record & Average Attendance

Record Attendance: 76,962 Wolves v Grimsby, FA Cup Semi-final, March 25th, 1939.
Modern All Seated Attendance Record: 76,098 v Blackburn Rovers, Premier League, March 31st, 2007.
Average Attendance: 2011-12: 75,387 (Premier League)

Ground Name: Riverside Stadium
Capacity: 35,100 (all seated)
Address: Middlesbrough, Cleveland, TS3 6RS
Main Telephone No: 0844 499 6789
Ticket Office No: 0844 499 1234

Year Ground Opened: 1995
Pitch Size: 115 x 75 yards
Team Nickname: Boro
Home Kit Colours: All Red
Official website: www.mfc.co.uk

What's The Ground Like?

The Club moved to the Riverside Stadium in 1995 after leaving its former home of Ayresome Park where it had played since 1903. The stadium is totally enclosed, after the previous open corners to either side of the West Stand were 'filled in' with seating in 1998. All the stands are two-tiered, although the West Stand is slightly larger than the other three sides, which makes the overall appearance of the stadium look somewhat imbalanced. This stand also has a row of executive boxes running across its middle and has the players tunnel and team dugouts in front. The roof around the stadium is raised up above the seating areas to allow more light to get to the pitch, through perspex panels located between the roof and the back of the seating areas. There is also an electric scoreboard mounted onto the roof at each end of the stadium.

Although the stadium looks a little bland on the inside, externally it looks great. This is especially so at night, when the stadium is illuminated and is visible from some miles around. Outside the main entrance you will find a pair of statues dedicated to two former Boro greats; George Hardwick & Wilf Mannion. In between the statues are the old entrance gates to Ayresome Park, which is a nice link with the Club's history.

What Is It Like For Visiting Supporters?

Away supporters are housed in the South Stand at one end of the stadium, where up to 4,500 fans can be accommodated. The turnstiles are electronic which means that you have to insert your ticket in a reader, to gain entry. Once inside then the leg room is okay and the view from the away section is excellent. However, the concourse running behind the stand is quite narrow, meaning that it can get quite crowded at half-time and before kick-off. There is a betting outlet available and there are a number of flat screen televisions, showing Sky Sports (and the match itself once it has kicked off). The catering had the usual fayre on offer of; Pies, Burgers, Hot Dogs, Pizza and Chips. Atmosphere on my visits has not been that great, but on the plus side I have not recently experienced any hassle there (well at least not for some years now).

One thing to point out is that there is very little in the way of pubs or eating establishments nearby, so you will need to head into the town centre for these.

Where To Drink?

Chris Taylor, recommends Doctor Browns, 10 minute's walk away from the ground at the bottom of Corporation Road, in the city centre. This pub serves real ale, has SKY TV and on my last visit had a good mix of home and away fans, both inside and outside of the pub. On the corner opposite the pub, is also a sandwich bar, which was doing a brisk trade in among other things, trays of roast potatoes and gravy. To find this pub; If you were standing outside the stadium with the main entrance behind you, head over to your left and turn right down the road, going under a bridge. A little way down this road on your left, there is an underpass (there is usually some programme and fanzine sellers standing by its entrance). Go down through the underpass and as you emerge on the other side turn right and go down the road and through another underpass. You will emerge in a small retail park (there is a McDonalds over on your right), which you walk through until you come to a main road. Turn right along this road and you will see the Doctor Browns pub over on your left. Otherwise, alcohol is available inside the stadium.

Directions & Car Parking

It is quite easy to find. Just follow the A66 (signposted Teesside from the A1) past Darlington's new ground and on into Middlesbrough. Carry on up the A66, through the centre of Middlesbrough and you will pick up signs for the Riverside Stadium. There is a small amount of parking available at the stadium itself (in Car Park E). It costs £6 per car and spaces can be booked through the ticket office. Otherwise there are a number of private parks located (mostly on waste land) nearby, costing in the region of £4. Also when you reach the turn off the A66 (as signposted) for the stadium, then rather than at the top of the slip road turning left towards the stadium, instead if you turn right to go back across the A66, then there is plenty of street parking available in this area. It is then about a 15-20 minute walk to the away turnstiles.

By Train

The ground is around a 15-20 minute walk from Middlesbrough railway station which is located on Albert Road. Although there is a direct train service from the North West, fans travelling from other parts of the country, will most likely find themselves changing at Darlington, for Middlesbrough.

If you come out of the main station entrance, turn left onto Zetland Road. Then left again into Albert Road and proceed under the railway bridge. Turn immediately right into Bridge Street East, going past the Bridge pub (not recommended for away fans) and then take the next right into Wynward Way. The stadium is down this road. If you come out of the rear station entrance, turn right onto Bridge Street East. Go straight past the Bridge pub and then take the next right into Wynward Way for the ground. The stadium is visible in the distance along most of this route.

Thanks to Glenn Brunskill for providing the directions.

Programme & Fanzine

Official Programme: £3.

Fly Me To The Moon Fanzine: £1

Record & Average Attendance

Record Attendance: 35,000 England v Slovakia, Euro 2004 Qualifier, June 11th, 2003.

For A Middlesbrough Game: 34,836 v Norwich City, Premier League, December 28th, 2004.

Average Attendance: 2011-12: 17,558 (Championship League)

Ground Name: The Den
Capacity: 20,146 (all seated)
Address: Zampa Road, London SE16 3LN
Main Telephone No: 020 7232 1222
Ticket Office No: 020 7231 9999

Year Ground Opened: 1993
Pitch Size: 105 x 68 yards
Team Nickname: The Lions
Home Kit Colours: Blue With White Trim
Official website: www.millwallfc.co.uk

What's The Ground Like?

The Club moved the relatively short distance to what then was called the New Den after leaving their original Den ground which was their home for 83 years. This was the first new major football ground to be constructed in London since before the Second World War. The stadium is made up of four separate two-tiered stands that are of the same height and look fairly similar. On one side is the Barry Kitchener Stand (named after a former player) which has the players tunnel and team dugouts at its front. This simple looking stand, has the same characteristics as both ends with windshields to either side in the upper tier and with the upper tier slightly overhanging the lower tier. The Dockers Stand on the other side, is slightly different having a row of executive boxes running across its middle. Between the East & North Stands in one corner is a large video screen.

What Is It Like For Visiting Supporters?

Away fans are located at one end of the ground in the North Stand (usually in the upper tier only). Around 4,000 away fans can be accommodated in this end. Like the general improvement in football, a trip to Millwall is not as threatening as it once was. However, it is hardly a relaxing day out and I found the Den to be quite intimidating. The large police presence at the match I attended did nothing to dampen this feeling. I would advise that you exercise caution around the ground and not to wear club colours. The most popular method of travel for away fans to the Den, is by official club coach, or by train from London Bridge. The Police are well drilled in dealing with the coaches and supporters arriving by train. Once inside the ground you will generally find the stewards helpful and friendly.

Luke Fern, a visiting Bolton Wanderers fan informs me; 'Inside the ground the concourse is mostly concreted and looks very dull. It is also very cramped with little space available for fans to get around those queuing for food and drinks. However, the view from our seats was excellent and the stewards were very tolerant and friendly. We had travelled by official Club coach and had to wait 45 minutes after the game had ended before we were allowed to exit the stadium car park'. Richard Langran a visiting Leicester City fan adds; 'We chose to drive down to Millwall and park away from the stadium. It was somewhat intimidating walking to and from the ground and the Leicester fans were kept back inside the stadium for quite a long time after the final whistle'.

Where To Drink?

There are not many pubs located near to the stadium and those should be avoided by away supporters. If travelling by train then it is probably best to grab a beer around London Bridge before moving onto the ground. I would advise keeping any colours covered, even when drinking in the London Bridge area.

On the Borough High Street by London Bridge is Barrow Boy & Banker, which is a Fullers pub and has the benefit of a large screen showing SKY Sports. Further down the High Street is the Borough Market, which on nearby Stoney Street is situated the legendary Market Porter pub. This pub is also a regular listing in the CAMRA Good Beer Guide and always has nine real ales on tap. Mick Hubbard adds; 'Also on Borough High Street is the George Inn, which is owned and leased by the National Trust. It is an outstandingly beautiful building, and the pub itself retains its wooden flooring and wall panelling. It serves its own George Ale which went down nicely'.

Chris Lynskey a visiting Scunthorpe United fan recommends; 'The Shipwright Arms on Tooley Street, near London Bridge. Come out of London Bridge tube station, turn right and it's only 200 yards down the road on your right-hand side. A lovely little pub which also serves food. We left the pub at 2.15pm to go and catch the train to the stadium and made it comfortably for kick-off'. Otherwise alcohol is available inside the stadium.

Directions & Car Parking

There are a number of ways of getting to the ground, but the most straightforward, if not the shortest in distance is to follow the A2 into London from Junction 2 of the M25. The A2 actually passes the ground. Once you go past New Cross Gate tube station on your right the ground is about a mile further on. The only awkward bit is about halfway in between New Cross Gate and the ground where the road splits into two. Keep to the right following the signs A2 City/Westminster. You will come to the stadium on your right. Street parking can be found on the small estate on your left just past the ground. There are no sizeable car parks around the ground itself.

By Train/Tube

It is probably best to go by rail, as South Berm-ondsey Railway Station is only a few minutes walk from the ground. There is a direct walkway specifically built for away fans which takes you directly to the away end and back to the station afterwards. This has made the Police's job of keeping rival supporters apart so much more manageable.

There are also two London Underground stations in the area, Surrey Quays & New Cross Gate, which are both on the East London Line. They are about 15-20 minutes walk away from the ground.

Programme & Fanzines

Official Matchday Programme: £3
No One Likes Us (NOLU) Fanzine: £1
The Lion Roars (TLR) Fanzine: £1.50

Record & Average Attendance

Record Attendance: 20,093 v Arsenal, FA Cup 3rd Round, January 10th, 1994.
Average Attendance: 2011-12: 11,484
(Championship League)

Ground Name: stadium:mk
Capacity: 22,000 (all seated)
Address: Denbigh, Milton Keynes, MK1 1ST
Main Telephone No: 01908 622 922
Ticket Office No: 01908 622 900

Year Ground Opened: 2007
Pitch Size: 115 x 74 yards
Team Nickname: The Dons
Home Kit Colours: All White
Official website: www.mkdons.co.uk

What's The Ground Like?

The Club moved to the new stadium in 2007. At a cost of around £50 million, the 22,000 all seated stadium, certainly looks a quality one and one that does look a bit different to other new stadiums that have been built. It was designed by HOK, the same firm of architects responsible for the Emirates & Wembley stadiums. From the outside it has a modern look, with good use of silver coloured cladding and a large amount of glass on view. The most striking feature of the stadium is its roof, which sits high up above the football ground with a large gap between it and the back row of seating. This allows more natural light to reach the pitch. The stadium is totally enclosed and has a bowl like design.

It is two-tiered, with three sides having a large lower tier being overhung by a smaller upper tier. The upper tier is mostly unused being devoid of seating, apart from on the West side where there is a Director's Box, plus executive and corporate hospitality areas. Unusually the concourse areas at the back of the lower tier see directly into the stadium, so there is what seems a noticeable gap between the lower and upper tiers where the concourse is located.

What Is It Like For Visiting Supporters?

Away supporters are located in the North East corner of the stadium where around 3,000 fans can be accommodated. On the plus side the stadium is a quality one i.e. it has not been built on the cheap, so the facilities are first class. The stadium has such creature comforts as big 'Emirates Style' comfy seats and the ability to continue to watch the game in progress, while eating a burger on the spacious concourse. The view of the playing action and leg room are both good and the atmosphere not bad. The stadium also has electronic turnstiles, so no paying at the gate here. Instead you gain entrance by putting your tickets into a bar code reader to gain entrance.

Alan Burgess, a visiting Sheffield Wednesday fan adds; 'the seating is marvellous both for comfort and leg room, the concourses very impressive and the sight lines fantastic. The food was the standard football ground offering but at least the serving areas were plentiful and well organised; there wasn't a bad atmosphere either from a crowd of 6,500 (though the PA system is deafening) and I can't end without a tribute to the toilets – separate, wide entrances and exits, plenty of space, soap and hot running water – luxury! A cut above almost all of the modern football stadiums'.

In keeping with the infamous concrete cows of Milton Keynes, the Club have a mascot called Mooie, while the South Stand is called the 'cowshed'. No wonder that the locals have christened the stadium 'The MooCamp!'

Where To Drink?

Ian Townsend informs me; 'There is a hotel connected to the stadium, of which some of the rooms have views of the pitch. But more importantly it also has the Red Dot Bar, into which away fans are usually welcomed provided any colours are kept reasonably discrete. This bar also shows Sky Sports.' The nearest pub to the ground is the Inn on the Lake (previously called the Beacon) which is around a 10 minute walk away, in the nearby Mount Farm area. This pub offers food and has recently been refurbished. Otherwise alcohol is available inside the stadium.

Directions & Car Parking

Leave the M1 at Junction 14 and head towards Milton Keynes. Go straight over the first roundabout and at the next (where there is a Total Garage on the corner) turn left onto the V11 Tongwell Street. Proceed across one roundabout and at the next turn right onto the H8 Standing Way (A421). Continue along the Standing Way going across a number of roundabouts. On reaching the Bleak Hall Roundabout turn left into the V6 Grafton Street. At the next roundabout, turn right and the stadium entrance is further down on the left.

There are 2,000 car parking spaces at the stadium, which cost £7 per vehicle. Otherwise you can street park in the Denbigh West industrial estate. Don't be tempted to park at the adjacent Asda Store as it is patrolled on matchdays and you may end up with a parking ticket for your trouble.

By Train

The nearest station is Fenny Stratford which is just over a mile away from the stadium. As you exit the station turn right and at the top of the road turn right onto the main Watling Street. Just go straight along this road and you will see the stadium over on your right.

There is also Bletchley railway station which is around about two miles away from the ground, while Milton Keynes Central is four miles away. There is a shuttle bus service which costs £1 each way, from both Bletchley and Milton Keynes Central Stations to the football stadium, which commences two hours before kick-off, running every 30 minutes. Surprisingly taxis are scarce outside Bletchley station so best to pre-book one in advance (Skyline 01908 222111 are a local taxi firm).

Programme

Official Programme: £3

Record & Average Attendance

Record Attendance: 21,309 Northampton Saints v Ulster, Heineken Cup Quarter-final, April 10th, 2011 **For an MK Dons game:** 19,506 v Queens Park Rangers, FA Cup 3rd Round, January 7th, 2012 **Average Attendance:** 2011-12: 8,659 (League One)

Ground Name: Globe Arena
Capacity: 6,476 (Seating 2,173)
Address: Christie Way, Westgate,
Morecambe LA4 4TB
Main Telephone No: 01524 411 797
Ticket Office No: Same as main number

Year Ground Opened: 2010
Pitch Size: 110 x 76 yards
Team Nickname: Shrimps
Home Kit Colours: Red & White
Official website: www.morecambefc.com

What's The Ground Like?

After 89 years at Christie Park the Club have moved to a new purpose-built stadium. At a cost of around £12 million, the Globe Arena (which is named after the company Globe Construction that built the stadium) was opened in 2010. The stadium is dominated by the Peter McGuigan Stand one side. This stand which is named after the current Club Chairman, has a capacity of just under 2,200 seats. This all seated, covered stand, has a box like feel, with a corporate glassed area to the rear. It is though free of supporting pillars and has wind-shields to either side, essential for a football ground located near the coast.

Opposite is the North Terrace, which is a very small open terrace that is only a few steps high. The terrace is split into two separate parts, with a large gap between them located around the halfway line. Behind this gap in the terrace is a service entrance, while above is perched a television gantry. Although reminiscent of the Car Wash Terrace at Christie Park, it does detract from the overall look and feel of the stadium. Both ends are covered terraces. The West Terrace is for home supporters and houses 2,234 fans, while the

East Terrace is substantially smaller and is for the away support. In the North East corner of the stadium, adjacent to the away terrace is a Police Control Box. Also located in this area, attached to a wall beside the Control Box is a small electronic scoreboard.

What Is It Like For Visiting Supporters?

Away fans are mostly housed in the East Terrace at one end of the ground, where just under 1,400 supporters can be accommodated. In addition the Club also make around 300 seats available in the Peter McGuigan Stand, which is shared with home fans. As you would expect with a new stadium the facilities and the view of the playing action are good. Although a new modern stadium, my only grumble was that the walkway at the back of the away terrace was very narrow (you could literally stand in the middle of it, hold your arms out wide and touch either side). Considering that the refreshment kiosk has a serving window opening out onto this walkway and further along were the entrances to the toilets, then this got rather uncomfortably crowded to say the least. On a positive note though, the acoustics of the away terrace were good, meaning that a good atmosphere was generated.

Where To Drink?

The closest bar that admits away supporters is on the Regent Leisure Holiday Park. This is situated just a few minutes walk away from the stadium along Westgate (with the stadium entrance behind you, turn right, cross over to the other side of the road and the Regent Park entrance is down on the left). David Foster, a visiting Chesterfield fan adds; 'I had a drink across at the Regent Caravan Park. This was fully accessible, offered a decent pint and food, had Sky television on a big screen and generally had a good atmosphere.' Otherwise if you turn left out of the stadium entrance then around a 10 minute walk away (located opposite a Lidl supermarket on Westgate) is the William Mitchell pub, which also shows Sky Sports.

Maybe a better bet (as we are at the seaside after all) is to take a 15 minute walk down to the seafront (out of the stadium entrance and turn right) and then on reaching the promenade turn right. There are a few more bars here, including Davy Jones Locker in the basement of the Clarendon Hotel, as well as a cafe, for those feeling peckish. Continuing to walk for about another five minutes you will reach the Ranch House pub. Good real ale on offer, hot pies at reasonable prices, large screen TV showing Sky Sports and an adjoining small amusement arcade to keep the kids happy, then what more would you want? If arriving by train then you may care to try a Wetherspoons outlet in the town centre, called the Eric Bartholomew on Euston Road or on the sea front the Station Promenade pub, which also has a Wacky Warehouse for the young children.

Directions & Car Parking

Exit the M6 at junction 34, then take the A683 towards Lancaster and take the A589 towards Morecambe. Go straight across two roundabouts passing a McDonalds outlet on your left. At the next roundabout (where there is a Toby Carvery) take the first exit into Westgate Road (signposted West Promenade, Sandylands). Continue along this road for about one mile and you will reach the stadium on your right. Parking at the stadium is for permit holders only so it is a case of finding street parking. If you continue along Westgate passing the stadium on your right, then on the other side of the railway bridge there is plenty of street parking to be had in the side roads on either side.

By Train

Morecambe railway station is around a 25-30 minute walk away from the ground. As you come out of the railway station turn left down Central Drive past Frankie and Benny's, a Morrisons superstore and a KFC outlet and you will reach the sea front. Turn left along the promenade passing the Ranch House pub on your left and then take the 5th left into Regent Road. Proceed straight up Regent Road and continue along into Westgate. You will reach the stadium on your left-hand side, just over the railway bridge. Morecambe is served by trains from Lancaster.

David Foster adds; 'From near Morecambe train station you can get a bus number 6 or 6A, from the bus stop located opposite Frankie & Benny's. This drops you right outside the stadium. Coming back there is a bus stop outside the ground, the bus then goes into town along the sea front and then onto the railway station.'

Programme

Official Programme: £3

Record & Average Attendance

Record Attendance: 5,003 v Burnley, League Cup 2nd Round, August 24th, 2010
Average Attendance: 2011-12: 2,144 (League Two)

Ground Name: Sports Direct Arena (But will always be known to many as St James' Park)
Capacity: 52,401 (all seated)
Address: St James' Park,
Newcastle-upon-Tyne NE1 4ST
Main Telephone No: 0191 201 8400

Ticket Office No: 0844 372 1892
Year Ground Opened: 1892*
Pitch Size: 114 x 74 yards
Team Nickname: The Magpies or The Toon
Home Kit Colours: Black & White
Official website: www.nufc.co.uk

What's The Ground Like?

The ground was largely rebuilt in the 1990s and is now unrecognisable from the St James' Park of old. On approaching the ground, it looks absolutely huge, as it appears to have been built on raised ground. I particularly like St James' Park as it is totally enclosed and has a great atmosphere. With the completion of the additional tier to the Milburn & Leazes (Sir John Hall) Stands in 2000, the capacity has been increased to over 52,000. These stands have a huge lower tier, with a row of executive boxes and a smaller tier above. This development has created the largest cantilever structure in Europe and has a spectacular looking roof, which allows natural light to penetrate through it (and hence is good for the pitch). However, the ground now looks somewhat imbalanced with one half of the ground being significantly larger than the other two sides. These remaining two sides the Gallowgate End and East Stand are both of the same height and are two-tiered. The stadium is also totally enclosed with all four corners being filled with seating.

What Is It Like For Visiting Supporters?

Away fans are housed on the far side of the Sir John Hall Stand, in the top tier. Up to 3,000 supporters can be accommodated in this section for League games and a larger allocation is available for cup games. Be warned though that it is a climb of 14 flights of stairs up to the away section and you are situated quite far away from the pitch. If you are scared of heights or have poor eyesight then this may not be for you. On the plus side you do get a wonderful view of the whole stadium, plus the Newcastle skyline and countryside in the distance. Also the leg room and height between rows are one of the best that I have come across and the facilities on offer are pretty good. The concourse is spacious and there is a fair selection of pies on offer, plus the usual burgers and hot dogs, all served in Newcastle United branded packaging (which made me wonder if their sales are affected when playing Sunderland!). There are also televisions on the concourse, showing live the game being played, with separate refreshment areas which serve alcohol, again in Newcastle United branded plastic glasses.

Jeremy Gold a visiting Leyton Orient supporter

adds; 'The visitors' section is on level seven at the top of the stand. The view is a long way from the pitch, although it is still good. If you suffer from vertigo, don't go! The stewarding at the game I went to was fairly strict. However, people were being warned against gesturing before they were thrown out. Unfortunately some people didn't take the hint and about five or six made the long trip back down the fourteen flights of stairs!'

The atmosphere in St James' Park can be electric and it is certainly one of the best footballing stadiums in the country. I personally found the Geordies friendly and helpful and a trip to Newcastle can be one of the better away trips in the Premier League.

Where To Drink?

The ground is one of the few remaining in the country that is literally right in the centre of the city. You are only a few minutes walk from the main shopping areas of Newcastle. There are plenty of bars to choose from in the city centre, but most away fans tend to favour the pubs opposite and around Newcastle Railway Station. The A Head Of Steam, The Lounge and O'Neills are all recommended, but some of these bars will only admit fans if colours are covered and none of them admitted children. Also nearby is a Wetherspoons outlet called the Union Rooms. Alternatively there is Idols which has strippers and is popular with both home and away fans. Alcohol is also served within the ground.

On my last visit I went to the Bodega on Westgate Road and had no problems. This pub is listed in the CAMRA Good Beer Guide and had a friendly atmosphere. Closer to the ground (and just around the corner from China Town which is good for a cheap lunch) is the Newcastle Arms on St Andrews Street. This pub is also in the Good Beer Guide, but unless you arrive very early and have no colours you are unlikely to gain entrance. Just down the road is The Backpage book shop, which is an oasis of football books, DVD's, programmes and memorabilia.

Directions & Car Parking

At the end of the A1(M) continue on the A1 and then the A184 towards Newcastle. Continue along this road, bearing left onto the A189. Continue over the River Tyne on the Redheugh Bridge, from which the ground can be clearly seen. Carry on straight up the dual carriageway (St James Boulevard). This leads directly to the Gallowgate end of the ground. As the ground is so central there are a number of pay and display car parks in the vicinity.

By Train

Newcastle Central Railway Station is half a mile from the ground and takes 10-15 minutes to walk. Claire Stewart informs me; 'You can also get the metro from inside the train station up to the ground, which has its own "St James' Park" stop. Go on the metro from the railway station to Monument Metro Station where you need to change trains to go to St James' Park. You can also walk up to the ground from Monument Station. It's pretty easy to find, and if you do happen to get lost, then just follow the black and white crowd'!

Programme & Fanzines

Official Programme: £3
The Mag Fanzine: £3
True Faith Fanzine: £2.50

Record & Average Attendance

Record Attendance: 68,386 v Chelsea, Division One, September 3rd, 1930.
Average Attendance: 2011-12: 49,936 (Premier League)

* Although the Club didn't move in until 1892, the land had been used for football since 1880.

Ground Name: Sixfields Stadium
Capacity: 7,653 (all seated)
Address: Sixfields Stadium, Northampton, NN5 5QA
Main Telephone No: 01604 683 700
Ticket Office No: 01604 683 777

Year Ground Opened: 1994
Pitch Size: 116 x 72 yards
Team Nickname: The Cobblers
Home Kit Colours: Claret and White
Official website: www.ntfc.co.uk

What's The Ground Like?

The Club moved from their old County Ground to the Sixfields stadium in October 1994. This neat all seater stadium is located on the outskirts of Northampton. It has three small covered single tier stands, and another larger single tier covered West Stand (capacity 4,000), at one side of the pitch. Away supporters are housed at one end in the South Stand. Apart from a set of four modern looking floodlights the corners of the stadium are largely open. A large hill is situated behind the North Stand and overlooks the ground, where small numbers of fans can be seen watching the game free, even though they can only see half the pitch!

What Is It Like For Visiting Supporters?

Away fans are located in the South End of the stadium where 800 supporters can be accommodated. If demand requires it, then an additional 300 seats can also be made available in the Alwyn Hargrave Stand. One slight pain about Sixfields is that you can't pay at the turnstiles. You have to buy your ticket first from a Portakabin and then you have to queue again. Some away fans have got caught out by this when arriving late. However, I have received a number of reports comple-

menting the standard of stewarding, other club officials and the Northampton fans themselves. Please note that if your club has a large away following to make sure that you have a ticket before travelling as it has not been unknown for away fans turning up on the day, to find that the away section has sold out.

Having lived in Northampton for a year and watched Northampton Town win the old fourth division (giving away my age now…), I have a soft spot for them. The fans themselves are quite passionate and this makes for a great atmosphere especially at cup games. Robert Dunkley informs me; 'outside the West Stand there is a used programme stall stocking a wide range of programmes from different clubs and seasons'.

Where To Drink?

The ground is built on a leisure complex on the outskirts of Northampton. This consists of a couple of fast food and eating establishments (including a KFC, McDonalds and a Pizza Hut), a cinema, a bowling alley and the stadium itself. There is just one pub on this site called the Sixfields Tavern, which is part of the Hungry Horse chain so offers meals and is family friendly. It also contains a Sports Bar, which shows Sky Sports, but it is primarily for home fans and bouncers man the entrance on matchdays. A better bet may be the Tenpin Bowling Alley which contains a bar, admits away fans and shows Sky Sports too.

Carl Brown adds; 'I found myself drinking in a T.G.I. Friday's outlet opposite the Main Stand. Maybe not your stereotypical pre-match watering hole but very convenient for a drink, plus there were a wonderful array of fine waitresses on display, serving the goods!' There is also a Frankie & Benny's nearby.

Kevin Roberts informs me; 'For those supporters travelling from the North and leaving the M1 at Junction 16 and taking the A4500 towards Northampton, then you will pass on your left the recently refurbished Turnpike pub, which as far as I am aware is still welcoming away supporters'.

Kevin continues; 'In Northampton town centre, there are several notable real ale pubs in addition to the usual Wetherspoons etc. A particular favourite for those looking for a decent pint near the train station is the Old Black Lion (turn left from station and 100 yards on right up the hill), or the Malt Shovel Tavern, which is possibly the best real ale pub in Northampton, having 14 hand pumps and is also listed in the CAMRA Good Beer Guide'.

Directions & Car Parking

From The South:
Leave the M1 at Junction 15A and take the A43 towards Northampton and you will come to the ground on your right.

From The North:
Leave the M1 at Junction 16 and take the A45 towards Northampton and you will come to the ground on your right.

The Sixfields stadium is well signposted around the area. There is a fair sized car park located at the ground, which costs £3. Make sure though that you arrive early as it has been known for it to get full for the more popular games. Parking in the nearby cinema and restaurant car parks is not allowed, and parking there will probably result in your car being given a £60 ticket, or worse still clamped! So make sure that you only use the official football parking provided at the ground.

By Train

Northampton train station is over two miles from the ground, so it is probably best to hire a taxi. However, if you feel like braving the 25-30 minute walk then Dave Brown provides the following directions; 'Come out of the main station entrance, go across the car park, up the steps and then turn right onto Black Lion Hill. Go over the railway bridge, and straight on along St James' Road. At the HSS Hire outlet (and the handily placed Thomas A. Beckett pub on the opposite corner) turn left onto St James' Mill Road. After about 400 yards turn right at the Fabric Warehouse (opposite Jewson) onto Harvey Reeves Road, which further on becomes Edgar Mobbs Way. After about a mile this road brings you out at Sixfields Stadium, with the South (away) Stand over on your right.

Liz Williams adds; 'From the railway station you can take the D2 bus towards Daventry, which also goes by the Sixfields retail park and stops about 200 yards from the stadium. The buses go from the bridge over the railway at the south end of the station. To return, get on at the same stop, but make sure to check which direction the bus is heading as the same stop serves both directions. The trip takes 10-20 mins depending on traffic (which can be heavy if there is a Saints rugby match on the same day)'.

Programme & Fanzine

Official Programme: £3

HotelEnders Fanzine: £1

Record & Average Attendance

Record Attendance: 7,557 v Manchester City, Division Two, September 26th, 1998.

Average Attendance: 2011-12: 4,809 (League Two)

Ground Name: Carrow Road
Capacity: 27,220 (all seated)
Address: Carrow Road, Norwich, NR1 1JE
Main Telephone No: 01603 760 760
Ticket Office No: 0844 826 1902

Year Ground Opened: 1935
Pitch Size: 114 x 74 yards
Team Nickname: The Canaries
Home Kit Colours: Yellow & Green
Official website: www.canaries.co.uk

What's The Ground Like?

Carrow Road has been steadily redeveloped since the late 1970s, with all four sides of the ground having new stands. The newest of these is the Jarrold South Stand at one side of the pitch which was opened in 2004. It is an impressive looking cantilever, single tier, all seated stand, that can house up to 8,000 supporters. It is unusual in having not one, but three separate television gantries suspended beneath its largely perspex roof. This stand was further extended in 2005 and now surrounds the corner of the ground where it joins the Norwich & Peterborough Stand, 'filling in' that area. The rest of the ground is also all seated and all stands are covered. Both ends look particularly smart, being large two-tiered affairs, complete with a row of executive boxes and distinctive pairs of large floodlight pylons protruding from their roofs. The first of these to be built was the River End in 1979 (it was later re-named the Norwich & Peterborough Stand), with the Barclay End opposite opening in 1992. On the remaining side is the Geoffrey Watling City Stand. Named after a former club president and opened in 1986, this single-tiered stand is smaller than both ends and houses among other things the Directors Box and Press Area. This stand extends around to meet the ends at both corners, giving the ground an enclosed look on that side. In one corner in between the Barclay End and Jarrold South Stand, the stadium is overlooked by a sizeable Holiday Inn Hotel. David Westgate adds; 'The corner in-fill between the Barclay Stand and the Geoffrey Watling City Stand is affectionately known to Norwich fans as the "Snake Pit!"'

What Is It Like For Visiting Supporters?

Away fans are housed on one side of the new Jarrold South Stand, on one side of the ground. As you would expect from a modern stand the facilities and view of the playing action are good. The normal allocation in this area is 2,500 fans although this can be increased further for cup games. If you are located at the very back of this stand then you can enjoy some fine views across the city, including Norwich Cathedral. The Club I found to be particularly friendly and relaxed. I certainly would rate it as one of the better away days, even though it seems an eternity to get there. As Delia Smith is on the board of Norwich City, the food available within the ground has been spruced up a fair bit and is very good. The Club even bake their own pies which not only include the usual array such as steak & kidney, chicken & mushroom, but also a number of 'matchday specials' (which change from game to game) such as beef in red wine gravy & cheese, mushroom and garlic.

Where To Drink?

The main pub for away fans is the Compleat Angler, which is located opposite the railway station. It is situated on a river bank and has a nice outside terrace overlooking the river. The pub itself is a bit basic but offers food and is away fan friendly. It is about a 10 minute walk away from Carrow Road. Otherwise Norwich has a number of pubs located in its centre, in fact on one visit I found a number of good pubs situated in between the train station and the ground, that were friendly. In fact I almost ended up being a pub crawl before the match had begun!

Rob Emery informs me; 'Not far away from the ground and towards the City Centre a new leisure complex called the Riverside has opened. This has a number of drinking and eating establishments, including a Wetherspoons Lloyds No.1 outlet. While Nicholas Mead suggests; 'the Coach and Horses on Thorpe Road brews its own beer and is around a 10 minute walk away from the ground'.

Directions & Car Parking

The ground is well signposted from the A11 and A47. From the southern bypass (A47) take the A146 into the city. At the traffic lights turn right towards the city centre on the A1054. At the next roundabout stay in the left hand lane and continue towards the city centre along the A147. At the next set of traffic lights, turn right into King Street. This street as it bends around to the right and crosses the river becomes Carrow Road, the ground is further down on the right.

David Clarke informs me that 'The best car park for away fans is Norfolk County Hall, which is well signposted on the left of the A146, as you follow signs towards the ground from the Southern Bypass. It is currently £3 and can hold about 2,000 cars, and does usually fill up by 2pm for games

where the away team bring loads of fans'. Martyn Swan adds; 'It's advisable to get to the car park before 1pm if you want a decent spot, otherwise you may get stuck in spaces at the back, and it can then take ages at the end of the game to exit'.

By Train

The ground is walkable from Norwich train station. If you ignore all those wonderful pubs it should take you no more than 10 minutes to walk to the ground. From the station turn left and head for the Morrisons supermarket and you should see the ground behind that.

Programme & Fanzine

Official Programme: £3
HotelEnders Fanzine: £1

Record & Average Attendance

Record Attendance: 43,984 v Leicester City, FA Cup 6th Round, March 30th, 1963.
Average Attendance: 2011-12: 26,606 (Premier League)

Ground Name: City Ground
Capacity: 30,576 (all seated)
Address: City Ground, Nottingham, NG2 5FJ
Main Telephone No: 0115 982 4444
Ticket Office No: 0871 226 1980

Year Ground Opened: 1898
Pitch Size: 115 x 78 yards
Team Nickname: The Reds
Home Kit Colours: Red & White
Official website: www.nottinghamforest.co.uk

What's The Ground Like?

The ground from a distance looks quite picture-squesque sitting on the banks of the River Trent. Both ends were redeveloped during the 1990s, much improving the overall appearance. At one end, the Bridgford Stand houses away fans in the lower tier; it is odd because one third of this stand was built lower than the rest, due to a local Council planning requirement to allow sunlight through to the houses in nearby Colwick Road. Opposite, the Trent End, is the most recent addition to the ground. It is a large two-tiered stand that looks quite smart. One unusual feature of the stand, is that running across the middle are a number of rows of seating enclosed within a covered shaded glass area. On one side there is a similarly impressive two-tiered stand, with executive boxes in between, which was built in 1980. Once called the Executive Stand, it was recently renamed the Brian Clough Stand in honour of their greatest manager. Facing this is a smaller and much older Main Stand (built in the mid 1960s) that now looks quite tired in the company of its shiny new neighbours.

What Is It Like For Visiting Supporters?

Up to 4,750 away fans can be accommodated in the lower tier of the Bridgford Stand, where the facilities and view of the action are good. I personally did not have any problems at the City Ground, but I have heard of away fans getting some hassle; for example it has not been unknown for the odd object to be thrown down on away fans from so called Forest fans seated above. Don't be surprised also if the stewards keep asking you to sit down if you stand in the seated areas, which can get annoying. There is also an element of Forest supporters in the 'A' Block of the Main Stand nearest to the away supporters, who feel it is their duty to continually berate away fans during the game, which can be unsavoury. It is also advised to keep colours covered around the ground, especially if you support another Midlands team. The good news though is that away fans can really make some noise from this stand, so make the most of it!

Where To Drink?

Nearly all pubs near to the ground are for home fans only. Audrey MacDonald, a visiting Hartlepool fan informs me; 'After trying to no avail to find a pub near to the ground that would allow in away fans, the Police directed us to the Meadow Club which is the Notts County Supporters Club, which was okay'. Carl Fitzpatrick, a visiting Coventry City adds; 'Very near to the ground on the banks of the River Trent, we came across the Nottingham Rowing Club, which displayed a banner outside saying that away fans were welcome. They charged £1 entry and the beer was good and very reasonable, plus the Forest fans that we met inside were chatty and friendly'.

Simon Phillips recommends the Stratford Haven, just down the road from the Larwood & Voce, 'it has great beer and food, it bustles and is used by both home and away fans'. This pub is located in a largely residential area where there is street parking available, if you arrive early.

Adrian Taylor a visiting Birmingham City fan adds; 'If travelling by train, then there are numerous pubs with character in and around the city centre including the Olde Trip To Jerusalem, The Castle (in Castle Street), Salutation Inn (on Hounds Gate), and my favourite, The Round House (in Royal Standard Place)'. Another pub worthy of mention is the Canal House; It is housed in a listed building, serving Castle Rock beers and it even has part of canal inlet running through the inside of the pub! I have received reports of fans getting some hassle in pubs near to the station, so use your discretion and keep colours covered. Otherwise, alcohol is available inside the ground.

Directions & Car Parking

From The North:

Leave the M1 at Junction 26 and take the A610 towards Nottingham and then signs for Melton Mowbray. Cross the River Trent and you will see the ground on your left. Alternatively as you approach Nottingham on the A610 you will pick up signs for 'football traffic'. Although following these seems to take you all round the outskirts of Nottingham you do eventually end up at the City Ground, along the A6011.

From The South:

Leave the M1 at Junction 24 and take the A453

towards Nottingham. Then take the A52 East towards Grantham and then onto the A6011 into Nottingham. The ground is situated by the A6011.

There is a large car park at the ground, otherwise there is some street parking to be had, especially in the roads near to the Meadow Lane ground across the river. Steve Barratt informs me; 'regarding the parking at Forest, the council operate a car park on match days on the Victoria Embankment, located near to the cricket ground. They charge £5 but it is only a two minute walk to the stadium'. The council also provide parking at their Eastcroft depot (NG2 3AH) at £4 a car. The depot is a 10 minute walk from the City Ground, located just off London Road (A60), opposite Hooters.

By Train

Nottingham railway station is located one mile from the City Ground and takes around 20 minutes to walk. As you come out of the main station entrance, turn left and then left again. Follow the road down to the dual carriageway and then turn right. The ground is about three quarters of a mile down the dual carriageway on the left, just over Trent Bridge.

Programme & Fanzine

Official Programme: £3

HotelEnders Fanzine: £1

Record & Average Attendance

Record Attendance: 49,946 v Manchester United, Division One, October 28th, 1967.

Average Attendance: 2011-12: 21,970 (Championship League)

Ground Name: Meadow Lane
Capacity: 20,300 (all seated)
Address: Meadow Lane, Nottingham, NG2 3HJ
Main Telephone No: 0115 952 9000
Ticket Office No: 0115 955 7204

Year Ground Opened: 1910
Pitch Size: 114 x 76 yards
Team Nickname: The Magpies
Home Kit Colours: Black & White
Official website: www.nottscountyfc.co.uk

What's The Ground Like?

During the early 1990s the ground was completely rebuilt, creating an attractive all seater stadium. Although the ground comprises four separate stands, it is quite smart looking. Both sides are single-tiered stands, the larger of which is the Derek Pavis Stand. This is the Main Stand containing the Directors Area and having the players' tunnels and team dugouts at its front. Opposite is the Jimmy Sirrell Stand which has a gable on its roof reminiscent of those old grounds, where they were once a common sight. At one end is the large Kop Stand, which can house up to 5,400 supporters. Again this is a modern stand with excellent facilities. The other end is the smaller, covered Family Stand. This stand has one sizeable solitary supporting pillar, which may affect your view as it is situated right at the front of the stand in the middle. This stand also has a small electric scoreboard on its roof. The stadium is completed with a set of four modern floodlight pylons.

What Is It Like For Visiting Supporters?

Away fans are housed on one side of the Jimmy Sirrell Stand, located on one side of the ground. The normal allocation for this area will be around 1,300, although this can be increased for cup games. On my last visit I was very impressed with the new stands and had a pleasant day out. The views were generally good as were the catering facilities. The local fans seemed friendly enough. The only disappointments were that the substantial supporters club didn't allow in away supporters and that the ground generally lacked atmosphere, however, this may improve with home fans now once again back in their traditional home end of the Kop, which previously was occupied by visiting supporters.

Andy McLaren, a visiting Hartlepool United fan adds; 'The stewards at the back of the away section let us stand and even joined in with some friendly banter. There was a reasonable number but they kept a low profile and let the fans enjoy themselves. Overall they were a credit to the club and made the day enjoyable!'

Where To Drink?

There are a few pubs around the ground that let away supporters in and are quite friendly and serve good real ale. Steve from the Pie Fanzine website informs me; 'On the main London Road, just across from the hump back bridge over the canal, is the newly refurbished and renamed Globe. A comfortable open-plan pub with good food and five ever-changing real ales and is listed in the CAMRA Good Beer Guide (however, no children are allowed). Just the other side of Trent Bridge is the Southbank Bar, the Globe's sister pub. It also serves excellent food and has sport on the numerous televisions; three real ales are offered here including one from the tiny local Mallards brewery. Just across from the front of the station down Queensbridge Road is the Vat and Fiddle situated next door to the Castle Rock micro-brewery. It offers 10 real ales and hot and cold food. Children are welcome'. It is also listed in the CAMRA Good Beer Guide.

Chris Rhoades recommends; the 'Trent Bridge Inn on Radcliffe Road, which is a Wetherspoons outlet'. While Tim Cooke, a travelling Millwall fan has a different angle (so to speak); 'definitely one for the lads! Hooters (on the main road A6011, on the outskirts of the city centre, you can't miss it!) has very nice waitresses wearing just enough to cover things up, serves lovely beer, and great food. Take my advice, make a weekend of it, Nottingham is a top city!'

If you are arriving by train and have a bit of time on your hands, then I would suggest that you check out the Olde Trip To Jerusalem. This historic pub dates back to the 12th century and some of the rooms are 'cave like' having been carved out of the rock that Nottingham Castle is situated upon. Add real ale, food and a small beer garden, then it is certainly worth a visit. It is about a five minute walk away from the train station. As you come out of the station turn right. At the top of the road turn left and then take the second right into Castle Road. Just tucked away on the left is the pub.

There is also the Waterfront complex of bars (including a Wetherspoons outlet) which is a short walk from the train station. As you come out of the station turn right and cross over to the other side of the road (as you cross the bridge going over the canal you can see the complex). At the top of the road turn left and the Waterfront complex is just down on the left, located behind the buildings on the main road. Otherwise alcohol is also available within the ground.

Directions & Car Parking

Leave the M1 at Junction 26 and take the A610 towards Nottingham and then follow signs for Melton Mowbray. Turn left before the River Trent into Meadow Lane. Parking is available at the Cattle Market (opposite the away end) which costs £3 a car or at Nottingham City Council's Eastcroft depot (NG2 3AH) at £4 a car. The depot is a five minute walk from Meadow Lane, located just off London Road (A60), opposite Hooters. The entrance is signposted with banners and is manned by security guards throughout the match. Otherwise there is plenty of street parking.

By Train

The ground is a 10 minute walk away from Nottingham railway station. As you come out of the main station entrance, Turn left from the station across the car park and then turn right at the traffic lights. The ground is about a quarter of a mile down the dual carriageway on the left.

Programme

Official Programme: £2.50.

Record & Average Attendance

Record Attendance: 47,310 v York City, FA Cup 6th Round, March 12th, 1955.
Average Attendance: 2011-12: 6,808 (League One)

Ground Name: Boundary Park
Capacity: 10,638 (all seated)
Address: Boundary Park, Oldham, OL1 2PA
Main Telephone No: 0161 624 4972
Ticket Office No: 0161 785 5150

Year Ground Opened: 1906
Pitch Size: 106 x 72 yards
Team Nickname: The Latics
Home Kit Colours: Blue With White Trim
Official website: www.oldhamathletic.co.uk

What's The Ground Like?

The ground is comprised of just three sides, as the Club demolished the Broadway (Lookers) Stand on one side of the stadium in 2008. This was in preparation for the building of a new 5,200 capacity Main Stand, however, this has yet to materialise.

At one end is the comparatively new Rochdale Road End, a good sized all seater covered stand with an excellent view of the pitch. It has windshields to either side and an electric scoreboard on its roof. Part of this stand is given to away supporters. The other end, the Chadderton Road Stand (also known as the 'Chaddy End'), is a medium sized all seater covered stand. Again there are windshields to either side, but the elderly nature of this stand is apparent from the supporting pillars running across the front of it. On one side there is the old two-tiered Main Stand. This used to have terracing in front, but has since been filled with seating. There is still some old unused terracing on one side of this stand. The ground also benefits from four large traditional floodlight pylons, leaving the visitor in no doubt that this is a football ground.

What Is It Like For Visiting Supporters?

Away fans are housed on one side of the Rochdale Road Stand at one end of the ground. This stand is shared with home supporters. It is divided into sections, the larger of which holds 3,000 fans and the smaller 1,600 fans. The predicted size of the away support, dictates which section is allocated, but for most games it is the smaller area.

The sections are separated by a large moat like gap, which certainly makes for a lot of banter across it. The facilities in this modern stand are fairly good, as are the acoustics. If you get a chance, make sure to try one of the pies; Cottage, Steak & Pepper, plus Cheese & Potato. Some fans reckon that this is the best part of a visit to Boundary Park! Make sure you wrap up well though as the location of Boundary Park on the edge of the Pennines, means that it always seems to be cold, with a biting wind that goes right through you. Generally a friendly day out.

Where To Drink?

The closest pub is the Clayton Green, which is a Brewers Fayre outlet and can be found two hundred yards from the corner of the Main Stand and the Chaddy End, on Sheepfoot Lane. There is also the Greyhound pub, which is across Broadway down Holden Fold Lane.

Chippy Lees, an exiled Latics fans in Cornwall, recommends the following; 'The Old Grey Mare on Rochdale Road is worth a visit. If you walk to the top of Sheepfoot Lane and turn left at the newspaper shop, the pub is about 100 yards down the road on the right. There's a varied selection of beers available, and again a warm welcome is assured. Further down on the right is The White Hart'.

Directions & Car Parking
Leave the M62 at Junction 20 and take the A627(M) towards Oldham. Take the second slip road off the A627(M) following the signs for Royton (A663). At the top of the slip road you will find a large roundabout that around it has a McDonalds and a KFC. Turn left at the roundabout onto the A663 towards Royton (beware though of 30mph speed cameras on this stretch). You will be able to see Boundary Park over on your right. Take the next right-hand turn into Hilbre Avenue which will take you up to the large Club car park, situated behind the demolished stand. The cost of the car park is; cars £5, minibus £10, coaches £15.

If you want to go straight to the Club main entrance, then at the roundabout take the second exit onto A627 Chadderton Way (signposted Oldham). After around 300 yards take the first left into Boundary Park Road and at the end of the road turn right into Sheepfoot Lane.

By Train/Metro
The new Metrolink line from Manchester to Oldham has recently been completed. The closest Metrolink station to the ground is Freehold which is around a 30 minute walk away from Boundary Park.

On exiting Freehold Metro Station turn right along Agnes Street. At the bottom of this street turn left into Robinson Street, then the third right into Gordon Street and then right onto Denton Lane. Crossover the road and at the roundabout turn left into Walsh Street. Where the road forks, bear right into Peel Street. Cross over Middleton Road (A669) into Garforth Road. At the end of Garforth Road turn right onto Burnley Lane and the left along the A627 Chadderton Way (you should be able to see the floodlights over on the right). Take the next right at the traffic lights into Westhulme Way and then Westhulme Way for the ground.

The nearest railway station is Oldham Mills Hill, which again is around a 30 minute walk away from Boundary Park. George Sutcliffe a visiting Sheffield United fan informs me; 'On leaving Mills Hill station descend the ramp then turn right. Then bear left into Haigh Lane which becomes Chadderton Hall Road and then Burnley Lane (although it is the same road) this takes you to the Toby Carvery at the M627 roundabout from where the ground is visible. Apart from a handful of Blades and a few Manchester based Latics hardly anyone took this route. There was also a large JW Lees pub called the Rose Of Lancaster on Haigh Lane 200 yards from Mills Hill Station which served food and had Sky Sports'.

Jon Brierley adds; 'Alternatively, rather than getting a train from Manchester to Oldham, you may find it easier to take a bus from Manchester Piccadilly Bus Station. Services numbers 24, 181 & 182 make the 25 minute trip to Oldham and go past the ground. They operate six buses an hour on Saturday afternoons, with three an hour on evenings and Sundays. Alternatively, fans from the Yorkshire direction might like to consider taking a train to Rochdale (direct services from York, Leeds, Bradford & Halifax) and then continuing to Boundary Park on bus 409 (every 10 minutes Saturday daytime, journey time 25 minutes)'.

Programme
Official Programme: £3

Record & Average Attendance
Record Attendance: 47,671 v Sheffield Wednesday, FA Cup 5th Round, January 25th, 1930.
Average Attendance: 2011-12: 4,433 (League One)

Ground Name: Kassam Stadium
Capacity: 12,500 (all seated)
Address: Grenoble Road, Oxford, OX4 4XP
Main Telephone No: 01865 337 500
Ticket Office No: 01865 337 533

Year Ground Opened: 2001
Pitch Size: 112 x 78 yards
Team Nickname: The U's
Home Kit Colours: Yellow & Blue
Official website: www.oufc.co.uk

What's The Ground Like?

The club moved to the Kassam Stadium in 2001, after leaving the Manor Ground, which had been its home for 76 years. The stadium is named after the former Club Chairman Firoz Kassam. It was built at a cost of around £15 million and is located on the outskirts of Oxford. It has only three sides, with one end remaining unused. Each of the stands are of a good size, are all seated, covered and are roughly of the same height. The South Stand on one side of the pitch, is a two-tiered stand with a row of executive boxes. This is a particularly impressive looking stand with police control and press boxes situated at the back. Opposite is the single-tiered North Stand, primarily given to away supporters. This has a number of strange looking floodlights protruding from its roof. At the one end is the Oxford Mail Stand, which is also single-tiered. There is a special type of pitch, one of the first to have artificial grass woven into the live turf. One disappointment is the large gaps in the corners, which sets the stands back from the playing surface and means cold winds whistling through in winter.

What Is It Like For Visiting Supporters?

Away fans are normally housed on one side of the North Stand, towards the open end of the ground. This stand may be shared with home supporters, or if demand requires it, then the whole of this stand can be allocated providing just over 5,000 seats in total. The facilities within and the views of the playing action are excellent, and there is also good leg room. The atmosphere within the ground is not bad, with the home fans in the Oxford Mail Stand doing their best to raise it. There is not much around the ground in terms of pubs and eating establishments, although refreshments inside the stadium are okay, although if there is a large away support, then it can take quite a while to get served. With one end of the ground being open, there is always the remark 'of watch my car' as another wayward shot flies into the car park behind. On the whole I found the Kassam Stadium to be an enjoyable and a largely friendly day out.

Where To Drink?

The nearest Public House is The Priory which is just behind the car park at the open end of the ground. This pub is quite historic looking from the outside and is generally fine for away fans, but as you would expect, it can get quite crowded. It boasts a large screen for SKY TV and also offered food, in the form of a wide range of pies and filled rolls. If the weather is good then the pub also do a barbecue prior to the match. Andy Wraight adds, 'There is the Holiday Inn Express Hotel on the corner behind the Oxford Mail and South Stand, which has a fair sized bar. The bar welcomes football supporters and has Sky Television. Kim Rockall informs me; 'There is a cinema and bowling alley complex located adjacent to the stadium, called Ozone. Inside the bowling alley there is a bar, which also has SKY TV and a fast food outlet'. Alcohol is also available inside the stadium.

Directions & Car Parking

The stadium is quite well signposted from the main routes into Oxford, with brown football signs pointing the way. The stadium can be found in between the Oxford Science Park & Blackbird Leys Estate. From the A423 Ring Road, take the A4074 towards Reading. After the roundabout with Sainsbury's on one corner, take the left turning signposted Cowley/Wallington/Oxford Science Park and you eventually come to the ground on your left.

There are 1,600 car parking spaces at the stadium itself, which are free. However, the car parks tend to fill up fast, so try and arrive early if you can (at least 75 minutes before kick-off). An additional 400 car parking spaces are available at the Ozone cinema and bowling alley complex adjacent to the stadium, which are also free to use. John Attwood a visiting Gillingham supporter adds; 'when arriving at the stadium, ignore the first stadium car park entrance that you come to and go up to the second entrance as the first will have you parking at the "open" end. There is a roundabout by the second entrance, which will take you back to the first entrance if the other half is full. I was also heavily delayed in trying to leave the car park after the game as there were only two exits available'. If you do end up arriving late at the stadium and find that the stadium car parks

are full, then don't get tempted to park on a grass verge as you may well end up with a parking ticket for your trouble.

By Train

Oxford railway station is over four miles from the ground and it is really not advisable to try to walk it. So either get a taxi or go by bus to the stadium. You can get the Oxford Bus Company Service, Number 5, from Oxford Railway Station (use bus stop R2) via the city centre to Knights Road in Blackbird Leys, which is a short walk away from the ground. On Saturday afternoons the bus runs every five minutes and on midweek evenings every 8-10 minutes. Journey time to the stadium is around 30 minutes.

Tim Rigby informs me; 'The 106 bus from Thames Travel departs the station forecourt (just to the left of the main entrance) at 12:30pm and winds its way through town and down to the ground for 12:55pm, and again at 1:30pm. It drops you off right outside the Main Stand, and picks up again from the same stop at 5pm and 6pm.

Programme

Official Programme: £3

Record & Average Attendance

Record Attendance: 12,243 v Leyton Orient, League Two, May 6th, 2006.

Average Attendance: 2011-12: 7,451 (League Two)

Ground Name: London Road
Capacity: 15,314
Address: London Road, Peterborough, PE2 8AL
Main Telephone No: 01733 563 947
Ticket Office No: 01733 865 674

Year Ground Opened: 1934
Pitch Size: 112 x 76 yards
Team Nickname: The Posh
Home Kit Colours: Blue & White
Official website: www.theposh.com

What's The Ground Like?

On one side of the ground is the Norwich & Peterborough South Stand, which was opened in 1996 and replaced a former open terrace. Encased in supporting tubular steelwork, the 5,000 capacity stand is an impressive sight. The two-tiered stand, is covered and all seated. There is also a row of executive boxes running across its middle. Opposite is the much older Main Stand that was opened in 1957. It is a two-tiered covered stand that is all seated. Originally it had a terraced area to its front but this was made all seated in the early 1990s. Both ends are covered terraced stands that look almost identical. Dating back to the early 1950s, they had their roofs replaced around 10 years ago. In one corner of the ground between the Norwich & Peterborough South Stand and the London Road Terrace, is a Police Control Box. On either side of the Main Stand are two tall, old fashioned looking floodlights. The ground had a set of four at one time, but two were taken down when the South Stand was built.

What Is It Like For Visiting Supporters?

With Peterborough now in the Championship, where all seater stadia is a requirement (clubs on promotion who have terracing are given a period of time to bring their grounds up to standard), then for many followers of other teams, it is a rare chance to get to stand once again on a real covered terrace. Just under 4,000 away fans can be accommodated in the Moyes Terrace, with a further 800 seats being made available to away fans in the Main Stand. If however, only a small away following is expected, then the terrace is kept closed and away supporters are housed just in the Block A seats of the Main Stand.

The Moyes Terrace has several supporting pillars, running along the front of it, which may obstruct your view, but the acoustics of the covered terrace are good, lending to a good atmosphere. If intending to sit in the Main Stand, then please note that the leg room can be a bit tight. Although the stewards are visible, they are pretty laid back and don't get involved unless needed. The only real downside to the terrace is that the facilities are inadequate if a big crowd is in attendance, with just one male toilet block and one refreshment serving hatch (with just two staff serving) being available. For the eagle eyed, then over to the right of the terrace in the distance, Peterborough Cathedral can be clearly seen. On the whole on each of my visits, I have found Peterborough to be a good and fairly relaxed day out, with some good pubs in the locality too.

Where To Drink?

The Cherry Tree pub on Oundle Road is popular with both home and away fans. It is about a 15 minute walk away from the visitors' turnstiles. It is a friendly pub that is listed in the CAMRA Good Beer Guide and also offers a range of reasonably priced matchday food, such Chilli & Chips, Curry & Chips, Burgers etc. which are served from a separate area to the rear of the pub. You can also park in their car park at a cost of £2.50 per car and £5 per minibus.

Near to the ground is Charters, which is certainly worth a visit and is also listed in the CAMRA Good Beer Guide. This former Dutch barge, is moored on the River Nene, just a few minutes walk away from London Road, on the left-hand side of the bridge, going towards the city centre. Upstairs is a Chinese restaurant, but downstairs there is a bar, which had on my last visit 12 real ales on tap. It was friendly enough and fans were able to take their drinks out onto the river bank, which makes it quite pleasant, when the weather is good. Alternatively, the ground is in walking distance (10 minutes) of the city centre (which is very pleasant and complete with a cathedral) where there are plenty of good pubs to be found.

Directions & Car Parking

The ground is located on the outskirts of the city centre, on the A15 London Road. The ground is fairly well signposted around the city centre.

From the North/West:

Drive into the city centre, follow signs for Whittlesey (A605) which will lead you onto the London Road. The South Stand roof is quite visible from some distance away, so keep a lookout.

From the South:

Leave the A1 at the junction with the A15. Take the A15 towards Peterborough, you will eventually come to the ground on your right.

There is a car park at the ground or otherwise there is a council pay & display car park just off London Road (on your left as you pass the ground going towards the city centre). This costs £4.40 for four hours. Otherwise there is street parking to be found on side streets further up Oundle Road (A605). Please though check for any parking restriction signs on lamp posts, as the side streets nearest to the ground operate a residents only parking scheme.

By Train

Peterborough station is around a mile away from the ground. Turn right out of the station and follow the main road, passing an Asda store on your right. At the traffic lights near to the Rivergate Shopping Centre, turn right. Go over the bridge and you can see the floodlights of London Road, over on your left. It takes about 20 minutes to walk from the station to the ground. Thanks to Andrew Dodd for providing the directions.

Programme & Fanzine

Official Programme: £3
Blue Moon Fanzine: £2

Record & Average Attendance

Record Attendance: 30,096 v Swansea City, FA Cup 5th Round, February 20th, 1965.
Average Attendance: 2011-12: 9,111 (Championship League)

Ground Name: Home Park
Capacity: 18,000 (all seated)
Address: Home Park, Plymouth, PL2 3DQ
Main Telephone No: 01752 562 561
Ticket Office No: 0845 872 3335

Year Ground Opened: 1901*
Pitch Size: 112 x 73 yards
Team Nickname: The Pilgrims
Home Kit Colours: Green & White
Official website: www.pafc.co.uk

What's The Ground Like?

During 2001 Home Park was transformed, with three sides of the ground being completely re-built. This included both ends and one side of the ground. They were replaced by single-tiered, covered all seated stands, that are of the same design and height. The corners between these stands were also filled with seating so that the ground is totally enclosed on those sides, making an impressive sight. There is a gap between the roof and the back of these stands, which is filled with a perspex strip to allow more light to get to the pitch.

The Grandstand at one side of the pitch is the only remnant of the old Home Park. This classic looking stand dates back to 1952, although its appearance makes it look much older. Although it is much older than the other sides, it is still taller than the other stands and is still the focal point at Home Park. It is a two-tiered stand, with an upper tier of seating and a lower tier of terracing, most of which is uncovered by the stand's roof. This roof is supported by four large pillars that run across the front of upper tier. For a couple of seasons, while the Club was in the Championship League, the terrace was filled with temporary seating to comply with League regulations.

Although the seating has since been removed this area is unused by spectators on matchdays. There are a couple of modern floodlight pylons situated on either side of the Grandstand.

In keeping with the naval tradition of the area the teams emerge to the Marines tune of Semper Fidelis. Home Park is the most westerly and southerly League Ground in England.

What Is It Like For Visiting Supporters?

Away fans are housed in the Barn Park End, which is all seated and covered. As you would expect from a modern stand the facilities and views of the playing action are both good. The normal allocation for visiting supporters in this area is 1,300 seats, although this can be increased to 2,022, if demand requires it. The atmosphere is normally good and even though I have received a number of reports of the stewarding being somewhat over zealous in the away end, on my last visit it was fine. No problems were encountered outside the ground and on the whole it was a good day out. The only down side was that the concourse was a bit cramped and if there is a good away support then it can get uncomfortably crowded.

Where To Drink?

Probably the best bet is the Britannia which is a sizeable Wetherspoons pub and is around a 10 minute walk away from the ground (from the car park outside the football ground, turn left and the pub is down the road on the right-hand corner). For most matches the pub which is busy normally, has a queue of fans waiting to get in outside, but this is controlled by the security staff, so you don't normally have to wait too long to gain entrance. Although away fan friendly, the pub doesn't tolerate away supporters singing their clubs songs and any who do are quickly ejected from the premises, so you have been warned. Near to the pub is normally a van selling pasties, which looked to be doing a roaring trade on my last visit. Opposite the Britannia is the Embassy Club which is best avoided by away fans. Otherwise alcohol is available within the ground.

Directions & Car Parking

Take the M5 to the South West and at the end of the motorway continue onto the A38 (The ground is well signposted from the outskirts of Plymouth on the A38). On entering Plymouth, turn left onto the A386 (towards Plymouth). When this road splits into two, keep on the left-hand side (again signposted Plymouth) and after about a mile you will see the ground on your left. The ground is well signposted 'Plymouth Argyle Home Park' on the way into Plymouth.

There is quite a large car park at the ground, which is free. It is operated on a 'first in before the game, first out after the game basis'. If you are last in, then on average it takes around half an hour to clear. The car park is normally full by 2.30pm on matchdays. There is some street parking if you drive past the ground, heading away from the city centre.

By Train

Plymouth railway station is about one and a half miles away, so either grab a taxi or embark on the 20 minute walk. As you come out of the station turn right and down the hill and under the railway bridge. Just keep walking straight along this road (A386) and you will eventually reach the ground on your right.

Alternatively (except for night games) then Andrew Chapman suggests a more picturesque route: 'Finally I would recommend turning right into Central Park Avenue, at the roundabout just downhill from the station on the A386. Then take the second left into Holdsworth Street, which will lead you up a steep hill into Central Park, where you'll see the ground as soon as you reach the top of the hill. It is a lot nicer route than following the roads – after all (apart from Aldershot) there are no other League clubs situated in a public park!' Chris Bennett adds; ' It's a much nicer walk than going up Alma Road and quicker as well'.

Programme & Fanzine

Official Programme: £3

Rub Of The Greens Fanzine: £1

Record & Average Attendance

Record Attendance: 43,596 v Aston Villa, Division Two, October 10th, 1936.

Average Attendance: 2011-12: 6,915 (League Two)

* The ground was originally built in 1893, the Club took it over in 1901.

Ground Name: Vale Park
Capacity: 18,947 (all seated)
Address: Hamil Road, Burslem,
Stoke-on-Trent, ST6 1AW
Main Telephone No: 01782 655 800
Ticket Office No: 01782 655 832

Year Ground Opened: 1950
Pitch Size: 114 x 77 yards
Team Nickname: The Valiants
Home Kit Colours: White & Black
Official website: www.port-vale.co.uk

What's The Ground Like?

The ground has a good mixture of the old and the new, it is just let down overall by the fact that the Lorne Street Stand, which was partly opened in 1999, is still yet to be fully completed. This stand which is two-tiered has a row of executive boxes situated between its large lower tier and much smaller upper tier. With a planned capacity of 5,000 it is of a good size and I'm sure it would look quite smart when finished. However, the outstanding works include half the lower tier towards the Hamil Road End. This area is currently empty of seating and is largely just a concrete base. On a positive note the original clock that was seen on the old stand has been incorporated into the new construction, above the players tunnel and Directors area in the centre of the stand.

On the opposite side is the Railway Stand which was opened in 1954. It is a fair sized stand that is covered to the rear. It has a number of supporting pillars that run across the middle of the stand. Originally it had a large paddock terrace in front, but this was subsequently filled with seating in the 1990s. At one end is the Hamil Road End, which is a good sized single-tiered stand. It

also has an electric scoreboard situated just below its roof. Again it has a number of supporting pillars (although fewer in number than the Railway Stand), plus it has windshields to either side. Opposite is the Bycars Road End, which although old looking was built in 1992. It also is partly covered to the rear and has some supporting pillars to either side. Situated in one corner, in between the Bycars & Railway Stand is an odd looking two-tiered structure that looks if it has been 'wedged' into the stadium. Filled with seating it is currently used as a Family Stand. The pitch is also one of the widest in the League.

What Is It Like For Visiting Supporters?

Up to 4,500 away supporters can be accommodated in the Hamil Road End, where the view and facilities located on the concourse behind the stand are good. Even a relatively small number of away fans can really make some noise from this stand, as the acoustics are excellent. However, the slope is quite shallow, which might affect your view should a tall person be seated in front. Normally though, you could still move to another seat if necessary. The PA within the ground is quite deafening at times and there is no escape, even in the toilets, as it is piped through! Please note that cash is not accepted at the away turnstiles, you have to buy a ticket from the portakabin in the car park by the away end. This portakabin is 'cash only'. If you wish to pay by credit or debit card you will need to purchase tickets from the Main ticket office.

Where To Drink?

Unfortunately the choice of pubs for away supporters to drink in near to the ground or in the town centre is very limited as Nick Williams a visiting Plymouth Argyle fan informs me; 'Apart from the Bull's Head, which was very welcoming, every other pub in the town that we found had signs up saying Home fans only'. Luckily the Bull's Head which is located in St John's Square, is a cracking pub. It is the local outlet for the nearby Titanic Brewery and is listed in the CAMRA Good Beer Guide. It is friendly for away fans and has up to nine real ales on offer as well as one traditional cider. To find this pub: From the outside of the away end, turn right and go down to the bottom of Hamil Road (passing the Vine Pub on your left). Turn right at the t-junction and then go straight across the traffic lights at the crossroads. Proceed past KFC, Wades and the New Inn on the right and then if you look over to your left, you will see a square with the Bull's Head, which is located on the right of this square. It is about a 10 minute walk. Otherwise alcohol is served inside the ground.

Directions & Car Parking

The ground is located in the town of Burslem, one of the six towns comprising Stoke-on-Trent. Leave the M6 at junction 15 or 16 and take the A500 towards Stoke-on-Trent. Follow A500 until the A527 Tunstall/Burslem exit, where you take the A527 towards Tunstall/Burslem. At the next island just past the Price Kensington factory turn right for Burslem town centre. Continue on this road up the hill, crossing another island and into Burslem town centre. Continue straight on over the traffic lights at the cross roads and then take the first road on

the left which takes you down to the ground. There is a large car park located outside a superstore next to the ground which costs £4, otherwise street parking.

By Train

Longport station is the closest to the ground, but is a good 25-30 minute walk away and is not well served by trains as Stoke-on-Trent station is. Therefore most fans end up at Stoke-on-Trent railway station, which is over four miles away and then take a taxi up to the ground.

John Midgley, a visiting Huddersfield Town fan informs me; 'Services run hourly from Crewe, Stoke & Derby to Longport. Cross over the line (if travelling from Stoke/Derby) and walk along Station Street. At the mini-roundabout follow the main road round to the left going up the hill. After a couple of minutes take the first major left onto Newcastle Street (B5051). Enter Burslem. Pass the Bull's Head pub at St. John's Square. Bear left onto Market Place. Shortly after cross the main road onto Jenkins Street which becomes Hamil Road. The ground will soon be visible on the left. Turn left into Lorne Street'.

Programme & Fanzines

Official Programme: £2.50
Vale Park Beano Fanzine: £1
Derek I'm Gutted Fanzine: £1

Record & Average Attendance

Record Attendance: 49,768 v Aston Villa, FA Cup 5th Round, February 20th, 1960.
Average Attendance: 2011-12: 4,820 (League Two)

Ground Name: Fratton Park
Capacity: 20,700 (all seated)
Address: Frogmore Road, Portsmouth, PO4 8RA
Main Telephone No: 02392 731204
Ticket Office No: 0844 847 1898

Year Ground Opened: 1898
Pitch Size: 115 x 73 yards
Team Nickname: Pompey
Home Kit Colours: Blue, White & Red
Official website: www.portsmouthfc.co.uk

What's The Ground Like?

Fratton Park is a traditional looking ground and one which oozes character. Both side stands are two-tiered and originally had terracing at the front, which has now been replaced with seating. The South Stand dates back to 1925 and was originally designed by Archibald Leitch who also designed a number of grounds and stands around this period. Although showing its age in parts, it has plenty of character with an old fashioned looking media gantry perched on its roof and raised team dugouts at its front. Opposite, the North Stand opened in 1935, looks somewhat plain and functional. Both the North & South Stands are two-tiered and have a number of supporting pillars.

At one end is the Fratton End, which is a more modern single-tiered stand that was opened in 1997. It is of a good size and is the tallest stand at the ground. Opposite is the recently covered Milton End, which is all seated. Part of this stand is given to away fans. On one corner of this stand by the away supporters is a Police Control Box that also has a large video screen perched upon its roof. The ground is completed with a superb looking set of tall floodlights that were first used in 1962.

If you get chance to wander around the outside of the ground beforehand then make sure to go down towards the home end to look at the mock tudor facade in Frogmore Road.

What Is It Like For Visiting Supporters?

Away fans are housed on one side of the Milton End (on the North Stand side) where around 2,000 fans can be accommodated. Although this end now benefits from having cover, the facilities within are pretty basic and the leg room tight, as this stand was a former terrace that has been converted to all seating. There are also some supporting pillars along the front of the stand that may impede your view. On a positive note, away supporters can really make some noise from this stand, further contributing to what is normally a great atmosphere, which is further aided by a drummer and bell ringer in the Fratton End.

Although this end is shared with home supporters, the Pompey home support get behind their team but generally in a non-intimidatory way towards the away contingent. Fans were literally separated by a netted area only three seats wide, but on my last visit there were no problems whatsoever. Entrance to the stand is gained by inserting your ticket into a bar code reader. If you have not pre-purchased a ticket for the game, then allow yourself plenty of time as the ticket booth is located at the opposite end of the ground to the away end. On the whole though try to sit back and enjoy Fratton Park, such older grounds now are becoming few and far between with the advent of new stadia being built.

Where To Drink?

On my last visit I went to the Good Companion pub, which is on the main A2030 about a five minute walk away from the ground. It is a large pub serving real ales and had a good mix of home and away support. I also noticed that it was doing a brisk business in food. Ian Pratt suggests the Brewers Arms which is 'always popular with away fans'. Steve Yeoman, a visiting Manchester United fan informs me; 'just outside the ground at the north east corner a large enclosed white marquee has been erected for away fans. It has a bar, televisions and was free to enter. There is also a handy burger van located outside'.

Directions & Car Parking

Go along the M27 (ignoring the M275 turn off for Portsmouth town centre) and continue on to the A27. At the junction with the A2030 turn right towards Southsea/Fratton and just continue straight along the A2030 and eventually you will see the ground in front of you, just slightly to your left.

There is a large car park behind the Fratton End, but this is for home supporters only. So it is mostly street parking for away fans. The good news is that there are few parking restrictions in place close to the ground. So if you arrive early enough, you can park only a few minutes walk away. When I have visited, I have parked in one of the side streets, found on the right hand side of the A2030 before you reach the Good Companion pub.

By Train

The nearest local train station is Fratton, which is a 10 minute walk away. Portsmouth train station is at least a 25 minute walk away.

On arrival at Fratton by train you pass the ground on the left. Fratton station has a footbridge as the only way out. At the top of the stairs from the platform turn left onto the footbridge (from which you can see the floodlights of Fratton Park) and exit into Goldsmith Avenue. (Note that if the gate on the footbridge is closed you need to turn right on the footbridge and exit via Platform 1, turn left as you exit the station, walk 30 metres and go back over the footbridge to Goldsmith Avenue.) Turn left along Goldsmith Avenue and walk about half a mile passing straight around a small round-about (by the Pompey Centre). Then turn left into Frogmore Road and the entrance to the Fratton End and South Stand is 100m ahead. For the Milton End stay on Goldsmith Avenue for another 100m and turn left into Apsley Road. Thanks to Peter Coulthard for providing the directions.

Programme & Fanzine

Official Programme: £3
Park Life Fanzine: £1.50

Record & Average Attendance

Record Attendance: 51,385 v Derby County, FA Cup 6th Round, February 26th, 1949.
Average Attendance: 2011-12: 15,016
(Championship League)

Ground Name: Deepdale
Capacity: 23,408 (all seated)
Address: Sir Tom Finney Way, Preston, PR1 6RU
Main Telephone No: 0844 856 1964
Ticket Office No: 0844 856 1966

Year Ground Opened: 1875*
Pitch Size: 110 x 77 yards
Team Nickname: The Lilywhites
Home Kit Colours: White & Navy
Official website: www.pnefc.net

What's The Ground Like?

With the addition of the new Invincibles Pavilion Stand in 2008, it now means that Deepdale has now been completely rebuilt in recent years. What was a great looking stadium, is now an even better one as the new stand completely fills the remaining side of what was the Pavilion side of the ground.

Three sides of the stadium are composed of some excellent looking all seater stands, complete with some spectacular looking floodlights. They are of the same height and style and are all large, covered, single-tiered stands. Each has a likeness of a past player outlined on the seats and is named after that player. Tom Finney, Bill Shankly and goalkeeping legend Alan Kelly, are all honoured and this makes a welcome change from the boring letters outlined on most new stands. The first of these stands to be built was the Tom Finney Stand in 1995. This was followed by the Bill Shankly Kop in 1998 and the Alan Kelly Stand in 2001. The fourth new stand, the Invincibles Stand (named after the legendary Preston team of 1888/1889 who went through the whole season unbeaten and were also the first in that season to win the League and FA Cup double), cost in the region of £9 million to build.

The design of this stand is slightly different to the other three. Even though it is of the same height and has a similar roof, it has a smaller tier of seating, with 22 executive boxes sitting above. Alas I presume that there was not enough space to incorporate another player image on the seating so instead we have to make do with the letters 'PNE FC' instead. Outside the stadium is a statue of former Preston legend Tom Finney.

What Is It Like For Visiting Supporters?

Away fans are housed in the modern Bill Shankly Kop at one end of the pitch. Normally the allocation for away fans is approximately half of this stand (3,000 seats) and it is shared with home supporters. However, for teams with a large away support, then the whole end can be allocated, raising the allocation to 6,000.

The views of the playing action and facilities within this stand are excellent. The stand is particularly steep, meaning that fans are kept relatively close to the pitch. On the concourse there are TVs by the refreshment serving areas showing the game live and with the bars being open during the game, this is too much of a temptation for some! James Prentice adds; 'I would recommend getting a 'Butter Pie' inside the ground, which is a bit of a local delicacy. It is just a normal pie but with a filling of very buttery mashed potato and onion. I was attracted to it by a flag at the top of the new Invincibles Stand that read 'True Prestonians Love a Butter Pie!' I particularly enjoyed my last visit as the fans, stewards and even police all seemed to be fairly friendly and there was a good atmosphere being generated within the stadium.

Where To Drink?

There is not a great deal in the way of pubs in close proximity to the ground. Further up Tom Finney Way (which used to be called Deepdale Road) from the stadium, is Sumners. This pub normally has a good mix of home and away supporters, although for certain high profile games and local derbies the pub does not admit away supporters. There is a good sized beer garden & car park at the pub. The pub does charge for parking (£3) but this can be redeemed against a purchase at the bar. Good food is available and children are allowed in.

There are also a couple of nearby clubs that welcome away fans. First there is St Gregory's Catholic Club, which is around a five minute walk away on Blackpool Road. The Club offers reasonably priced drinks, hot pies, plus has SKY television. You can also park at the Club at a cost of £3. Secondly, there is the Fulwood Conservative Club, situated around 10 minutes walk away from Deepdale, at the junction of Blackpool Road and Garstang Road across from Moor Park. Parking is available at the Club at a cost of £3 per car and non-members are admitted free into the club on matchdays. Otherwise alcohol is served within the ground.

Directions & Car Parking

Leave M6 at Junction 31 and follow signs left for Preston. Go up a steep hill (often a police speed trap on the hill, so stick to 30) and follow the road down to a mini-roundabout (speed camera by the BP garage on the left). At the roundabout with the

Hesketh Arms turn right into Blackpool Road. Go straight on over three sets of lights and just before a fourth set, the ground appears set slightly back on the left. Parking is mainly in the streets surrounding the ground.

By Train

Preston railway station is around a mile and a half from the ground and takes around 25 minutes to walk, although you will pass some good pubs on the way. Leave the Preston railway station via the main entrance, and head right at the top of the drive. This is the main High Street. Continue along the High Street, passing all the regular big name shops. The High Street (or Church Street/Fishergate as it's known) is about a mile long, and you will pass a church as you come to its end. Simply carry on walking along this street, and when you reach the ring road, you head straight over the large traffic lights, heading towards Preston Prison. Turn left at the Prison into Church Street, then left into Deepdale Road. Continue straight along Deepdale Road and after about a mile you will reach the ground. Thanks to Kevin Wrenn for supplying the directions.

Programme

Official Programme: £3

Record & Average Attendance

Record Attendance: 42,684 v Arsenal, Division One, April 23rd, 1938.

Average Attendance: 2011-12: 11,820 (League One)

* The ground was opened in 1875 as an athletics, rugby and cricket ground. Football was first played later on the site in 1881.

Ground Name: Loftus Road Stadium
Capacity: 18,360 (all seated)
Address: South Africa Road, London, W12 7PA
Main Telephone No: 020 8743 0262
Ticket Office No: 08444 777 007

Year Ground Opened: 1917
Pitch Size: 112 x 72 yards
Team Nickname: The Superhoops
Home Kit Colours: Blue & White Hoops
Official website: www.qpr.co.uk

What's The Ground Like?

Loftus Road has a compact feel, as the ground is totally enclosed, with supporters being close to the pitch. An unusual aspect is that all four stands are roughly the same height, their roofs meet at all four corners with no gaps. The South Africa Road Stand on one side, has a larger upper tier, compared to the lower tier, with a row of executive boxes running across the middle. There are a couple of supporting pillars in this stand. The other side, the Ellerslie Road Stand, is single-tiered, with a television gantry suspended below its roof. Both ends are similar looking two-tiered stands. On one of these, the School End (where the away fans are located) there is a large video screen located on the centre of its roof. Below this and situated between the lower and upper tier is a small electric scoreboard. The ground oozes character and there is nothing similar in the League.

What Is It Like For Visiting Supporters?

Away fans are situated in the upper tier of the School End, where around 1,800 fans can be accommodated. If demand requires it then the lower tier can also be allocated, increasing the number of places available to about 2,500. If the away club only takes the upper tier allocation, then the lower tier is allocated to home supporters. Alan Griffiths, a visiting Barnsley fan informs me; 'the entrance for away fans to the School End upper tier is no longer in South Africa Road, but on the opposite side of the ground in Ellerslie Road (turnstile block 2).'

I must say that on my three visits, I have found the stadium lacking a little in atmosphere. Also the leg room between rows of seats was a little tight. There is normally quite a large police and steward presence, and you should expect to be searched before you enter the away end. However, on the plus side I have never experienced any problems there, as it is generally relaxed and friendly. Dan Markham a QPR fan disagrees with me; 'It is virtually impossible to have such a small compact enclosed stadium, and not have a tremendous atmosphere. You are close to the pitch, close to the visiting fans and most importantly close to the action'. Another plus point was that the food that was served within the ground was quite good and the service prompt. Entrance to the stadium is gained by inserting your ticket into a bar code reader.

Where To Drink?

There are no pubs for away fans in the immediate vicinity around the stadium. Most away fans head over to nearby Shepherds Bush Green where the Walkabout and O'Neills are both popular with away supporters. The Walkabout has the benefit of Sky Sports & ESPN, serves food and is the Police designated away pub. To find Shepherds Bush Green; exit Shepherds Bush Market Underground Station (the Hammersmith & City line station), turn left out of the station and the green is a short way down the road on the right. Diagonally across Shepherds Bush Green opposite the Central line entrance to Shepherds Bush Underground Station, is a retail complex called Vue, which upstairs includes a Wetherspoons outlet. Otherwise alcohol is available in the away end.

On the eating front David Frodsham adds; 'On my travels to many football grounds, I have yet to find a wider selection of food available than on the Uxbridge Road. The cosmopolitan inner city nature means that you can almost eat your way around the world. From the normal range of cafes, burger bars, fried chicken outlets and chippies, there are Indian, Chinese, Thai & Jamaican outlets. There are Lebanese and Indian kebab shops, the latter selling "doner" kebabs made with Indian spices!'

Directions & Car Parking

From The North/West:

At the end of the M40, take the A40 towards Central London. At the point where the A40 becomes the A40(M), turn off onto the A40 towards White City/Shepherds Bush and turn right into Wood Lane, turn right into South Africa Road for the ground.

There is not much in the way of parking near to the ground. Matt Garside from Southampton suggests; 'It's probably easiest to just park on the road in this area as it costs £6.60 for three hours parking'. Some of these areas are free after 5pm. However, there are a number of restricted parking zones around the stadium so be careful where you park.

By Train/Tube

The nearest London Underground station is White City on the Central Line, which is about a five minute walk away. Also nearby (a little further along Wood Lane opposite the BBC Television Centre) is the recently opened Wood Lane Station, which is on the Hammersmith & City line. It is around a seven minute walk away from Loftus Road.

Otherwise there are two other tube stations close by; Shepherds Bush Market on the Hammersmith & City line and Shepherds Bush on the Central Line. The former is about a 10 minute walk away from the ground, while the other is about 15 minutes. Personally I tend to use Shepherds Bush Market tube station, simply because there seems to be more pubs around this area, especially around Shepherds Bush Green. Leaving both Shepherds Bush tube stations; turn right and the ground will come into view further down on the right. Please note that Queens Park tube station is nowhere near the ground!

The nearest train station is Shepherds Bush, which is adjacent to the tube station. However, it is not directly served by any of the major London mainline stations. However, trains from Watford Junction and Clapham Junction both stop there.

Programme & Fanzine

Official Programme: £3
A Kick Up The R's Fanzine: £2.50

Record & Average Attendance

Record Attendance: 35,353 v Leeds United, Division One, April 27th, 1974.
Average Attendance: 2011-12: 17,295 (Premier League)

Ground Name: Madejski Stadium
Capacity: 24,200 (all seated)
Address: Bennett Road, Reading, RG2 0FL
Main Telephone No: 0118 968 1100
Ticket Office No: 0844 249 1871

Year Ground Opened: 1998
Pitch Size: 112 x 76 yards
Team Nickname: The Royals
Home Kit Colours: Royal Blue & White
Official website: www.readingfc.co.uk

What's The Ground Like?

This Club moved to the stadium in 1998, after spending 102 years at their former home of Elm Park. The stadium is of a fair size and is totally enclosed, with all four corners being occupied. Three sides are single-tiered, while on one side the West (Main) Stand is two-tiered, including a row of executive boxes. This stand has a curve in its roof and the team dug outs are located in front. Unlike the West Stand, the other stands have a more conventional look to their roofs, although there is a gap between the roofs and the back of the stands, that contains perspex, to allow more light to reach the pitch. The ground has been designed with the supporter in mind as the fans are housed very close to the pitch and the acoustics are very good. The stadium also has a video screen in the South East corner. The stadium, named after Reading's chairman John Madejski is shared with London Irish Rugby Club.

What Is It Like For Visiting Supporters?

Away fans are located in one end of the stadium, in the South Stand, where just over 2,300 fans can be accommodated (4,300 for cup games). The facilities in this stand are good with plenty of leg room and the views of the pitch are superb, as there is good height between rows. Away fans can really make some noise in this stand, so make the most of it. The atmosphere is also boosted by a drummer in the home section. Entrance to the stadium is by ticket only and if tickets are still available for away supporters then they can purchase them on the day at the South Stand ticket office located between gates 9 and 10. You enter the stadium by inserting your ticket into a ticket reader which scans the bar code on the ticket and gives you a green light to go in.

Where To Drink?

There are no pubs as such near to the stadium. However, I did locate a Holiday Inn on Imperial Way which was around a 15 minute walk away. The hotel had a small bar inside it, but then attached had a larger Irish themed separate bar area, called Callaghans. This bar had Sky Television, but as you would expect was very crowded with away fans and served drinks at what I can only term as 'hotel prices'. Across the road from the hotel is a very good fish & chip shop. There is also The World turned upside down pub on Basingstoke Road. This chain pub normally has a mixture of home and away fans and also was popular for food. It is around a 15 minute walk from the stadium.

Otherwise it may be an idea, especially if you are making the journey by train, to drink in the centre of Reading before the game. Dave McKerchar adds; 'The Three Guineas on the station approach has been designated as an away fans pub. It offers a range of eight real ales and is listed in the CAMRA good beer guide. It has a big screen Sky TV and it also does food'. Alcohol is also available inside the stadium.

Directions & Car Parking

If you are travelling along the M4 from the West you can see the stadium on your left. Leave the M4 at Junction 11, bear left on to the A33 relief road which leads you directly to the stadium. The Madejski Complex is well signposted from Junction 11.

If you arrive early enough then there is street parking to be had along Imperial Way. There is also parking available at the Old Depot by the Courage Brewery on the A33/Imperial Way roundabout at a cost of £7 per car. There is some limited parking available at the stadium itself for a cost of £8, but it can be a bit of lengthy process to get out of the car park at the end of the game. Richard Buckingham adds; 'You can also park on the site of the now demolished greyhound track, close to the stadium. From the M4 at Junction 11 take the A33 towards Reading town centre. Follow the dual carriageway past the stadium and McDonalds, KFC and Pizza Hut outlets, then look for the 'Alternative Parking' signs ahead. On the left you will reach a small slip road into the parking site (which incidentally is an official stadium car park). It is also £8 to park there. It is stewarded and has the advantage of a quick post-match exit either back to J11 or towards Reading. The car park is a 5-10 minute walk away from the ground.'

Alternatively the Club operate a 'Park & Ride' scheme at Foster Wheeler at Shinfield Park. This costs for the return shuttle bus; Adults £3.50, Children £2. From Junction 11 of the M4, take the B3270 towards Earley and then follow the signs to 'Football Car Park C'. The car park opens at 1pm for Saturday afternoon games with the first bus departing at 1:30pm.

By Train

Reading railway station is situated just over three miles away from the Madejski Stadium. Probably the easiest way to get to the ground is to catch the No 79 'Football Special' bus, which leaves just down from the station, commencing at 1pm for Saturday afternoon games. As you come out of the main station entrance turn right and the buses are about 200 yards down the road on the opposite side – there is normally one waiting. The fare is £3.50 return for adults and £1.75 for children and normally takes about 15 minutes to get to the ground. A single fare costs £3 for adults, so don't lose that ticket!

Programme

Official Matchday programme: £3

Record & Average Attendance

Record Attendance: 24,135 v Manchester United, Premier League, January 19th, 2008.
Average Attendance: 2011-12: 19,219 (Championship League)

Ground Name: Spotland
Capacity: 10,249
Address: Sandy Lane, Rochdale, OL11 5DR
Main Telephone No: 0844 826 1907
Ticket Office No: Same as main number

Year Ground Opened: 1906
Pitch Size: 114 x 76 yards
Team Nickname: The Dale
Home Kit Colours: Blue & Black
Official website: www.rochdaleafc.co.uk

What's The Ground Like?

The ground has benefitted greatly with the construction of three new stands during the 1990s and year 2000. It is quite picturesque, with a number of trees being visible behind the stands. The last of these new stands to be opened was the smart looking Westrose Leisure Stand at one side of the pitch, which was opened in 2000.

This single-tiered stand replaced a former terrace and has a capacity of 4,000. On the other side is another single tier, the all seated Main Stand. This has a number of supporting pillars and some executive boxes at the back. At one end the Pearl Street Stand is the third of the new stands. This is also all seated and serves as a Family Stand. It has a couple of supporting pillars that are right at the front of the stand. The Thwaites Beer (Sandy Lane) End is the only terraced area remaining. It is on the small side but does at least benefit from having a roof. There is a Police Control Box located in one corner, between the Main & Pearl Street Stands. Spotland is shared with the Rochdale Hornets rugby league team.

What Is It Like For Visiting Supporters?

Away supporters are housed in the Willbutts Lane Stand on one side of the ground, where up to 3,650 supporters can be accommodated. Normally away fans are confined to the centre of the stand. If required, then this stand can be split between home and away fans. The view of the action and facilities within, are both pretty good. The acoustics are excellent, so away fans can really make some noise from within it. This, coupled with both home ends singing, makes for a good atmosphere. If Rochdale do score then 'Samba de Janeiro' blasts out around the ground from the PA system.

I would say that Spotland in my book, is one of the best footballing days out in the country. Friendly and knowledgeable fans, good stewards, good facilities, a couple of pubs located at the ground, a great range of pies on offer and not a bad atmosphere to boot. In other words all the right elements to make for a great day out. Add a pretty lady on my arm, my team winning six nil and I'll think that I have been transported to heaven!

Teresa Jewell a visiting Sheffield Wednesday fan adds; 'The ground is homely, with the staff being helpful and polite. The pies on sale were worth every penny. Parking though looked pretty bad, so I would advise getting there early if you want to park near to the stadium. The club house to the front of the ground is welcoming to away fans. There is also a chip shop facing the away end for something more substantial to eat, which does a roaring trade on matchdays'.

Where To Drink?

At the ground itself, there are two bars to choose from, Studds & the Ratcliffe Arms. Studds is located underneath the Pearl Street Stand and is worth a visit, if only to sample the large range of tasty pies and pasties on offer at £2.50 (which are also available inside the ground). No real ales here, but the bar has lots of memorabilia/pictures on the walls and some lovely looking barmaids which softens the blow. The Ratcliffe Arms is located at the car park entrance to the ground, on Sandy Lane. This pub has SKY TV and on my last visit had a mixture of home and away fans.

If you arrive early, the Cemetery Hotel, located at the bottom of Sandy Lane and on the corner with Bury Road, is also worth a visit. This comfortable historic pub has a range of real ales on offer and again friendly clientele. Otherwise alcohol is available inside the ground.

Directions & Car Parking

Exit the M62 at Junction 20 and take the A627(M) towards Rochdale. At the end of the A627(M) you should be in the left-hand lane to turn left at the traffic lights. Now follow the road and with Tesco on your left, go straight through the next set of lights (approach in the middle lane) into Roch Valley Way. At the next crossroads (where the Cemetery pub is on the corner) go straight onto Sandy Lane, where the ground can be found on the right after approx three quarters of a mile.

Car parking at the ground is now for permit holders only, so it is a case of finding some street parking. However, this may be a bit of a distance from the ground as there is a "residents only" parking scheme in operation in streets around Spotland. So if not careful you could end up with a parking ticket for your trouble, so check first to see if there are street parking restriction signs, before deciding to park up.

By Train

Rochdale Railway Station is located just under two miles away from the ground. The station is around a 35-40 minute walk from Spotland, so best jump in a taxi, rather than walking. If you have time on your hands however, and decide to walk – here's how:

On leaving the main entrance proceed straight on at the roundabout in front into Maclure Road. Follow this street (passing a fire station on your right) to the end and turn left at the T-junction onto Drake Street (A640). Follow this right to the end until you reach Manchester Road (A58) which is a dual carriageway. Turn right and walk along the righ-hand side of the road. At the major junction, which has traffic lights turn left (crossing Manchester Road) into Dane Street (A6060). Just after passing ASDA on the right, bear right onto Mellor Street (still the A6060 – here Dane Street bears left). Follow this road right to the end and bear left onto Spotland Road which soon becomes Edenfield Road (A680), bearing round to the left. Take the second left onto Willbutts Lane for the ground. Thanks to John Midgley for providing the directions.

Programme

Official Programme: £3

Record & Average Attendance

Record Attendance: 24,231 v Notts County, FA Cup 2nd Round, December 10th, 1949.

Average Attendance: 2011-12: 3,109 (League One)

Ground Name: New York Stadium
Capacity: 12,000 (all seated)
Address: Main Street, Rotherham, S60
Main Telephone No: 0844 4140733
Ticket Office No: 0844 4140737

Year Ground Opened: 2012
Pitch Size: 110 x 72 yards
Team Nickname: The Millers
Home Kit Colours: Red & White
Official website: www.themillers.co.uk

What's The Ground Like?

After spending four years at the Don Valley Stadium in Sheffield, the Club have returned home to Rotherham. The new stadium, which cost in the region of £20 million to build, is located close to their old Millmoor ground where they played for 101 years. The area of Rotherham where the ground is located is historically known as New York (hence the stadium name) and is built on the site of the old Guest & Chrimes factory. Set beside the River Don, the stadium from the outside looks far larger than its 12,000 capacity and is quite striking in its design. It is totally enclosed and all seated.

On one side is the West (Main) Stand. This is the largest of the four single-tiered stands. It is unusual in so much that the middle seated area of the stand is situated at a lower level than either of the wings. There is an executive area at the back with seating outside. Above this is a television gantry, set into the red panelled wall. The other sides of the stadium are much smaller in size. Both ends are virtually identical, except that the South Stand has a small electric scoreboard situated at the back of it. On the remaining side is the East Stand, which is slightly less tall than both the ends. This simple looking stand has two large areas built into the front of the stand for the use of disabled supporters.

The most interesting feature inside the stadium is the roof. This descends down from the West Stand over the ends in large 'steps' eventually meeting the East Stand. A large amount of transparent perspex has been used in the roof to allow more light to reach the playing surface and improve their overall look. On the roof of the East Stand are two futuristic looking floodlight pylons that are supplemented by a row of lights above the Main Stand.

What Is It Like For Visiting Supporters?

Away fans are housed in the South Stand at one end of the stadium, where around 2,500 supporters can be accommodated. As it is a new stadium you would expect the facilities and the view of the playing action to be good. The angle of the stand is quite steep, meaning that supporters are situated close to the pitch.

Unlike most new stadiums which are situated way out of town in the middle of nowhere, the New York Stadium is located close to the town centre. This not only means good transport links, but also a fair choice of eating and drinking outlets.

Where To Drink?

There are a number of pubs in the nearby town centre, which are only a few minutes walk from the stadium. Very close to the railway station is the Bridge Inn (turn right out of the station and the pub is across the road on the left). This pub which is listed in the CAMRA Good Beer Guide serves beers from the Old Mill Brewery as well as guest beers and a real cider. There are also three Wetherspoon pubs in Rotherham town centre. One of these, the Bluecoat (on the Crofts) is also Good Beer Guide listed.

Directions & Car Parking

From the North:

Leave the M1 at Junction 34 and take the A6178 towards Rotherham. At the third roundabout called Ickles Roundabout take the first exit onto the A630 Centenary Way (signposted Doncaster), you will see the stadium on your right. You will pass the floodlights of Millmoor on your left and at the next roundabout (called the Masbrough roundabout with the Liquid night club on one corner) turn right onto Main Street and the entrance to the stadium is down on the right.

From the South:

Leave the M1 at Junction 33 and take the A630 towards Rotherham. After around two miles and crossing over three roundabouts you will reach the stadium on your right. You will pass the floodlights of Millmoor on your left and at the next roundabout (called the Masbrough roundabout with the Liquid night club on one corner) turn right onto Main Street and the entrance to the stadium is down on the right.

Car parking at the stadium is for permit holders only. However, there are a number of pay & display car parks located around the town centre. Otherwise there is some street parking available around the area of the Millmoor ground.

Postcode for Sat-Nav: S60 1QY (nearby Police Station on Main Street)

By Train

The station is located almost directly behind the stadium. As you come out of the main station entrance turn right along Bridge Street. Opposite the Bridge Inn is a footpath that goes along one side of the River Don down towards a Tesco Superstore. Walk along this footpath and then head towards the Tesco car park entrance. Turn left going up over the bridge across the river and then take the next right into Market Street. At the bottom of Market Street turn right into Main Street and the stadium entrance is down this road on the left.

Programme

Official Programme: £2.50

Record & Average Attendance

Record Attendance: At Millmoor: 25,170 v Sheffield United, Division Two, December 13th, 1952.

Average Attendance: 2011-12: 3,498 (at the Don Valley Stadium – League Two)

Ground Name: Glanford Park
Capacity: 9,183
Address: Doncaster Road, Scunthorpe, DN15 8TD
Main Telephone No: 0871 221 1899
Ticket Office No: Same as main number

Year Ground Opened: 1988
Pitch Size: 111 x 73 yards
Team Nickname: The Iron
Home Kit Colours: Claret & Blue
Official website: www.scunthorpe-united.co.uk

What's The Ground Like?

The club left the Old Show Ground and moved to the new Glanford Park in August 1988. When opened, it was the first new League football ground to be built since the Second World War. It is a somewhat simple affair with all four stands being of equal height and similar in appearance. The ground is totally enclosed, although the corners are not used for spectators. The home end is terracing, while the other three sides of the ground are all seated. The main downside is the many supporting pillars running along the front of the stands that may impede your view. There is a small electric scoreboard suspended below the roof of the South Stand. The stadium is completed with a modern looking set of four floodlight pylons.

What Is It Like For Visiting Supporters?

Away fans are housed in the AMS Stand (aka the South Stand) at one end. This is all seated and can house 1,650 supporters. If demand requires it, then extra seats can be made available in the south corner of the West Stand. Although there are a couple of supporting pillars in this stand, the view is generally okay. A good selection of refreshments are available including Bacon Butties ('the best in the world!' according to Torquay United fan Tim Porter).

James Broadbent adds; 'the ground is very easy to find on the edge of town. Scunthorpe is generally a friendly place to visit, where you can have decent banter and a good day out. To help boost the atmosphere the club allow drums and musical instruments to be brought into the stadium'.

On my last visit the atmosphere was good inside the ground and no problems were encountered. It was on this visit that I witnessed an amusing incident, when in the League Cup tie against Birmingham City, the stewards tried to insist that away fans sat down rather than standing up. Of course this met with chants of; 'Stand up, if you love the Blues!' to which the stewards looked somewhat dismayed, with many Birmingham fans continuing to stand up. One poor steward was dispatched to sort this 'problem' out. I have to say he used a unique and an effective approach, during a lull moment in the away fans singing, a voice from the back of the stand, was heard singing; 'Sit down and watch the game! Sit down and watch the game!'.

You guessed it, it was the lonely steward singing! Still it had the desired effect! Well for a while anyhow...

Where To Drink?

Right by the ground there is The Old Farmhouse pub, which does admit away fans providing though that they are not wearing team colours. There is another pub near the ground called the Berkeley, which is also popular with away supporters. To find this Sam Smiths pub go past the ground (or park there first) and follow the main road towards Scunthorpe and it is on the left-hand corner of the first roundabout you reach. On my last visit this 1930s/40s art deco pub/hotel had a pleasant mixture of home and away supporters and served good beer in a comfortable atmosphere. The only draw back was that it seemed that you could only park in their car park if you were staying at the hotel, as there was an automated barrier across its entrance.

If coming by train, then the Honest Lawyer on Oswald Road is well worth a visit. Although a modern pub inside, it has been listed in the CAMRA Good Beer Guide and has a number of beers on offer. Also on Oswald Road is the Blue Bell which is a Wetherspoons outlet. Otherwise alcohol is available inside the stadium.

Directions & Car Parking

The ground is on the outskirts of Scunthorpe, making it easy to find from the motorway. Leave the M180 at Junction 3 and take the M181 for Scunthorpe. At the end of this motorway, you will see the ground on your right. Turn right at the first roundabout onto the A18 and right again into the large car park at the stadium, which costs £3.

By Train

Scunthorpe railway station is over two miles away from the ground. Either get a taxi from the station, or if you have time on your hands and are feeling fit... Turn left out of the station and head towards the crossroads (facing a church) and turn right into Oswald Road, going past a set of traffic lights and the Honest Lawyer and Blue Bell pubs. At the next traffic lights turn left into Doncaster Road (where there are a number of fast food outlets). Then just go straight down this road and you will eventually reach Glanford Park on your left. Otherwise as you pass the Blue Bell pub on your left, turn left onto Doncaster Road where you can catch Bus Number 909 (every 20 minutes to the hour, does not run on Sundays) down to the ground.

Programme

Official Programme: £3

Record & Average Attendance

Record Attendance: 8,921 v Newcastle United, Championship League, October 20th, 2009.
Average Attendance: 2011-12: 4,339 (League One)

Ground Name: Bramall Lane
Capacity: 32,702 (all seated)
Address: Bramall Lane, Sheffield, S2 4SU
Main Telephone No: 0871 995 1899
Ticket Office No: 0871 995 1889

Year Ground Opened: 1862*
Pitch Size: 112 x 72 yards
Team Nickname: The Blades
Home Kit Colours: Red, White & Black
Official website: www.sufc.co.uk

What's The Ground Like?

Bramall Lane has to me been one of the most underrated grounds in the country. The construction of three large modern looking stands, plus the filling in of the corners (albeit one corner is filled with administrative offices), makes it a great ground and one that has character. Both sides of the ground are large single-tiered stands. While the South Stand is a fairly plain looking stand, the Visit Malta Stand which sits opposite, is probably the smartest looking stand at Bramall Lane. This stand, which was opened in 1996 has had the corners to either side of it filled in, by offices on one side and a family seated area on the other. At the back of the stand are a row of executive boxes and on its roof is a small gable, reminiscent of when many older grounds featured them. At one end is the Kop Stand, which is slightly disappointing as it has two large supporting pillars. Opposite is the 188BET (Bramall Lane) Stand, which during the Summer of 2006 was extended around one corner of the stadium to meet the South) Stand. Also the roof was replaced with a new cantilever structure, allowing the supporting pillars of the old roof to be removed, giving fans more cover and an unimpeded view of the playing action. This stand is two-tiered and also has an electric scoreboard, perched between the two. The stadium is balanced, with all four stands being of the same height.

Outside the stadium behind the South Stand is a statue of former Club Chairman Derek Dooley and another of former playing legend Joe Shaw. Dave Croft adds; 'a lot of Blades fans sentimentally call the ground – Beautiful down town Bramall Lane'.

What Is It Like For Visiting Supporters?

Away fans are housed in the lower tier of the Bramall Lane Stand at one end of the ground, where around 3,000 supporters can be accommodated. For cup games if the demand requires it, then the upper tier can be made available too. Bramall Lane is a great place to watch football as the stands are located close to the pitch, the views are generally good, as well as the atmosphere too. Chris Bax adds; 'Any tickets still available for the away end can be purchased from two dedicated away ticket windows just up from the turnstile entrances'. On the concourses there are television screens showing the game going on inside as well as a betting outlet. The Club have automatic turnstiles, meaning that you have to insert your ticket into a bar code reader to gain admittance. Prepare though to be searched on entry into the ground by the stewards. The United fans are particularly passionate and vocal about their club. This makes for a great atmosphere at games, but also can make it somewhat intimidating for the away supporter.

Where To Drink?

Nick Turrell, a visiting Brighton fan adds; 'About a 10 minute walk away on Queens Road is The Earl pub, which on our visit was okay for away fans to drink in'. About 15 minutes walk away on Wellington Street is the Devonshire Cat. This pub has around 12 hand pulled beers on offer, serves food, has a large screen tv, welcomes families (until 7pm) and is listed in the CAMRA Good Beer Guide. Although there are bouncers on the doors, away fans are allowed into the pub wearing colours.

Near to the railway station is the Globe, which Simon, a visiting Chelsea fan informs me: 'I found that the Globe pub around a five minute walk from the station and a 15 minute walk from the ground welcomed home and away fans as long as there was no singing'. Simon Cumming a visiting Barnsley fan recommends 'The Howard which is a good pub for away fans. Service was very good and it's well policed'. This pub is also located near to the railway station, on Howard Street opposite. While Dave Barraclough informs me; 'In the station itself is the Sheffield Tap which serves real ales and is run by the Thornbridge Brewery' (please note though that no football colours are allowed). Otherwise alcohol is available inside the ground.

Directions & Car Parking
From The North:
Leave the M1 at Junction 36 and follow the A61 into Sheffield. Follow the A61 into Sheffield passing Hillsborough Stadium on your right. Continue along the A61, which becomes the ring road around the western side of the city centre. You will eventually reach a roundabout at the junction with the A621. At the roundabout turn right onto the A621 Bramall

Lane. The ground is a short way down on the left.
From The South:
Leave M1 at Junction 33 and take the A630 into Sheffield City Centre. On reaching the inner ring road follow signs for A621 Bakewell, the ground is about a quarter of a mile the other side of the city centre. It is located on the A621 (Bramall Lane). Street parking.

By Train
The ground is walkable from Sheffield mainline train station, (10-15mins). As you come out of the station, walk left along the main road. Where the road splits take the right fork which is Shoreham Street and continue down this road to the ground.

Programme
Official Programme: £3.

Record & Average Attendance
Record Attendance: 68,287 v Leeds United, FA Cup 5th Round, February 15th, 1936.

Average Attendance: 2011-12: 18,702 (League One)

* The ground originally opened as a cricket ground in 1855, but the first football match was not played there until December 1862, when Sheffield FC (who are the oldest club in the world, being formed in 1857) played Hallam. This makes Bramall Lane the oldest professional football ground in the world!

Ground Name: Hillsborough
Capacity: 39,812 (all seated)
Address: Hillsborough, Sheffield, S6 1SW
Main Telephone No: 0871 995 1867
Ticket Office No: 0871 900 1867

Year Ground Opened: 1899
Pitch Size: 115 x 75 yards
Team Nickname: The Owls
Home Kit Colours: Blue & White
Official website: www.swfc.co.uk

What's The Ground Like?

Although the ground has not had the level of new investment some other clubs have recently received, it is still a beautiful ground oozing character. It has four large separate stands, all of which are covered and are roughly the same height, giving a uniform feel to the stadium. On one side is the North Stand. This large single-tiered stand was opened in 1961. It was hailed as an architectural marvel, as at the time it was the largest cantilever stand ever built in Britain and only the second such type of stand to have been constructed (the first was at the Old Showground in Scunthorpe). The two-tiered South Stand on one side of the ground is the largest of the stands and is superb looking. It was originally opened in 1914 and was designed by the famous football ground architect Archibald Leitch. A second tier and new roof were added in 1996. In keeping with the original look of the stand, a triangular gable incorporating a clock adorned with a copper football was placed on the new roof. The stand has a large lower tier with a small upper tier above. At the back of the lower tier is a row of executive boxes. The team dugouts and Directors Box are located on this side.

At one end is the Spion Kop. This was previously a huge open bank of terrace that was at one time the largest in Britain. It gained a roof in 1986 and was made all seated in 1993. Opposite is the West Stand or Leppings Lane End. This two-tiered stand was opened in 1966.

Like the Kop, it has a number of large supporting pillars. One corner of the ground is filled with seating between the North & West Stand, this area is uncovered. On the other side of the West Stand is an electric scoreboard, under which is tucked a Police Control Box. Unusually for such an old ground, it doesn't have a set of floodlight pylons. Instead the stadium is illuminated by lights running across the front of the stand roofs.

Outside the ground near the main entrance is a memorial to the 96 fans who died at Hillsborough in 1989, at the FA Cup semi-final and& Nottingham Forest.

What Is It Like For Visiting Supporters?

Away fans are normally placed in the upper tier of the West Stand (the Leppings Lane) end of the ground, where up to 3,700 away supporters can be accommodated. If there is a particularly large following (or for an FA Cup Tie) then the corner described above may also be made available, plus the lower tier of the West Stand. This can take the allocation up to 8,000. There are a number of supporting pillars in the West Stand, which could impede your view. Alternatively if a small away support is expected then the open corner between the Leppings Lane & North Stand is only made available. The concourses are showing their age a little and the refreshments are served from behind a metal mesh, which gives the area a prison like feel. There are also a number of supporting pillars in the West Stand, which could impede your view.

Where To Drink?

Mark Doyle informs me; 'A pub that caters for away supporters is the New Bridge Inn on Penniston Road, which is the main A61 that runs by the stadium. Walk up the A61 in the opposite direction to Sheffield City Centre (Meadowhall & M1) and you will reach the pub on the same side of the road just before a railway bridge'. It is probably about a 10 minute walk away. Although a small pub it is welcoming and serves real ale, although like anything on matchday you need to get there early.

Also I did pass a couple of pubs (the Norfolk Arms & The Red Lion) on the way into Sheffield on the A61 from the M1, where away fans were drinking. Bill Harris, a visiting Millwall fan adds; 'I found an excellent Pub called The New Barrack Tavern on the A61 just before McDonalds on the way to the ground, from the city centre. Although on my own I was made to feel very welcome and spent a good couple of hours talking football to the locals'. The pub is roughly 15-20 minutes walk from the ground. This pub is owned by the Castle Rock Brewery and is listed in the CAMRA Good Beer Guide.

Please note that alcohol is not made available to visiting supporters in the away section of the ground.

Directions & Car Parking

Leave the M1 at Junction 36 and follow the A61 into Sheffield. Continue along the A61 for approximately eight miles. You will see Hillsborough Stadium on your right. This is not the shortest route to the ground, but this is definitely the easiest and avoids Sheffield City Centre. There is some street parking to be had if you arrive early, otherwise there are some unofficial car parks along the A61 that charge in the region of £4.

By Train/Tram

Sheffield Railway Station is located over three miles away from the ground. Either get a taxi up to the ground, or bus from the bus station which is a one minute walk away (as you leave the railway station entrance turn right). Cross over at the pedestrian crossing, and follow the signs. Then head for the far side of the terminus. Bus no. 53 to Ecclesfield runs regularly to the ground (every 10 minutes), the journey time is about 30 minutes. Jeremy Dawson informs me; 'if arriving by train, by far the easiest way to get to the ground is by tram, which run every 10 minutes during the day. Leaving the station on a blue tram, you can change to a yellow one in the city centre, which takes you to Leppings Lane'. The journey time of the tram is around 20 minutes.

Programme

Official Programme: £3

Record & Average Attendance

Record Attendance: 72,841 v Manchester City, FA Cup 5th Round, February 17th, 1934.
Average Attendance: 2011-12: 21,336 (League One)

Ground Name: Greenhous Meadow
Capacity: 9,875 (all seated)
Address: Oteley Road, Shrewsbury, SY2 6ST
Main Telephone No: 01743 289177
Ticket Office No: 01743 273943

Year Ground Opened: 2007
Pitch Size: 115 x 77 yards
Team Nickname: Shrews, Salop, Town or Blues
Home Kit Colours: Blue, Amber and White
Official website: www.shrewsburytown.com

What's The Ground Like?

After 97 years of playing at their Gay Meadow ground, the Shrews have moved to a new stadium on the outskirts of the town. The Greenhous Meadow as it is currently called, has a capacity of 9,875 seats. It is comprised of four separate stands and at first glance looks similar in design to some other new stadiums that have been recently built. Yes it is smart looking, functional and tidy, but lacks that certain something to make it stand out from the others.

Each of the stands are simple single-tiered stands, that are covered. Below the roof at the back of the stands is a sizeable strip of perspex that runs along the length of the stands. This is to allow more light into the stadium to facilitate pitch growth. Each of the stands are 18 rows high, with the Roland Wycherley Stand (named after the Club Chairman) on one side, being the 'Main Stand'. This stand has a slightly different layout to the others with a press area and eight corporate boxes at its rear, the type of which that you can sit outside of. The North Stand at one end of the stadium where the away fans are located also houses a prominent looking Police Control Box. Four small floodlight pylons are present on the

roofs of the side stands. An unusual feature of the stadium is that the areas for disabled fans are high up at the very back of the stands and are accessed by lifts. There is also a small electric scoreboard next to the away end.

What Is It Like For Visiting Supporters?

Away fans are located in the North Stand at one end of the ground. Leg room is good and the stands are quite steep keeping the fans close to the action and there is good height between rows. The concourses are quite well laid out, although the swing doors at the entrances to the toilets were met with a bit of trepidation. Although they were clearly marked one for entrance and one for exit, the inevitable occurs with fans piling out of each. The catering is provided by a local company called Jennys and I have to say that my steak pie was very tasty, one of the better that I have had on my recent travels. There are also large plasma screens on the concourses showing Sky Sports throughout the afternoon.

I had a pleasant visit to the Greenhous Meadow and was surprised by the reasonable atmosphere inside. This is boosted by a drummer in the home end, while most of the Shrewsbury singers tend to congregate close to the right of the away supporters in the West Stand. Even though I was at a local derby, the atmosphere was not hostile and I encountered no problems around the stadium.

Where To Drink?

David Matthias informs me; 'There are a couple of pubs within walking distance of the stadium. Firstly there is the 'Brooklands Hotel', just off Meole Brace Island, about five minutes walk away. Big screens and catering on matchdays. Also handily located just up from the BP Garage across the road is the 'Flippin Fish' Fish & Chip Shop.

There is also the Charles Darwin Pub; 10 minutes walk away, with 70 car parking spaces. There is also a good chippy opposite called the Tasty Plaice. Peter de Courcy, a visiting Macclesfield Town fan adds; 'The Charles Darwin pub now charges £5 to park, but you get one free drink at the bar with the parking ticket, even if it's the most expensive drink in the round, so it can be a good deal! It also has a good selection of ales, a very welcoming landlord and friendly local fans.'

The Brooklands Hotel is situated on Mill Street. From the stadium turn left along the B4380 Oteley Road. Head around the large roundabout towards Shrewsbury Town Centre. Then turn left into Roman Road and then left again into Mill Street. The hotel is down on the right.

The Charles Darwin Pub is in the opposite direction. From the stadium turn right along the B4380 Oteley Road. Take the second left into Sutton Road and the pub is down on the right.

Otherwise alcohol is available to away fans within the stadium before the game but the bars close 15 minutes before the kick-off, before opening again at half-time.

Directions & Car Parking

At the end of the M54 continue onto the A5. After about seven miles, there is a traffic island which is at the junction with the A49. Bear left at this island still following the A5. At the next roundabout take the 3rd exit onto the B4380 (Thieves Lane).

Continue along Thieves Lane going straight over two roundabouts and this will lead you into Oteley Road. You will reach the stadium down further down Oteley Road on the left.

There is a large car park at the stadium, holding almost 700 cars, however, this is for permit holders only (although I have received reports of fans turning up early and being admitted for £7). Parking is prohibited in the nearby Retail Park and nearby streets, so to find some street parking you may have to drive a bit further away. Check though for any parking restrictions detailed on posts, before parking up. Otherwise there is a car park costing £5 at the Brooklands Hotel, or for the same price at Pritchards Van Hire, opposite the hotel (100 spaces, entrance by the BP garage). Also nearby is the Meole Brace Bowling Club, which also offers parking at £5 per car and has a bar on site too. It can be found at Meole Rise (Off Upper Road, SY3 9JF).

By Train

Shrewsbury train station is around two miles away from the stadium. So it should take around 40 minutes to walk. Otherwise you can grab a taxi up to the ground, or take a bus from the town centre bus station (service numbers 8, 16, 23, 25 & 544/546 all stop near to the stadium). There are also plans to introduce a dedicated bus service on matchdays. Shrewsbury train station is served by trains from Birmingham New Street, Manchester Piccadilly, Crewe and Newport (Gwent).

Programme

Official Programme: £3

Record & Average Attendance

Record Attendance: 9,441 v Dagenham & Redbridge, League Two, April 28th, 2012.
Average Attendance: 2011-12: 5,770 (League Two)

Ground Name: St Mary's Stadium
Capacity: 32,689 (all seated)
Address: Britannia Road, Southampton, SO14 5FP
Main Telephone No: 0845 688 9448
Ticket Office No: 0845 688 9288

Year Ground Opened: 2001
Pitch Size: 112 x 74 yards
Team Nickname: The Saints
Home Kit Colours: Red & White
Official website: www.saintsfc.co.uk

What's The Ground Like?

The Club moved from The Dell to the new St Mary's Stadium in 2001. In some ways this saw the Club returning to its roots as it was originally founded as 'Southampton St Marys', hence the club nickname 'The Saints'. To be truthful the stadium looks, quite simply, superb. The stadium is completely enclosed, with all corners being filled with seating. There are also two great looking screens sitting on the roofs at each end. Running around three sides of the stadium, just below the roof, is a transparent perspex strip which allows more light and facilitates pitch growth. On the remaining side there is a row of executive boxes. The crowd are set well back from the playing action, as firstly there is a cinder track surrounding the playing surface and secondly the pitch itself must be the largest in the League (although the playing area does not use all of it). Outside the stadium behind the Itchen Stand is a statue of former Southampton legend Ted Bates.

What Is It Like For Visiting Supporters?

Away fans are located in the Northam Stand at one end of the stadium, where normally up to 3,200 fans can sit. For cup games this allocation can be increased to 4,750. The view of the playing action and the facilities within this stand are excellent. Leg room is good, although the width of the seating seemed to be a bit narrower than other grounds (either that or I am putting on weight!). The sizeable concourse behind the stand features a betting outlet, has TVs which show the game as it is played and a number of eating and drinking outlets. There are plenty of staff and the queues never seemed to get particularly long, which was a pleasant surprise. There is also a 'Pie & Pint' outlet that as the name suggests, only serves beer and pies. Perhaps they should rename it as 'Heaven'!

I have thoroughly enjoyed my visits to St Mary's and would happily return. The stadium has a great atmosphere and the facilities are first class. I particularly commend the Club for the friendliness of their staff, from the stewards to the catering staff. Even as I left the stadium, a steward wished me an enjoyable journey home! Considering that away supporters are almost treated with contempt at some other clubs, this was a refreshing change. Coupled with the relaxed attitude of the home supporters and the excellent facilities, then this to me makes a visit to St Mary's one of the better days out in the League.

Where To Drink?

There are not many pubs located close to the stadium, so the choice for away fans is limited. Derek Hall, a visiting Hartlepool United fan recommends the King Alfred pub on Northam Road. 'It is a good pub to visit, just a few minutes walk away from the stadium. Simply head towards the railway line to the right of the away end, then go up and over the railway bridge. The pub is a minute's walk away to your left. There is a small pay and display car park adjacent'. The pub also shows Sky Sports and has a barbeque on match-days.

There is the Waterfront Bar in William Street, which is an area called Shamrock Quay. Nic Hallam a visiting Wolverhampton Wanderers fan adds; 'In the Ocean Village we found The Admiral Sir Lucius Curtis public house. This large establishment had an excellent choice of beers, friendly bar staff and a convivial mix of both home and away fans'.

Most fans seem to end up in the city centre before the game, where there are plenty of pubs to choose from. Paul Hunt, a visiting Bristol City fan adds; 'On our last visit the Standing Order Wetherspoons outlet was for home fans only, with bouncers on the door. We ended up in Yates Wine Lodge in the central shopping area'. Otherwise alcohol is served within the ground.

Directions & Car Parking

From the M3 take the A33 into Southampton. Continue on the A33 until you reach the junction with the A3024 Northam Road and turn left onto this road towards Northam. Then turn right onto the B3038, Britannia Road for the stadium.

There is hardly any parking available at the stadium for away fans and there are parking restrictions in force for the local area. Most fans seem to be just heading for the city centre car parks and then embarking on the 15-20 minute walk to the stadium. I did this and parked in an NCP car park, which cost £5. I should point out though, that after the game the roads around the city centre become almost gridlocked. It took me over an hour to get away afterwards.

Alternatively, on my last visit I noticed a number of fans parking around the Marina area and then taking the 10 minute walk to the ground. Parking in this area has the advantage that at the end of the game, you can avoid the city centre gridlock, by heading along the coast on the A3024 and then onto the M271/M27.

Park & Ride

Gavin Ellis, a visiting Arsenal supporter informs me; 'There is a park and ride scheme in operation specifically for away supporters. This is situated just off junction 8 of the M27. The traffic in Southampton really made London look provincial, and I'd definitely not recommend people driving into the centre'. This facility costs £8 per vehicle.

By Train

The stadium is located around one and a half miles away from Southampton station (where there is also quite a large car park), which should take about 30 minutes to walk. There is also a shuttle bus in operation taking fans from the station to the ground. This operates from the Blechynden Terrace bus stop outside the station.

Programme & Fanzine

Official Programme: £3
Beautiful South Fanzine: £1

Record & Average Attendance

Record Attendance: 32,363 v Coventry City, Championship League, April 28th, 2012.
Average Attendance: 2011-12: 26,420 (Championship League)

Ground Name: Roots Hall
Capacity: 12,392 (all seated)
Address: Victoria Avenue, Southend-On-Sea, SS2 6NQ
Main Telephone No: 01702 304050
Ticket Office No: 08444 770077

Year Ground Opened: 1955*
Pitch Size: 110 x 74 yards
Team Nickname: The Shrimpers
Home Kit Colours: Blue With Sky Blue Trim
Official website: www.southendunited.co.uk

What's The Ground Like?

At one end of the ground is the relatively modern South Stand. This stand which was opened in 1994, replaced a former open terrace and greatly improved the overall look. It is a small 'double decker' type of stand, the upper tier hanging over the lower. It is all seated and covered, but unfortunately has a few supporting pillars. On its roof is a small clock, dedicated to former player, Director & Chairman, Frank Walton. There are a couple of blocks of flats that overlook the ground from behind this stand.

Opposite is the North Stand, which like the West Stand at one side of the pitch, is single-tiered and has an old looking 'barrel' shaped roof (that dates back to the 1950s), with the West Stand having a unique double barrel roof. The West Stand extends around to the North Stand so that one corner is filled with seating. It has a number of supporting pillars right at the front, which may hinder your view of the action. It also has the most precarious looking TV gantry that stands on stilts and is accessed by a long ladder. On the other side is the East (Main) Stand which is another single-tiered, covered stand, that has a row of executive boxes running across the back of it. At the front are some strange looking dugouts, which has the management team standing at the front

leaning on a wall, with the players sitting behind. The ground has four tall traditional looking floodlight pylons. In other words a proper football ground! The club have an unusual looking club mascot called 'Elvis J Eel', the 'J' standing for jellied!

What Is It Like For Visiting Supporters?

Away fans are normally housed on one side of the North Stand (on the Main Stand side of the ground), where up to 1,200 away supporters can be accommodated. This stand is normally shared with home supporters, but for the Cup games the whole stand can be allocated bringing the allocation up to 2,000 seats. The stand is covered, but there are a number of supporting pillars running across the front of the stand that could impede your view. The stand is a former terrace and like most former terraces that have had seats bolted onto them, the leg room and height distance between each row is less than desirable. One good thing for away fans in the North Stand, is that comparatively few numbers of fans can really make some noise from it and with the home fans in close proximity, it makes for a good atmosphere. Refreshments within the away area are served from a 'Transport Cafe' type establishment, complete with tables and chairs. Even though

Roots Hall is an older ground it has some rather modern electronic turnstiles, into which you insert your ticket to gain entrance.

Where To Drink?

Away fans tend to use the Blue Boar pub which is located on the main Victoria Road, just up from the ground (going towards Southend town centre) on one corner of the crossroads. David Wells informs me; 'There is the Bar Victoria Court, which is located further down the A127 from Roots Hall towards Southend. It is not a traditional football pub by any means but it is okay for pre-match pint'. This Bar is about a 10 minute walk away from the ground.

A bit further away is the 'The Bell', a large Toby Carvery, which you pass on your way into Southend on the A127. The town centre is around a 20 minute walk away, where there are plenty of pubs including a Wetherspoons outlet (the Last Post on Clifftown Road). There are also a number of bars along the seafront, which can be quite nice on a a sunny Saturday afternoon. Any Walden adds; 'The Railway Tavern which is outside Prittlewell station is also used by away fans.'

There is also a good fish and chip shop located across the road from the Blue Boar by the traffic lights, called the 'Fish House', which I found to be excellent. Judging by the amount of fans standing outside eating fish and chips (there is some seating inside as well), then I'm not the only one that thinks it is good. Please note that alcohol is not served to away fans within the stadium.

Directions & Car Parking

From the M25 take Junction 29 and follow the A127 to Southend. Continue towards the town centre, through the lights near to the Bell Pub. At the next roundabout turn right (3rd turning), continuing on the A127. The ground is on the right just past the next traffic lights. If you turn right as you reach the ground, this will put you behind the away end where there is plenty of street parking to be found. Otherwise there is a car park at the ground, behind the Main Stand which costs £5, or there is the Southend High School For Boys which also offers car parking for £5 per car (the school entrance is on Prittlewell Road).

By Train

The closest station to the ground is Prittlewell, about a five minute walk away. It is served by trains from London Liverpool Street. As you exit the station turn right, you will then come to a crossroads with traffic lights. On your right is the 'Fish House', fish and chip shop. Pass this and turn right. Walk about 100 yards and the ground is tucked away on your left.

If you happen to end up at Southend Central station (served by trains from London Fenchurch Street), you're about a 25 minute walk from the ground. The main bus station is close to Southend Central, and therefore it may be an idea to get a bus up to the ground, rather than walking.

Programme & Fanzine

Official Programme: £3
All At Sea Fanzine: £1

Record & Average Attendance

Record Attendance: 31,090 v Liverpool, FA Cup 3rd Round, January 10th, 1979.
Average Attendance: 2011-12: 6,000 (League Two)

* Football had been played on the site since 1906. The Club subsequently built a new ground at Roots Hall in the 1950s.

Ground Name: Lamex Stadium
Capacity: 6,546 (Seating 3,412)
Address: Broadhall Way, Stevenage, Herts, SG2 8RH
Main Telephone No: 01438 223 223
Ticket Office No: Same as main number

Year Ground Opened: 1980*
Pitch Size: 110 x 70 yards
Team Nickname: Boro
Home Kit Colours: Red & White
Official website: www.stevenagefc.com

What's The Ground Like?

To be honest, the ground doesn't look much from the roads running past it, as most of the stadium is obscured behind trees. Inside though, you will find a nice tidy stadium that although generally modern, still has a bit of character about it. Also those trees give the ground a pleasant green 'leafy' surround.

On one side is the all seated covered Main Stand that looks quite impressive and is single-tiered. It is unusual in so much that at the back of the stand on either side of it, there are large gaps between the back of the roof and the stand below. While in the middle of the stand at the back, there are a number of glass fronted areas to various Club offices. Opposite is the fair sized East Terrace, which is covered and quite steep. Even though like the rest ground, the stand is relatively new, it does have a gable with a clock sitting on its roof above the halfway line, which gives it a touch of character. Oddly though it has a sizeable service tunnel located towards the centre of the stand with the terracing extending around it.

At one end is the Buildbase South Stand, which is another single-tiered, all seated, covered stand. This stand which was opened in 2001 is given to away supporters. There is an electric scoreboard on the roof of this stand. Opposite at the North End of the ground, is a small covered terrace. This terrace is mostly covered (around three quarters) with a portion of open terrace to one side. A set of four new floodlights (one pylon in each corner) were installed for the start of the 2007/08 season.

On promotion to the Football League, the Club changed its name from Stevenage Borough FC, to Stevenage FC, which was its original name when founded in 1976.

What Is It Like For Visiting Supporters?

Away fans are located at one end of the ground in the Buildbase South Stand, where up to 1,400 supporters can be housed. As you would expect from a relatively new stand the facilities and views of the playing action are good. I found the public address system though within the away end to be particularly loud, which interrupted a few conversations. The atmosphere within the stadium is aided by a drummer on the home East Terrace, who keeps the Stevenage fans going throughout most of the game. If you are into plane spotting then from the away stand you can watch a steady stream of jets descending into Luton airport. Normally an enjoyable day out and one that fans of most other clubs look forward to.

Where To Drink?

There is a large Club House bar at the ground, behind the South Stand, which is popular with both home and away fans alike. However, for some high profile games, the bar will be open to home fans only, but this is only for a small minority of games. On my last visit, even though the bar was busy, I was served relatively quickly and it was a friendly atmosphere.

Otherwise there is not much in the way of pubs near to the ground. Still if you like your real ale then it is worth taking the 15 minute walk to the Our Mutual Friend pub in Broadwater Crescent. This pub which is listed in the CAMRA Good Beer Guide offers seven beers on hand pump, plus real cider and perry. If you have time on your hands then you can take the 15-20 minute walk into the town centre, where there are plenty of pubs to be found including a Wetherspoons outlet (called the Standard Bearer, which is located near to the Bus Station).

Across the roundabout from the ground there is a Retail Park that has various eating outlets such as Pizza Hut, McDonalds & Burger King, plus there is also a Harvester outlet called the Roaring Meg, which also has a bar.

Directions & Car Parking

Leave the A1 (M) at Junction 7 and take the A602 towards Stevenage. Go straight across the first roundabout and as you approach the next round-about you can see the floodlights of the ground over on the right. However, if you go straight acr-oss the roundabout then you will see the entrance on the left to the large official car park which is free. The car park though has only one ent-rance/exit, so this can lead to bit of a bottleneck after the game has finished.

By Train

Stevenage Railway Station is about one mile away from the ground. Leave the station booking hall and turn left towards the town. Take the stairs on the right before the bridge over the dual carriage way and head along the A602, Lytton Way. At the roundabout which has the police station on the right, take the second exit into Six Hills Way. At the next roundabout take the third exit (South) continuing along the A602, Monks-wood Way, passing a large Asda store on your right. After about three quarters of a mile (McD-onalds/Burger King etc. will be on your right) you will arrive at a roundabout and the ground will be opposite you on the other side of the A602. Thanks to Roger Dickinson and Gary Barker for providing the directions.

You can also get the Arriva No.5 Bus to the ground, from Stop E at the nearby bus station. The 10 minute journey costs £1.50 single, or £2.30 return. As the ground is not easily spotted in the distance, ask the driver to drop you off on Monks-wood Way, opposite the entrance to the retail park.

Programme & Fanzine

Official Programme: £3
The Broadhall Way Fanzine: £1

Record & Average Attendance

Record Attendance: 8,040 v Newcastle United, FA Cup 4th Round, January 25th, 1998.
Average Attendance: 2011-12: 3,559 (League One)

* Stevenage FC took over the ground in 1980. It had been previously used by Stevenage Athletic FC, who went out of business.

Ground Name: Britannia Stadium
Capacity: 28,383 (all seated)
Address: Stanley Matthews Way,
Stoke-on-Trent, ST4 4EG
Main Telephone No: 01782 367 598
Ticket Office No: 01782 367 599

Year Ground Opened: 1997
Pitch Size: 115 x 75 yards
Team Nickname: The Potters
Home Kit Colours: Red & White Stripes
Official website: www.stokecityfc.com

What's The Ground Like?

The Club moved to the Britannia Stadium in 1997, after playing for 119 years at their old Victoria Ground. The stadium looks imposing from afar, as it is perched upon a hill with hardly any buildings around it. It especially looks good at night when it is lit up. The ground is of a fair size. One large single stand, incorporating the Boothen End and Seddon Stand, completely surrounds half the pitch as it extends around one corner. While the other two stands on the other sides are 'free standing' having open corners to either side.

The largest of these is the Q-railing (West) Stand, which is the tallest at the Britannia. This imposing stand has a large lower tier of seating with a smaller tier above. Situated between the tiers is a row of Executive Boxes. There are quite large open areas to each side of this stand, which detracts from the overall look of the stadium. If these could be filled at some point, then the ground would benefit greatly. The Marstons Pedigree (South) Stand at one end of the stadium is partly given to away supporters. This simple looking stand is like the rest of the stadium, all seated and covered, with windshields to either side. It is

though quite steep, meaning that fans are kept close to the playing action. Unusually the teams come onto the pitch from one corner of the ground, between the Marstons Pedigree (South) Stand and the Q-railing (West) Stand. In the corner on the other side of the Marstons Pedigree (South) Stand is a large video screen. Outside the stadium there is the great looking statue of the legendary former player Sir Stanley Matthews

The Club also have a couple of unusual looking mascots, with a blue coloured hippo called 'Pottermus' and his white girlfriend 'Pottermiss', obviously this is what happens to hippos when they visit the Potteries!

What Is It Like For Visiting Supporters?

Away fans are housed on one side (towards the Players Tunnel and Main Stand) of the Marstons Pedigree (South) Stand at one end of the ground, where around 2,800 supporters can be accommodated. This stand is shared with home fans on the other side. At first I was quite perturbed by a large sign advising fans that persistent standing would result in ejection from the ground, however, the facilities and view of the action from this stand are good. The concourse is adequate and there is a large choice of refreshments available. The stadium is quite high up in an exposed position and the open corners can mean that a cold wind can whip through the stadium, so bear this in mind, especially in the winter months. I thought the inside of the stadium was a bit bland and lacking character, although I'm sure that this can be developed in time. Listen out though for the Stoke anthem 'Delilah' being sung by the home fans, they can still give a great rendition of that Tom Jones classic song.

It is also worth bearing in mind though that the Stoke fans are passionate about their club and this can make for an intimidating atmosphere, so it is best to keep colours covered around the ground. Don't be surprised if you are kept in after the game, in a fenced off compound to the rear of the away stand, while the Stoke fans are allowed to disperse.

Where To Drink?

Next to the stadium is a Holiday Inn and a Harvester Pub/Restaurant that do allow in away fans. You can also park at the Harvester itself for a cost of £3. A bit further away on Dennis Viollett Road (off Sir Stanley Matthews Way) is a Power League complex that also has a bar, which also allows in away supporters, shows SKY television and you can even park in their car park for £4.50. Otherwise alcohol is available at the back of the away end, but queues can be lengthy, especially if there is a big support.

Directions & Car Parking

Leave the M6 at Junction 15 and then go straight across the roundabout onto the A500 towards Stoke. Continue along the A500 passing the junction with the A34. Leave the A500 at the slip road following signs for the A50 towards Derby. At the top of the slip road turn right at the roundabout (still A50) and then move into the second from left lane (signposted Britannia Stadium). You can see the stadium over on your right. Turn right at the top of the slip road and then

right at the next roundabout for the stadium. The Britannia is quite well signposted. Car parking at the stadium costs £5.

By Train

Stoke station is just over two miles away from the stadium, so unless you are feeling fit, it maybe best to hire a taxi. Tim Rigby a visiting Wolves fan adds 'there are some shuttle buses than run from Glebe Street in Stoke up to the Britannia Stadium, which depart every 15 minutes before kick-off. There are return buses after the game back to Glebe Street from behind the Sentinel (East) Stand'.

Colin Bell adds; 'It took us less than 30 minutes to walk to the stadium from the station, using this route: Turn right from the station and head down Station Road. At the lights, turn right along Leek Road (A52), under the railway line and then left down on to the tow path of the Trent & Mersey Canal. Follow the tow path all the way until you are level with the stadium, where two footbridges take you over the canal and then the railway line, straight into the ground near the South Stand away end.'

Programme & Fanzine
Official Programme: £3
The Oatcake Fanzine: £1.20

Record & Average Attendance
Record Attendance: 28,218 v Everton, FA Cup 3rd Round, January 5th, 2002
Average Attendance: 2011-12: 27,226 (Premier League)

Ground Name: Stadium Of Light

Capacity: 49,000 (all seated)

Address: Stadium Of Light, Sunderland, SR5 1SU

Main Telephone No: 0871 911 1200

Ticket Office No: 0871 911 1973

Year Ground Opened: 1997

Pitch Size: 114 x 74 yards

Team Nickname: The Black Cats

Home Kit Colours: Red & White Stripes

Official website: www.safc.com

What's The Ground Like?

The Club moved to the stadium in 1997, after leaving their former home of Roker Park where they had played for 99 years. The stadium is of a good size, is totally enclosed and on the whole is quite impressive. It is composed of two three-tiered stands (at the North end and the West side of the pitch), while the others are two-tiered. The West (Main) Stand on one side also has a row of executive boxes (which you can sit outside if you wish), that are situated just below the top tier. Currently, with half the stadium being larger than the other, it looks a little imbalanced, when looking from the away section in the South Stand. However, if at some point the Club were to add an additional tier to the two remaining sides, then an even more remarkable stadium would emerge. There is also a large electronic scoreboard perched upon the roof at either end.

Outside the stadium there is a statue of former FA Cup winning manager Bob Stokoe, as well as some reminders of the former Wearmouth Colliery, on the site of which the stadium was built. Behind the West Stand there is a large red wheel, an emblem of the lifts that used to take the miners down to the mines. Also outside one corner of the stadium is a large miners lamp. If you feel a little mischievous, then ask the nearest Sunderland fan whether it is a Geordie Lamp. Don't worry you won't get any physical abuse, just a long lecture that the lamp is in fact a Davy lamp!

What Is It Like For Visiting Supporters?

Away fans are now housed in the Upper Tier of the North Stand at one end of the stadium, where around 3,000 fans can be housed. Although the facilities are fine in this area, you do have to climb a large number of flights of stairs to reach this top tier. It almost feels if this area has been 'tucked in' under the stadium roof, as it comes down over this section. It means that if you are sitting towards the back of the tier, then although you can see the pitch, you get a limited view of the majority of the rest of the stadium, giving the feeling of being a bit cut off from it all. For cup games where there is a larger allocation of tickets available (up to 7,000) then away fans will revert back to being housed in the South Stand for those matches.

When people ask me which grounds are 'the best' to visit, then Sunderland inevitably comes out as one of my top five recommendations. On its day the place can be rocking, the PA system deafening (especially when the classical piece 'Dance Of The Knights' from Prokofiev's 'Romeo & Juliet' is played before the players come on to the pitch at the start of the game) and the Sunderland supporters exceptionally friendly (I was even given a Sunderland shirt by one supporter!). Bear in mind though, that you are not allowed to swear inside the stadium, so if you persist you may find yourself being ejected from it!

Where To Drink?

Stephen Lundell informs me; 'There are two social clubs; the Sunderland Companions club, and the New Democratic Club, both on North Bridge Street (the road approaching the Wearmouth Bridge), which are about a five minute walk away form the stadium. Although they get very busy they do welcome away supporters, and serve reasonably priced beer'. Otherwise you are not that far from the city centre where there are plenty of pubs to be found. My pick would be the William Jameson (a Wetherspoons pub) on Fawcett Street, for a drink before or after the game, as it has a great atmosphere. Alcohol is also available inside the stadium.

Directions & Car Parking

Exit the A1 at Junction 62, the Durham/Sunderland exit and take the A690 towards Sunderland. After about eight miles, you will reach a roundabout, at which turn left onto the A19, signposted for the Tyne Tunnel. Stay in the left-hand lane and take the second slip road towards Sunderland (signposted Stadium Of Light, A1231 Sunderland). This takes you onto a bridge crossing over the River Wear. Turn right onto the A1231 following the signs for Sunderland. Go straight over four roundabouts into Sunderland.

Then go through two sets of traffic lights (keeping in the left-hand lane at the second set, going straight on towards Roker rather than the city centre) and you will see the Stadium car park on your right, about a mile after the traffic lights. However, there is only limited parking at the ground, so alternatively, you can park in the city centre and walk to the ground (about 10-15 minutes). The traffic for a couple of miles around the ground was solid when I went so allow plenty of time for your journey.

There is also a 'Park & Ride' scheme in operation on matchdays, free for both home and away supporters. This is situated at Sunderland Enterprise Park, which is well signposted just off the A1231. Buses run every five minutes, for 90 minutes before kick-off and continue after the game until everyone has gone.

By Train & Metro

Sunderland railway station in the city centre is walkable from the stadium (around 15 minutes). Paul Duck informs me; 'You will exit the station opposite Greggs. Turn right out of the station heading up towards a JJB Sports store and walk through the gap between JJB and a nail bar to the right of JJB. Keep walking straight ahead and within 100m you will see the Stadium Of Light rising up in front of you over the Wearmouth Bridge'.

Ashley Smith adds; "The Metro stations called the 'Stadium of Light' and 'St. Peters' both serve the stadium. Both stations are only a few minutes walk from the ground, although away supporters should alight at St Peters Station as that is closer to their entrance.

Programme & Fanzines

Red & White Review Official Programme: £3

A Love Supreme Fanzine: £2.50

Sex & Chocolate Fanzine: £1.50

The Wearside Roar Fanzine (TWR): £2

Record & Average Attendance

Record Attendance: 48,353 v Liverpool, Premier League, April 13th, 2002.

Average Attendance: 39,095 (Premier League)

Ground Name: Liberty Stadium
Capacity: 20,700 (all seated)
Address: Morfa, Swansea, SA1 2FA
Main Telephone No: 01792 616 600
Ticket Office No: 0844 815 6665

Year Ground Opened: 2005
Pitch Size: 114 x 74 yards
Team Nickname: The Swans or The Jacks
Home Kit Colours: White with black trim
Official website: www.swanseacity.net

What's The Ground Like?

The Club moved to the Liberty Stadium in 2005, after spending 93 years at their former Vetch Field home. Built by Interserve for a cost of around £30 million, it is located near to the former site of the Morfa Athletics Stadium on the West side of the River Tawe. The stadium was christened White Rock by the Swansea residents, but was renamed the Liberty Stadium under a 10 year corporate sponsorship deal.

Although fairly conservative in its design, the stadium is still impressive. It is completely enclosed with all four corners filled with seating. Each of the four stands is two-tiered and three are of the same height. The West Stand at one side of the pitch is slightly taller, having a row of 28 corporate hospitality boxes, situated above the upper tier. The Club's offices are also located behind this stand. An unusual feature is the great use of transparent roofing towards the South End of the stadium. This allows more natural light into this area, making for an interesting effect. Both ends have an electric scoreboard situated on the front of their roofs, although for some reason the scoreboard at the North End is larger than the one at the South End. Outside the stadium at the South

West corner, by the club shop and ticket office, is a statue of former Swansea legend Ivor Allchurch. The stadium is shared with Ospreys Rugby Union Club.

What Is It Like For Visiting Supporters?

Away fans are housed in the North Stand at one end of the stadium. Up to 2,000 fans can be accommodated in this area, although this allocation can be reduced to 1,000 for teams with a smaller following. The views of the playing action from this area are excellent as there is a good height between rows and the leg room is probably one of the most generous of any stadium that I have visited. The concourses are spacious, with food and beverage outlets, plus a number of television sets, for pre-match and half-time entertainment. As you would expect from a new stadium the facilities are good. Away fans are separated from home fans by two metal barriers, with a line of stewards and Police in between. Interestingly, the main singing contingent of home fans, have, in the traditions of the Vetch Field, situated themselves along one side of the pitch in the East Stand, rather than at the South end of the stadium and this helps contribute to a good atmosphere. However, I would exercise general caution around the area of the stadium and consider keeping colours covered.

Where To Drink?

Phil Weston a visiting Stoke City fan informs me; 'Stoke fans were drinking in The Harvester and Frankie & Benny's just outside the ground and a couple of the pubs just up from the stadium'. Otherwise it a choice of a drink on the way to Swansea, go into the city centre or drink inside the stadium, where alcohol is made available to away fans. The Club open the turnstiles 90 minutes before kick-off, so that fans have the option to eat and drink within the stadium itself.

Directions & Car Parking

Leave the M4 at Junction 45 and take the A4067 towards the City Centre (sign posted A4067 South). Stay on the A4067 for around two and half miles and you will reach the stadium on your left. Car parking at the stadium is for permit holders only and most of the immediate residential areas around the stadium now have 'residents only' parking schemes in place. However, away mini buses and coaches can park behind the North Stand in a fenced compound, at a cost of £20 per coach and £10 per minibus. Don't be tempted to park on the nearby Retail Park as you may well end up with a ticket, or worse still, clamped for your trouble!

Away Fans Park & Ride Facility

Away supporters are being encouraged to use the Park & Ride facility located at the Felindre old steel works site, which is signposted off Junction 46, shortly after leaving the M4. The cost of parking there including transport by bus to and from the stadium is £6 per car. Away supporters have their own separate buses to and from the stadium, with the buses waiting outside the away stand at the end of the game to take supporters back to the car park. Simon Wright, a visiting West Bromwich Albion fan adds; 'The park and ride is located in the middle of nowhere, but curiously has a high

fence. Apparently the facility is also used as a park and ride for the DVLA so the fencing may be for the benefit of their staff. There are toilets on the site although they do look rather ancient. All the staff were friendly and the buses frequent. After the game has ended, the park and ride buses leave the compound with the away coaches for fairly obvious reasons. In my case, this meant a wait of around 20 minutes'.

There is also some street parking to be had. If coming from the M4, you pass the stadium on your left and continue straight on towards Swansea, then after going under a bridge, there are a number of roads on the right, where street parking is available. It is then around a 10-15 minute walk to the stadium.

By Train

Swansea Railway Station is on the main line route from London Paddington. It is about two miles from the stadium. Regular local bus services (every 10 minutes: routes 4, 4a, 120, 122, 125, 132) and taxis (around £6) are available from the train station to the stadium. Otherwise if you have time on your hands then it should take about 25-30 minutes to walk.

Programme & Fanzines

Official Programme 'Jack Magazine': £3
Swansea Oh Swansea Fanzine: £1
A Touch Far Vetched Fanzine: £1

Record & Average Attendance

Record Attendance: 20,605 v Liverpool, Premier League, May 13th, 2012.
Average Attendance: 2011-12: 19,946 (Premier League)

Ground Name: County Ground
Capacity: 15,728 (all seated)
Address: County Road, Swindon, SN1 2ED
Main Telephone No: 0871 876 1879
Ticket Office No: 0871 876 1993

Year Ground Opened: 1896
Pitch Size: 110 x 70 yards
Team Nickname: The Robins
Home Kit Colours: Red & White
Official website: www.swindontownfc.co.uk

What's The Ground Like?

A traditional looking ground, that has an interesting mix of stands. Both sides are large two-tiered covered affairs that tower above the two smaller ends. The Main Stand is the Arkells Stand on one side. Built in 1971 the stand is a fairly simple affair and has the players tunnel and team dugouts in front. It has windshields to either side and a few supporting pillars. Opposite is the smarter looking Don Rogers Stand. Opened in 1994, this stand has a cantilevered roof, allowing spectators to have an uninterrupted view of the playing action. It has a large upper tier, with a much smaller lower tier. The Town End is a small covered stand, that is the traditional home end. Unfortunately it has a row of supporting pillars that run across the front of it. Oddly on one side, the base of one of the floodlight pylons is situated within the stand, with the pylon itself rising up through the roof of the stand. At the other end is the Stratton Bank Stand. This area is uncovered and open to the elements. It has a small electric scoreboard situated above it, next to which is a Rolex Clock. Apparently this is the only Rolex clock that can found within a football ground anywhere in the World. The ground also benefits by a striking set of four floodlight pylons.

What Is It Like For Visiting Supporters?

Away fans are located in the Arkells Stand at one side of the pitch, where up to 1,200 fans can be housed. This is an older stand with facilities to match, but at least you are under cover. If you are at the back of this stand there is one supporting pillar which may impair your view of the goal, otherwise it is fine. You even get a view of some of the rolling Marlborough Hills beyond one corner of the ground! There is a small kiosk at the back of stand serving among other things a range of pies, but be careful when taking them back to your seat. The entrances to the seating areas are through large solid doors, and to compound matters they open out towards you!

Teams with a larger away following can also be allocated the Stratton Bank End if required. A further 2,100 fans can be accommodated in this area, but the end has no cover and is open to the elements. Fine on a nice sunny day, but on a cold wet, winter's day, it can be grim. This area was a former terrace that has had seating bolted onto it, which meant that the height between rows is not great. I found Swindon to be a relaxed and fairly friendly day out, although the size of Police presence on my last visit seemed excessive.

Where To Drink?

Away fans are treated to their own bar, called Bar 71, which is located by the away turnstiles. Otherwise there is the Cricket Club, the entrance to which is further down County Road. As Mark Osborne from Swindon adds; 'On match days home and away fans can park at the cricket ground (for a small fee) and then have access to a drink in the cricket club. This is a very friendly (as well as cheap) club that always welcomes away fans'.

Audrey MacDonald, a visiting Hartlepool United fan, recommends The Merlin on Drove Road, near to the magic roundabout. 'Away fans are welcome and they have Sky Sports showing on 12 television screens and even in the gents (according to my husband)'. Alcohol is available within the ground to away fans in the Arkells Stand (but not in the open Stratton Bank End).

Directions & Car Parking

From M4 J15:

Follow the A4259 (Queens Drive) towards Swindon. Go across one roundabout and at the next take the first exit onto the A4312 (signposted Swindon /Football Traffic). You will see the floodlights of the County Ground over on the right, as you approach the large Magic Roundabout (so called as it is one large roundabout surrounded by five mini roundabouts). The County Ground is on the corner of this roundabout.

From the North A419 from Cricklade/ Cirencester/M5:

Continue on the A419 until reaching the top of the new three lane stretch of dual-carriageway, which runs uphill. (I would advise to stay in the inside lane on this climb as the exit approaches quickly). Take the exit at the top of the hill (Lady Lane Junction). At the lights go right, then almost immediately at the next set of lights go left. Follow this road through the next set of traffic lights (passing the Motorola building to the right), then branch left onto the A4311. From here follow this road, following signs for Town Centre. At Transfer Bridges roundabouts turn left at the first and then

straight over the second. The County Ground is on the left after the mini-roundabout. The County Ground is one of the few remaining football stadiums you can notice from a fair distance, due to the striking floodlights. Thanks to Robin Sharpe for supplying the directions.

If you survive the Magic Roundabout then there is some street parking. Otherwise park at the cricket club (take County Road off the Magic Roundabout, go past the County Hotel on your right, you will see a small sign further down on your right for football parking, just before the mini-roundabout). There is some parking available at the ground itself at a cost of £10.

By Train

The ground is walkable from Swindon train station and should take you around 10-15 minutes. Leave the station, cross the road and proceed up the road between the two pubs (Great Western and Queen's Tap), continuing to the end of the road. Turn left, proceed along Manchester Road, through traffic lights as far as you can go. At the junction turn right. The County Ground is about 300 yards up this road on the left. Thanks to John Bishop for providing me with the directions.

Programme

Official Programme: £3

Record & Average Attendance

Record Attendance: 32,000 v Arsenal, FA Cup 3rd Round, January 15th, 1972.

Average Attendance: 2011-12: 8,411 (League Two)

Ground Name: Plainmoor
Capacity: 6,500 (Seats 2,950)
Address: Plainmoor, Torquay, Devon, TQ1 3PS
Main Telephone No: 01803 328 666
Ticket Office No: Same as main number

Year Ground Opened: 1921
Pitch Size: 110 x 74 yards
Team Nickname: The Gulls
Home Kit Colours: Yellow, Blue & White Trim
Official website: www.torquayunited.com

What's The Ground Like?

On one side is a new stand which was opened in July 2012. This covered all seated stand has a capacity of 1,750 and cost in the region of £2 million to build. Called Bristow's Bench after a former Director of the Club, the stand also includes new dressing rooms, disabled facilities and a new press box. It is a fairly simple looking affair, although it has windshields to either side, situated below an elevated roof. The stand is raised above pitch level meaning that spectators have to climb a small staircase to enter it. Opposite is a newish, small covered terrace, called the Thatchers Popular Cider Terrace. It looks slightly odd, having a large television gantry perched on its roof.

At one end is the Yelverton Properties Family Stand, which is a neat, attractive, covered all seater stand that has a capacity of 1,200. Differing from other clubs, the Directors Box is situated in this stand, rather than being on one side of the pitch. The other end is a small covered terrace, built in 2000 to replace a former open terrace and is normally used to house away fans. To one side of this stand is Police Control Box. Outside the ground behind the home end and next to the Club shop is a programme shop which is worth a look.

The ground is completed by a set of four traditional looking floodlight pylons.

What Is It Like For Visiting Supporters?

Around 1,100 away supporters can be accommodated in the Marsh Toyota Away Stand, at one end of the ground. Additionally a number of seats are also made available in the Bristow's Bench Stand. The away terrace is covered and the acoustics are good, meaning that relatively few away supporters can still really make some noise from this area. Although the facilities are fairly basic, this was compensated by some good banter between the away fans and the stewards, plus the catering outlet was doing a roaring trade in selling hot pasties. All in all a good day out.

Where To Drink?

The supporters club Boots & Laces behind the main stand allows away supporters in and I found it quite pleasant and friendly. Simon Blogg recommends O'Connors near the ground. This Irish themed pub is around a five minute walk from the home end on Marychurch Road and was popular with away fans on my last visit. To find this pub; with the home end behind you, turn right and continue in this direction until you reach Mary-church Road. Turn left along this road keeping the supermarket on your right and you will see the pub further down on the left.

Neil Le Milliere, a visiting Exeter supporter adds; 'The George Inn on Babbacombe Road, was extremely welcoming, both before and after the game. The pub is around a 10 minute walk away from the ground'. Located handily around the corner in Princes Street is the Hanburys Fish & Chip shop which has on occasion won national awards. Further on at the bottom of Princes Street you will find the Buccaneer Inn. Not only a good pub serving St Austell Ales, but outside the front of the pub you can also enjoy some great views along the coast. (There is also plenty of street parking available in this area). Also on Babba-combe Road is the Dog & Duck which welcomes away fans and also shows matches broadcast on SKY television.

Directions & Car Parking

At the end of the M5 follow the A38 and then turn left onto the A380. On reaching Kingskerwell, take the first exit at the large roundabout (where there is a McDonalds and Sainsburys on one side) onto the A3022 towards Torquay. After one mile turn left towards Babbacombe (signposted Babba-combe (A379)). After a further mile turn left into Westhill Road for Warbro Road for the ground. Torquay United is signposted on nearing the ground. Street parking.

By Train

The ground is over two miles away from the main Torquay railway station and so a taxi may well be in order. Neil Le Milliere adds; 'Torre station (one stop before Torquay station but not all trains stop there) is closest to the ground. Walk up the hill opposite the station and it's around a 20-25 minute walk.

If you have time on your hands then you can walk to the ground from Torquay station in around 40 minutes: On leaving the station turn left into Rathmore Road. Follow the road down crossing

into Falkland Road. Proceed by way of Lucius Street and Tor Hill Road into Union Street. Take the St Marychurch Road and climb the Hill towards Babbacombe then take the third turning on the right into Bronshill Road. The floodlights of Plain-moor will be visible after a few minutes on the left. Thanks to Myles Munsey for providing the directions.

Programme & Fanzine

Official Programme: £3
Capital Gulls Fanzine: £1

Record & Average Attendance

Record Attendance: 21,908 v Huddersfield Town, FA Cup 4th Round, January 29th, 1955.
Average Attendance: 2011-12: 2,869 (League Two)

Ground Name: White Hart Lane
Capacity: 36,274 (all seated)
Address: Bill Nicholson Way, 748 High Road, Tottenham, London, N17 0AP
Main Telephone No: 0844 499 5000
Ticket Office No: 0844 844 0102

Year Ground Opened: 1900
Pitch Size: 110 x 73 yards
Team Nickname: Spurs
Home Kit Colours: White & Navy
Official website: www.tottenhamhotspur.com

What's The Ground Like?

I have always been a great fan of White Hart Lane ever since my first visit way back in 1987. It has always been one of my favourite grounds in London to watch a game. It is totally enclosed which really adds to the overall look of the stadium and can make for a great atmosphere. Both ends have huge 'Jumbotron' video screens, built into the roof, which are a unique feature. All the stands are two-tiered with a row of executive boxes situated along their middle. Only the East Stand on one side has a couple of large supporting pillars (which can be forgiven considering that the stand dates back to the mid 1930s), otherwise there are no obstructions to your view. A television gantry is also suspended from beneath the roof of this stand. Opposite is the West Stand which was opened in 1982. Although much newer compared to the East Stand, it is its older neighbour that takes the eye, with the famous emblem of the Club, the gold coloured Cockerel sitting proudly on its roof. Another unusual feature of the stadium is the Police Control Box suspended underneath the roof in the South West corner, looking like some kind of UFO!

What Is It Like For Visiting Supporters?

Away fans are housed in one corner of the ground in between the South and West Stands, where up to 2,900 supporters can be accommodated, in the lower and upper tiers. If you have a ticket for the upper tier then prepare yourself for quite a climb to reach the away area. You are though rewarded with a great view of the action from this section and the leg room is ample. The facilities in this modern stand are above average. On the downside there is little space between the away and home fans. As you would expect there is plenty of banter between the two, but the stewards tend to take a tougher line on the away support. On my last visit a number of fans were ejected from the ground, plus there were repeated warnings to away fans to remain seated.

One strange aspect of sitting in the upper tier is seeing the Police Control Box directly above you, where a number of uniformed faces can be seen peering down on the away supporters. Although I have not personally experienced any problems at White Hart Lane, it may be wise to exercise caution around the ground and you may consider keeping colours covered.

Where To Drink?

Due to a number of pubs going out of business in the area around the ground, the choice for away fans is now rather limited. Simon Hornby informs me; 'The best place for away fans to get a drink is the Harringey Irish club on the Pretoria Road which is opposite White Hart Lane station. It has two large bars showing Sky Sports, offers reasonably priced food and you can also park there for £10'.

Tim Pick, a visiting Wolverhampton Wanderers fan adds; 'We drank at the Elmhust on Lordship Lane, which is about a 10 minute walk away from the ground. It is large mock tudor style looking pub with four or five Sky Sports screens. There were home fans and away fans in colours mixing without any problems. Prices were okay too (for London)'.

It may be an idea to drink in Central London before the game and then take a train to White Hart Lane Station. There is a Wetherspoon outlet at Liverpool Street Station from where you get the train to White Hart Lane. If you decide to take the long walk from Seven Sisters tube station to the stadium, then there are a number of pubs along the way. Inside the ground alcohol is also available to away supporters before the game, but strangely not at half-time.

Directions & Car Parking

Leave the M25 at Junction 25 and take the A10 towards Enfield. Continue on the A10 through Enfield and at the roundabout with the Northern Circular (A406), turn left onto the A406 (Sterling Way). Turn right into Fore Road (the A1010) which becomes the High Road and you will come to the ground on your left.

On street parking is virtually non-existent around the stadium on matchdays as a Controlled Parking Zone (CPZ) is in operation which means that only local residents who have a parking permit and blue badge holders can park legally. The perimeter of the zone is up to a mile from the ground and this has led to some private car parks near to the stadium charging up to £15 for the privilege. If you do park around the area, make sure that you take notice of the advisory parking notices attached to lamp posts, as otherwise you may find that you car gets towed away.

By Train/Tube

White Hart Lane Station is the nearest to the stadium, which is only a few minutes walk away. It is served by trains from Liverpool Street. Located at Liverpool Street is a handy Wetherspoons pub, plus a Cornish pasties outlet opposite.

The nearest London Underground station is Seven Sisters which is on the Victoria Line. The ground is about a 20 minute walk away, but there are plenty of buses running up Tottenham High Road to the ground. Chris Knibs informs me; 'Although there are plenty of buses, not many of them go past the ground. Those that do mostly have numbers that end in a 9, so take 149, 249, 279 or 349. You can also get a normal overground train from Seven Sisters to White Hart Lane station.

Programme

Official Programme: £3.50

Record & Average Attendance

Record Attendance: 75,038 v Sunderland, FA Cup 6th Round, March 5th, 1938.

Average Attendance: 2011-12: 36,026 (Premier League)

Ground Name: Prenton Park
Capacity: 16,587 (all seated)
Address: Prenton Road West, Birkenhead, CH42 9PY
Main Telephone No: 0871 221 2001
Ticket Office No: Same as main number

Year Ground Opened: 1912
Pitch Size: 112 x 72 yards
Team Nickname: Rovers
Home Kit Colours: White, Royal Blue Trim
Official website: www.tranmererovers.co.uk

What's The Ground Like?

During 1994-95 the Club replaced three sides of the ground with new stands. Only the Main Stand on one side of the pitch was left intact. This stand is a fair sized all seated, covered stand, that was opened in 1968. It is two-tiered and contains a couple of supporting pillars. The ground though is dominated by the Kop Stand at one end of the stadium. This stand has a single tier which has a capacity of around 5,500 and dwarfs the rest of the ground (although interestingly the Main Stand has a larger capacity). It replaced a former open terrace. Opposite is the Cowshed Stand. This single-tiered stand looks a little strange as one side of it has more rows than the other, giving a sloping effect. It has an electric scoreboard on its roof. On the other side is the Johnny King Stand (formerly the Borough Road Stand and now named after a former manager), which is a small covered stand that runs the entire length of the pitch.

What Is It Like For Visiting Supporters?

Away fans are housed in the affectionately named Cowshed Stand at one end, where up to 2,500 fans can be accommodated. You will be relieved to know that the only connection with a real cow-

shed is the name, as the fairly new covered, all seated stand, has good facilities and unhindered views of the playing action. The concourses are of a good size and the acoustics of the stand good, meaning that away fans can really make some noise.

Where To Drink?

The main pub for away fans is the Prenton Park Hotel, which is situated just across the road from the away turnstiles. This normally has a good mix of home and away supporters.

There are also a number of other pubs within walking distance of the ground. The Mersey Clipper, behind the Main Stand tends to be for home fans only, while The Sportsmans Arms on Prenton Road East is more welcoming towards visiting supporters. Otherwise alcohol is available in the away end.

All fans please note, it is a criminal offence to drink alcohol on the streets of Birkenhead, you may find yourself being arrested if you do.

Directions & Car Parking

From M6/M56 join the M53 and exit at Junction 4 and take the B5151 Mount Road from the fourth exit of the roundabout (the ground is signposted from here). After two and a half miles when Mount Road becomes Storeton Road, turn right into Prenton Road West and the ground will be visible on the right-hand side.

Sue Warwick adds; 'An easier route to the ground is to leave the M53 at Junction 3 and take the A552 Woodchurch Road towards Birkenhead. You will pass a Sainsbury's and then as you reach the Halfway House pub turn right at the traffic lights onto the B5151 Mount Road. Take the first left for the ground'.

There is a car park at the ground, otherwise, street parking, but beware that there is a strict local residents parking scheme in operation around the ground. Further along Borough Road, going past the Kop Stand, is a sports ground which has parking spaces costing £3 per car.

I got hopelessly lost trying to find the ground and did actually end up at the Mersey admiring the views of Liverpool across the river. My frustrations were not eased, when on asking a local chap for directions to the football ground the guy replied 'Liverpool or Everton?' After asking about another three locals I finally found the ground after going round most of Birkenhead.

By Train

The closest railway stations are Rock Ferry and Birkenhead Central, both served by Liverpool Lime Street. Both stations are a fair walk from the ground. (15-20 minutes). Philip Jackman provides directions from Rock Ferry station; 'Upon leaving Rock Ferry turn right and walk up Bedford Road for a fair distance until you reach a roundabout. At the roundabout, turn right into Bebington Road and walk along this road until you reach the Sportsman pub. Then turn left into Prenton Road and you will reach the ground and away fans turnstiles on your left.'

While Adam Hodson provides directions from Birkenhead Central; 'On exiting the station cross the road, turn right, then at the roundabout turn left onto Borough Road (A552 towards) Heswall. Go through four sets of traffic lights passing a Shell Garage on the left-hand side and at the fifth roundabout (signposted B5152 Clatterbridge and Tranmere Rovers FC), walk straight through onto Borough Road and the Ground is on the right-hand side after passing the Prenton Park Pub. It took around 15 minutes from the station'. Alternatively you can get a bus to the ground from the nearby Conway Bus Station, by making your way through the Grange Shopping Precinct, which is located on the opposite side of the main roundabout outside Birkenhead Central Station.

Programme

Official Programme: £3

Record & Average Attendance

Record Attendance: 24,424 v Stoke City, FA Cup 4th Round, February 5th, 1972.

Average Attendance: 2011-12: 5,130 (League One)

Ground Name: Banks's Stadium
Capacity: 10,989 (all seated)
Address: Bescot Crescent, Walsall, WS1 4SA
Main Telephone No: 01922 622 791
Ticket Office No: 01922 651 414/416

Year Ground Opened: 1990
Pitch Size: 110 x 73 yards
Team Nickname: The Saddlers
Home Kit Colours: White & Red
Official website: www.saddlers.co.uk

What's The Ground Like?

The Saddlers moved to the then called Bescot Stadium in 1990 from Fellows Park, which had been their home for 104 years. A fairly simple affair, somewhat similar to Glanford Park in Scunthorpe, which was opened two years earlier, the stadium received a boost in 2003 with the opening of a huge stand at one end. This is a large two-tiered affair that completely dwarfs the rest of the ground. It is smart looking, with a glassed area running across its middle, which houses the concourse. Unusually, it has a slightly larger upper than lower tier. This end before it was redeveloped was previously called the Gilbert Alsop (a former Walsall playing great) Stand, but in a commercial sponsorship deal, was renamed the Floors 2 Go Stand and is now currently the Tilechoice Stand.

The rest of the stadium is totally enclosed with three of the stands being roughly the same height, giving it a 'box-like' feel. These stands are not particularly big, around 15 rows high. The corners are filled, but only for advertising hoardings. The Main Stand on one side has a small television camera gantry perched on its roof, as well as the players tunnel and team dug outs at its front. At the back of the stand is a glassed area, which I

presume is used for corporate hospitality. Opposite is the Family Stand which is a simple seated stand that has dedicated areas for wheelchair users at its front.

The main disappointment is the large number of supporting pillars in each of the older stands (the newer Tilechoice Stand is pillar free). As Walsall unfortunately very rarely fill the stadium, this is not a huge problem. However, for big games this can be very annoying if you are unlucky enough to get seated behind one. There are four floodlight pylons mounted on the roof of each side stand, plus there is also a small electric scoreboard situated on top of the Sign Specialists (William Sharp) Stand.

What Is It Like For Visiting Supporters?

Away supporters are housed in the Sign Specialists Stand at one end of the ground, where around 2,000 away supporters can be accommodated. There are a few supporting pillars at the front which could impede your view. The good news though, is that even a small amount of away fans can really make some noise and make a good atmosphere. A trip to Walsall can be disappointing in terms of trying to get there and the stadium itself, but is more than countered by the relaxed atmosphere around the ground and the friendliness of the Walsall fans themselves.

If you are a neutral supporter attending the game then I would recommend sitting in the Tilechoice Stand at one end of the ground. This is simply, that situated between the two tiers is a large enclosed area that overlooks the pitch. This contains two bars, refreshment kiosks and a giant television screen showing the latest scores. I was very impressed with the facilities.

Where To Drink?

There is the Saddlers Club situated just outside the stadium that is happy to admit away supporters on matchdays on payment of a £2 entrance fee, although under 16s are admitted free. The Club has two rooms, a smaller one at the front which is for home supporters and a larger function room at the back, which is for away fans. This area has seating for 300, has a large screen showing Sky Sports news, has food on offer, plus they offered real ale. But as you would expect if there is a large away following it can get full pretty quickly.

Otherwise, the nearest pub to the ground is the King George V on Wallowes Lane. It is okay, but again understandably busy which can make it a bit difficult to get served quickly. It is about a 15 minute walk away, opposite the Morrisons Supermarket. If you are walking from the stadium, go out of the official car parks and down towards McDonalds. Go past McDonalds on your right and take a left-hand turn into Wallowes Lane. At the end of the lane turn left onto the main road and the pub is just setback on the left. Otherwise alcohol is available inside the stadium.

Directions & Car Parking

The ground is right next to the M6, in fact you can see it from the motorway just north of the RAC Control Centre. Unfortunately, this stretch of motorway normally has a large traffic jam on both Saturday lunchtimes and early weekday evenings, so allow extra time.

From M6 South:

Leave the M6 at Junction 7 and take the A34 towards Walsall (beware though of speed cameras on this stretch of dual carriageway). At the end of the dual carriageway turn left at the Bell Inn public house into Walstead Road (sign posted Bescot Stadium, Bescot Station Park & Ride). Continue straight on this road for two miles, passing another pub called the Tiger on your left. You will come to Bescot Stadium and entrance to the away end on your right.

From The M6 North:

Leave the M6 at Junction 9 and take the A461 towards Walsall. Bear right on to the A4148 (Wallowes Lane) and turn right at the second set of traffic lights. You will see the ground on your left.

Car Parking:

There is a good sized car park located at the ground (cost £3) and behind the away stand, which lends itself to a quick getaway after the match. Bescot Railway Station also offers car parking for £2. Alternatively there is some street parking to be had off Wallowes Lane.

By Train

Bescot Stadium has its own Railway Station, situated behind the away end only a few minutes walk from the turnstiles. Trains run there on a local line from Birmingham New Street and the journey time is around 20 minutes. There is a regular service on Saturdays along this line and you should not have too many problems getting away after the game.

Programme

Official Programme: £3

Record & Average Attendance

Record Attendance: 11,049 v Rotherham United, Division One, May 9th, 2004

Average Attendance: 2011-12: 4,274 (League One)

Ground Name: Vicarage Road
Capacity: 19,900 (all seated)
Address: Vicarage Road, Watford, WD18 0ER
Main Telephone No: 0844 856 1881
Ticket Office No: Same as main number

Year Ground Opened: 1922
Pitch Size: 115 x 75 yards
Team Nickname: The Hornets
Home Kit Colours: Yellow & Black, Red Trim
Official website: www.watfordfc.com

What's The Ground Like?

Overall a tidy looking ground, that is somewhat let down by the old East Stand on one side. I am normally a fan of old stands, but the East side is a mish-mash of a couple of tired looking structures and an open seated area in one corner. Originally built in 1922 the Main Stand as it was known was extended with an adjoining structure in the late 1960s. The side has now been closed due to health and safety concerns and the roof of the Main Stand has been removed. Apart from the Directors Box, the stand remains empty of spectators. The players though will continue to use the dressing rooms in this stand. On the other side is the Rous Stand. This two-tiered stand has an interesting roof design, which allows light to penetrate through. It also has a row of executive boxes across the back.

The ground has had both ends re-developed during the 1990s along with the front of the Rous stand. Both ends are large single-tiered stands, with some strange looking floodlights perched on the roof. Away fans are housed in one of these ends in the Vicarage Road Stand. Opposite work had begun in 'filling' in the corner between the Rookery Stand and the Rous Stand, plus additional construction at the rear of this stand, but due to financial difficulties, work has been suspended, leaving a half finished shell. Vicarage Road is shared with Saracens rugby club.

What Is It Like For Visiting Supporters?

Away fans are housed in the Vicarage Road Stand at one end of the ground. This stand is normally shared with home supporters (with the obligatory 'no-mans land' comprised of empty seats covered in netting in between). Around 2,200 visiting fans can be accommodated in this area. The stand has electronic turnstiles, meaning that you have to place your ticket into a bar code reader to gain entrance. You should also then expect to be searched by the stewards on the way in.

I've always found this club friendly and the stewarding relaxed on my four visits and have never had any hassle, although at times there can be a heavy police presence around the ground and in the town centre. My only real gripe is that the size of the concourse at the back of the stand is one of the tightest that I have come across and is wholly inadequate when there is a large away following. There is also a betting outlet available.

On the first occasion that I visited Vicarage

Road, I met a Watford supporter in a pub who gave me a free ticket to that night's game against Luton. I was also impressed with this chap as at the time he had visited 91 League grounds with Watford. Perhaps he was in some part my inspiration for doing the '92'.

Where To Drink?

Christopher Harrison, a visiting Middlesbrough fan recommends the Odd Fellows in Fearnley Street; 'It is only a couple of hundred yards from the ground and they even had a barbeque in the beer garden'. The bar is situated off Cassio Road and is clearly visible when taking the route to Vicarage Road from the town centre via Market Street. The pub is only a few minutes walk from the away turnstiles. It has a large beer garden, with a covered area for smokers and offers from its barbecue, burgers and hot dogs. Even though it was very busy on my last visit, I was impressed with the service from behind the bar, getting served in reasonable time (even though it looked like you had no chance of getting near to the bar let alone being served!).

Otherwise the ground is in walking distance of the town centre, where along the High Street you will find a few pubs including a large Wetherspoons outlet called the Moon Under Water, an O'Neils and a Walkabout. Please note that alcohol is not sold in the away section.

Directions & Car Parking

Leave the M1 at Junction 5 and take the A4008 into Watford. If on nearing the town centre you can't see the ground over on your left, just go left around the inner ring road (follow signs for Watford General Hospital as this is behind the stadium) and you will soon spot it. There are also some private match day car parks available at some industrial units near the ground, as well as the Vicarage Road Girls School, which is close to the stadium and charges £5 per car. As the ground is almost right in the centre of town, then there are a number of car parks in walking distance.

By Train/Tube

The nearest station is Watford High Street, a 10 minute walk away from the ground. However, you are likely to come into Watford Junction train station, which is about a 20 minute walk. Either get a train to Watford High Street from Watford Junction or if you have time to walk to the ground then:

Leave the station and take the main road straight opposite (Clarendon Road) all the way (over Ring Road at lights) up to the High Street. Turn left and go past Wetherspoons (Moon under Water) on your right and then take the first right after 100 yards into Market Street. Continue along again crossing the Ring Road to the T junction and then left at an excellent chip shop. Vicarage Road is the next right turn. It should take around 15-20 minutes to walk. Thanks to Albert Fuller for providing the directions.

Watford also has its own London Underground station, which is on the Metropolitan Line and is situated just under one mile from Vicarage Road. However, overland trains from London normally have a shorter journey time.

Programme & Fanzines

Official Programme: £3

Record & Average Attendance

Record Attendance: 34,099 v Manchester United, FA Cup 4th Round Replay, February 3rd, 1969.
Average Attendance: 2011-12: 12,704 (Championship League)

Ground Name: The Hawthorns
Capacity: 26,500 (all seated)
Address: Halfords Lane, West Bromwich,
West Midlands, B71 4LF
Main Telephone No: 0871 271 1100
Ticket Office No: 0871 271 9780

Year Ground Opened: 1900
Pitch Size: 115 x 74 yards
Team Nickname: The Baggies
Home Kit Colours: Navy & White Stripes
Official website: www.wba.co.uk

What's The Ground Like?

With the completion of the East Stand in 2001, the Club achieved its objective in completely re-building the Hawthorns and making it a modern stadium. Not only has the ground received a much needed face lift, but it is now totally enclosed and all seated. The East Stand is an impressive, large single-tiered stand, which has been well integrated with the rest of the ground. It has a row of executive boxes running along the back, and to each side of the stand the previous open corners have been filled with corrugated sheeting. There is a thin supporting pillar on each side of the stand to support the corner structures. On the other side is the smaller Halfords Lane Stand. This stand which was opened in 1982 stretches around two corners of the ground. The home end, the Birmingham Road Stand is large, covered, and quite steep. At the other end away fans are housed in the Smethwick End. Both these ends were built in 1994-95. Two new video screens have been installed in opposite corners of the ground, one at the Smethwick End side of the East Stand and the other in the opposite corner of the Halfords Lane Stand.

An interesting feature of the ground is that in one corner of the ground (between the East Stand and Birmingham Road End) you will notice perched up on a wall, a large Throstle standing on a football. This has been kept over from the previous stand (it used to sit above the clock on the half-time scoreboard) and maintains the links with tradition. Outside the ground on the same corner are the 'Jeff Astle Memorial Gates' erected in tribute to the legendary striker. While just beyond the East Stand Car Park is a Memorial Garden.

One strange fact about the Hawthorns is that it is the highest ground in England (in terms of feet above sea level).

What Is It Like For Visiting Supporters?

Away fans are housed on one side of the Smethwick End, where the normal allocation is 3,000 seats. This means that this stand is shared with home supporters. For cup games, the whole of this stand can be allocated to away supporters, raising this figure to 5,200. The facilities and the view of the pitch in the Smethwick End are okay, although the leg room is a little cramped. I have been to the Hawthorns on a number of occasions and have always found it to be a fairly friendly place. The only thing against it, in terms of a day out is the lack of nearby pub for away fans, meaning that most elect to drink inside the ground instead. Considering that the concourse at the back of the Smethwick End is pretty small in comparison to its overall capacity, then it can have uncomfortable feel, especially when there is a capacity away support.

One tip on finding your seat in this stand, is to remember that although your ticket is marked with the letter of the row, say Row B Or Row LL, the plates indicating the row in the stand read B1 or LL1. As you would expect a number of fans get confused by the addition of the number 1 and start to wander around the stand looking for their seat. So you have been warned. Also in first gaining entry to the stand, the Club operate automatic turnstiles, where you have to put your ticket (which has a bar code on it) into a slot reader, which then allows the turnstiles to admit you. There are stewards on hand if you get a problem and on my last visit fans were also being searched before entering the ground.

Where To Drink?

The main pub for away fans is The Vine which is about a 15-20 minute walk from the ground. From Junction 1 of the M5 turn left towards West Bromwich town centre (opposite direction to the ground). Take the first left into Roebuck Street. The Vine is down on the left. You can also street park in this area and then walk to the ground. This pub also offers Indian food and has an indoor tandoori barbeque (from 1pm on Saturdays), plus has a beer garden with children's play area.

Dave Wilson recommends; 'The Park Hotel which is just off junction one of the M5 and a 10 minute walk to the ground. You can park on their car park for £5 and away fans are always welcome'. Sean Mowat, a visiting Sheffield United supporter adds; 'As you pass the ground on the right on the main Birmingham Road, carry on about another half a mile and there is a pub on the right set back off the road called the Royal Oak. The beer is okay and they also serve Asian food (try the chicken kebabs!). It had a friendly atmosphere on our visit'.

Directions & Car Parking

The Hawthorns is located on the A41 (Birmingham-West Bromwich Road). If approaching from outside the area the ground is about half a mile from Junction 1 of the M5. On leaving the M5 take the A41 towards Birmingham, the ground is on your right. Beware though of speed cameras on this stretch of the A41. Street parking or alternatively there are a few private matchday car parks at some local industrial units near the ground, or at Hawthorns station which costs £4.

By Train

The Hawthorns has its own railway and metro station which are about a five minute walk from the ground. It can be reached from Birmingham New Street, by first taking a train to Smethwick Galton Bridge and changing there for the Hawthorns. Total journey time is around 20-25 minutes. Alternatively the Hawthorns is also served by direct trains from Birmingham Moor Street and Birmingham Snow Hill. The metro line runs from Birmingham Snow Hill.

Programme

Official Programme: £3

Record & Average Attendance

Record Attendance: 64,815 v Arsenal, FA Cup 6th Round, March 6th, 1937.
Average Attendance: 2011-12: 24,793 (Premier League)

Ground Name: Boleyn Ground
Capacity: 35,333 (all seated)
Address: Green Street, Upton Park, London, E13 9AZ
Main Telephone No: 020 8548 2748
Ticket Office No: 0870 112 2700

Year Ground Opened: 1904
Pitch Size: 110 x 70 yards
Team Nickname: The Hammers or Irons
Home Kit Colours: Claret & Blue
Official website: www.whufc.com

What's The Ground Like?

On the whole the stadium is an impressive one, being of a good size and having three modern stands. On one side of the ground is the impressive looking Dr Martens West Stand that was opened in 2001. This large two-tiered stand (which is reputedly the largest League ground stand in London), has a capacity of 15,000. Located between the tiers are two rows of corporate executive boxes. Opposite is the East Stand, which was opened in 1969. This stand in comparison, although two-tiered, is rather on the small side and looks somewhat out of place compared to its larger shiny neighbours. Both ends are large, smart, two-tiered stands. In the North East and South West corners there are video screens installed as well as an electronic score board in the South West corner. Also in the South West corner is a large image of Booby Moore who overlooks the ground.

Probably the most striking feature of the stadium can only be seen externally, where an elaborate facade comprising of two castle turrets has been built around the reception area entrance. The turrets have been modelled on those appearing on the Club crest. It is nice to see a Club actually trying to instill some character into a new stand. Just outside the ground near the Boleyn Pub, is the handsome statue of England Captain Bobby Moore, holding aloft the World Cup Trophy which England won in 1966. The statue shows Moore being hoisted aloft by fellow West Ham players Geoff Hurst and Martin Peters with Everton defender Ray Wilson.

What Is It Like For Visiting Supporters?

Away fans are housed in one end, in the lower tier of the relatively modern Sir Trevor Brooking Stand. The usual allocation for away supporters is 2,200, but if demand requires, away fans can be allocated the whole of the lower tier of the North Stand, where up to 3,600 supporters can be accommodated. The ground is compact, with the fans seated close to the pitch. This coupled with the passionate support of the West Ham faithful can make for a vibrant atmosphere. However, this can be intimidating for away supporters, so exercise caution around the ground. If you find yourself seated on the far left of the away section (towards the East Stand) then as the pitch is situated towards the West Stand, you may experience some sight difficulties of the action going on, in and around the corner on the other side.

Entrance to the stadium is gained by inserting your ticket into an electronic bar code reader. Inside the ground the stewards are fine, however, the concourse is somewhat cramped, which leads to somewhat of a scrum at half-time. There are flat screen TVs on the concourse to keep fans entertained. Food on offer includes a range of Peter's Pies.

Where To Drink?

Kevin Hosking informs me; 'Probably the best option for away fans is the Wetherspoon outlet called Millers Well which is opposite East Ham Town Hall. It is though about a 20 minute walk away along Barking Road (although it may be an idea to travel to East Ham tube station before the game, go to the pub and then walk on to the stadium). Another good option is the Denmark Arms also on the Barking Road near the East Ham Town Hall; this is a large pub which shows all live football games'.

Directions & Car Parking
Directions from the M25:
Travel to M25 Junction 27, and go on to the M11 southbound. Follow the M11 south until it divides to join the A406 (North Circular Road). Take the left-hand fork signposted A406 South. Do not follow the signs for the City.

The end of the motorway joins the A406 from the left, creating a four lane road for a short distance. You need to be in one of the outside two lanes (this can be tricky if traffic is heavy). Proceed south (dual carriageway with slip roads) passing the junctions for Redbridge, and Ilford.

Leave the A406 at the Barking junction. At the roundabout at the bottom of the slip road, turn right, taking the third exit towards East Ham (Barking Road). Proceed West along Barking Road through several sets of traffic lights until you have passed the lights at East Ham Town Hall (big red Victorian building on the left just before the lights). Three quarters of a mile further, you pass the

ground on your right (behind a parade of shops, including the Hammers Shop). At the next lights (Boleyn Arms Pub on the right-hand corner), turn right into Green Street. The main entrance to the ground is 200 yards on your right. Thanks to Gareth Howell for providing the directions.

On Saturday matchdays, parking is very restricted with little or no off-road parking. The best areas to look for spaces are roads left off Barking Road, once you are past the lights at East Ham Town Hall.

By Train/Tube
The nearest tube station is Upton Park which is on the District, plus the Hammersmith & City Lines. The station is a short walk from the ground. Please note that West Ham tube station is nowhere near the ground. Steve Cook adds; 'the queue at Upton Park tube station after the game can be horrendous. You are better off going for a couple of pints and letting the queues die down'. Adam Long, a visiting Reading fan informs me; 'After the game you are probably best to walk up to East Ham, which will at least mean you will get a seat, before everyone else gets on at Upton Park'.

While Andrew Saffrey suggests; 'Forest Gate station is about 25 minutes walk from Upton Park, and it's much less busy than Upton Park Station after the final whistle. It is served by local Great Eastern trains from Liverpool Street'.

Programme & Fanzines
Official Programme: £3.50
Over Land And Sea: £2.50
On The Terrace Fanzine: £2

Record & Average Attendance
Record Attendance: 42,322 v Tottenham Hotspur, Division One, October 17th, 1970.
Average Attendance: 2011-12: 30,931 (Championship League)

Ground Name: DW Stadium
Capacity: 25,023 (all seated)
Address: Loire Drive, Wigan, WN5 0UZ
Main Telephone No: 01942 774 000
Ticket Office No: 0871 663 3552

Year Ground Opened: 1999
Pitch Size: 110 x 60 metres
Team Nickname: Latics
Home Kit Colours: Blue & White
Official website: www.wiganlatics.co.uk

What's The Ground Like?

The DW Stadium was opened in 1999 after the Club moved from its former home of Springfield Park, where it had been in residence since the Club's formation in 1932.

The DW is a functional stadium but overall it has somewhat of a bland look. In fact I would say that it looks more interesting from the outside from a distance than it does within. The four separate stands are of roughly the same height and are all single tiered. They are also quite steep meaning that fans are sat quite close to the playing action, although this is mitigated a little by the fact that the stands themselves are set back a fair distance from the pitch perimeter.

Both the side stands have large supporting steel frameworks visible above their roofs, while oddly both ends are different, having the steel framework located below the roof line. Unusually for a modern stadium, it does seem to be lacking in the number of corporate areas and executive boxes. There is an electric scoreboard above the Boston (East) Stand, on one side of the ground.

The stadium was originally named the JJB Stadium under a sponsorship deal that lasted for 10 years. This was replaced by a new deal in August 2009, which saw the stadium being renamed the DW Stadium in partnership with DW Sports Fitness. The stadium is also shared with Wigan Warriors Rugby League club.

What Is It Like For Visiting Supporters?

Away fans are located in the North Stand at one end of the stadium, where up to 5,400 visiting supporters can be accommodated. The stadium is functional and the facilities adequate, but it just seems to lack something to give it that memorable feeling. The view of the playing action and leg room are generally adequate. To the left of the away section is where the singing Wigan fans tend to congregate, who are aided by a drummer. On the concourse alcohol is available in the form of Tetleys and Carling. To try and bring some order, there is a queuing system in force which is overseen by the stewards (plus if I remember correctly you could only buy two beers per person). Apart from the beer, I did enjoy one of the best meat and potato pies that I have had in a long time.

Scott Carpenter, a visiting Newcastle fan adds; 'the concourses seemed too small for the large amount of away fans attending on my visit, which led to it being rather uncomfortably crowded at half-time'.

Where To Drink?

The traditional pub for away fans visiting the DW stadium is the Red Robin, which is only a few minutes walk away from the ground opposite the Cinema Complex.

Simon Wright, a visiting West Bromwich Albion fan informs me; 'Beside the away turnstiles is an entrance to a bar, specifically for the use of away fans. It has the usual bar, big screen television and sells pies, as well as teas and coffees. It's a great facility and welcomes families'. It is known as the Marquee Bar as it resembles one inside.

Otherwise in the centre of town is a Wetherspoons outlet called the Moon Under Water which was popular with away supporters on my last visit. Also worth a visit is the award winning Anvil pub, which is located next to the bus station. Both these pubs are listed in the CAMRA Good Beer Guide. Also worth a mention is the Berkeley on Wallgate (near the railway station). This fair sized pub, had a good mix of home and away supporters on my last visit, serves five ever changing real ales and shows Sky Sports on a huge screen.

Directions & Car Parking

From The South:

Leave the M6 to Junction 25 then take the A49 to Wigan. After around two miles you should pass an Aldi store on your left, before reaching a large roundabout, that is traffic light controlled. Turn left at this roundabout into Robin Park Road and continue into Scot Lane. The ground is down Scot Lane on your right.

From The North:

Leave the M6 at Junction 26 and follow the signs for Wigan town centre (this road meets the A49) then turn left into Robin Park and continue into Scot Lane. The ground is down Scot Lane on your right.

Car Parking:

There is a large car park at the stadium, specifically for the use of away supporters, which costs £5 per car or motorbike, £10 for mini buses and £20 for coaches. As you may expect though, there is sometimes quite a delay in getting out of this car park after the game, especially if there has been a larger than normal crowd in attendance. Make sure though that you avoid parking on the nearby Retail Park, as parking there is restricted to two hours and I have been informed of a number of fans who have ended up getting parking tickets (£50) because of this.

By Train

Wigan's central railway stations (Wigan North Western and Wallgate stations) are a good 20 minute walk from the ground. So either take a taxi, or break up the journey with a few pub stops on the way!

On exiting Wigan North Railway Station turn left and go down the road heading under a railway bridge. On leaving Wallgate station turn right and go down the road passing Wigan North station on your left and then proceed under the railway bridge. It is a fairly straight walk along Robin Park Road passing the Jacobs Well Pub (at Wigan Pier) on your left, which is okay for away supporters. When you reach the Seven Stars hotel, you should be able to see the stadium over on your right. Either at the Seven Stars Hotel turn right and follow the locals on a shortcut along a canal to the stadium, or take the next road on the right.

Programme & Fanzine

Official Programme: £3
Cockney Latic Fanzine: £1

Record & Average Attendance

Record Attendance: 25,133 v Manchester United, Premier League, May 11th, 2008.
Average Attendance: 2011-12: 18,634 (Premier League)

Ground Name: Molineux
Capacity: 31,700 (all seated)
Address: Waterloo Road, Wolverhampton, WV1 4QR
Main Telephone No: 0871 222 2220
Ticket Office No: 0871 222 1877

Year Ground Opened: 1889
Pitch Size: 116 x 74 yards
Team Nickname: Wolves
Home Kit Colours: Gold & Black
Official website: www.wolves.co.uk

What's The Ground Like?

The ground is dominated by the new Stan Cullis Stand at one end of the stadium. This impressive looking structure towers over the rest of Molineux and the roof steelwork can be seen from miles around on the Wolverhampton sky line. The stand is two-tiered, with a larger lower tier, with the upper tier having a large windshield on one side. The stand extends partly around one corner towards the Steve Bull Stand and some seats in the upper tier in that corner, will have a restricted view of the playing area, due to the roof of the Steve Bull Stand being directly in the line of sight. It is hoped that at some point the Steve Bull Stand will be replaced by a similar structure and will extend around to meet the new Stan Cullis Stand.

Both sides of the stadium are two-tiered covered stands, that have a row of executive boxes situated along the middle. They are unusual in being oval in shape, meaning that those sitting on the halfway line are furthest away from the playing action. The oldest of these is the Steve Bull Stand, which was opened in 1979, while opposite is the Billy Wright Stand which was opened in 1993. This stand is the Main Stand at Molineux, which contains the Directors area, team

dugouts in front and a television gantry below its roof. At one end is the Jack Harris Stand, which was also opened in 1993, four months after the Billy Wright Stand. This is a large single-tiered stand, part of which is given to away supporters. Situated in the corner between the Jack Harris and Billy Wright stands, is a temporary stand that has a capacity of 900 seats. The seats are green coloured which makes it look a little out of place to the rest of the stadium. This is affectionately known as the 'Gene Kelly' stand (or officially known as the Wolves Community Trust). That is because this area is open to the elements so you could end up 'singing in the rain'. There are a couple of video screens in two of the corners, but unfortunately these are no longer in operation. Outside the stadium is the impressive statue of former playing legend Billy Wright.

What Is It Like For Visiting Supporters?

Away fans are normally housed on one side of the Jack Harris Stand at one end of the stadium where around 2,000 fans can be accommodated. This stand is shared with home supporters which helps to boost the atmosphere. For games where there is a larger away following, then the away fans are not given an 'end' as such, but are instead housed in the lower tier of the Steve Bull Stand along the side of the pitch. Up to 3,200 away supporters can be housed in this area. Fans in this stand are sat quite far back from the playing area, which gives the illusion that the pitch is larger than at most other grounds.

Musical delights at the ground include just before kick-off, 'Hi, Ho, Silver Lining' with the crowd singing 'Hi, Ho, Wolverhampton!' On one visit I got talking to a couple of Wolves fans on the train up to Wolverhampton and they suggested going for a drink in the city centre before the game which I did. I had quite an enjoyable time and they even took me right up to the away supporters entrance, shook my hand and wished me luck! Very hospitable. I personally did not experience any problems on my visits, but I have received a number of reports of others that have not been so lucky. It is strongly advised that colours are kept covered around the ground and city centre (and that goes for your cars too).

Where To Drink?

There are a number of pubs near to the ground but they are for home fans only. Molineux is only a 10 minute walk away from the city centre where there are plenty of pubs to be found, however, by far the greater majority of these are also for home supporters and have bouncers on the doors. One exception is the Walkabout Bar on Queen Street as Tom Rice, a visiting Aston Villa supporter informs me; 'The Walkabout bar in the city centre, seems to be now the designated pub for away fans to drink in. The bouncers on the door, checked to make sure that we were Villa fans before entering'.

Directions & Car Parking

From The South:
Leave the M6 at Junction 10 and take the A454 towards Wolverhampton. Continue to follow the A454 right into Wolverhampton (be wary of speed cameras on the A454). On reaching the traffic island that intersects with the ring road, turn right.

As you approach the 2nd set of lights look for the signs for football parking. The ground is over the second set of lights on the right. Alternatively if you turn left into the city centre you may find a space in one of the many council run 'pay & display' car parks.

From The North:
Leave the M6 at Junction 12 and take the A5 towards Telford and then turn onto the A449 towards Wolverhampton. On reaching the traffic island that intersects with the ring road, turn right. Then as South.

By Train

Wolverhampton railway station is around a 15 minute walk away from Molineux. From the main station entrance proceed straight on towards the city centre and as you reach the inner ring road turn right. Just follow the ring road as it continues in a circular pattern around to the left. Eventually you will see the Molineux on the right.

Programme

Official Programme: £3

Record & Average Attendance

Record Attendance: 61,305 v Liverpool, FA Cup 5th Round, February 11th, 1939.
Average Attendance: 2011-12: 25,672
(Premier League)

Ground Name: Adams Park
Capacity: 10,300
Address: Hillbottom Road, High Wycombe, HP12 4HJ
Main Telephone No: 01494 472 100
Ticket Office No: 01494 441 118

Year Ground Opened: 1990
Pitch Size: 115 x 75 yards
Team Nickname: The Chairboys
Home Kit Colours: Navy & Light Blue
Official website: www.wycombewanderers.co.uk

What's The Ground Like?

On one side of the ground is the impressive looking Frank Adams Stand, opened in 1996. This was named in memory of the man who originally donated to the club their previous ground at Loakes Park. It is a large two-tiered stand, complete with a row of executive boxes and it dwarfs the rest of the stadium. The other three stands are smaller affairs, but are at least all covered. Only the Greene King IPA Stand at the home end remains as terracing. Opposite is the Dreams Stand, housing away supporters, a medium sized single-tiered stand, with windshields to either side. Along the other side of the ground is the Main Stand. This single-tiered stand has a raised seating area, meaning that fans access it by climbing a small set of stairs in front of it. There is a large video screen situated in one corner of the stadium, between the Dreams and Main Stands. The ground is currently shared with Wasps Rugby Club.

What Is It Like For Visiting Supporters?

Away fans are mostly located at one end of the ground in the Dreams Stand, where just over 2,000 supporters can be accommodated. For teams with a larger following then 350 seats are also made available in the Main Stand, increasing the total allocation to 2,350. I personally had an enjoyable day at Wycombe. The club has a relaxed friendly feel about it. The ground is situated in a nice setting with a wooded hill overlooking the ground (this normally has a small contingent of supporters watching the game for nothing) and with green fields surrounding the other sides. The standard football ground fayre of burgers, pies, pasties and hot dogs are available from the refreshments area.

David Abbott, a visiting Northampton Town supporter informs me; 'I have to say what an excellent ground Adams Park is. Good signposting around the ground, good organisation, good atmosphere, excellent view from the away end and friendly fans. It was a very pleasant visit and if all grounds and supporters were as welcoming and well-behaved as Wycombe the game would be all the better for it'.

Mike Jordan, a visiting Torquay United fan tells me; 'I found the home fans, stewards and staff of Wycombe to be friendly and welcoming towards away supporters. Also, for visitors interested in wildlife, at half-time or during dull moments, look out for Red Kites drifting over the ground!'

Where To Drink?

As the ground is on the edge of an industrial estate, there aren't many pubs around. Neil Young informs me 'The nearest pub to Adams Park is the Hourglass in Sands (about a 15 minute walk, from the end of the road up to the ground). Away fans are normally okay in small groups except for big games or local derbies'. Martin Redfern, a visiting Scunthorpe United informs me; 'we arrived early at the ground and were able to go into the Supporter's Club at the ground itself, which cost £2 to enter. The Club is one of the suites at the far end of the Main Stand. It was a spacious room with two bars and food. The atmosphere was extremely relaxed and friendly with both home and away supporters'.

Directions & Car Parking

The stadium is located on the outskirts of Wycombe on the Sands Industrial Estate. Leave the M40 at Junction 4 and take the A4010 towards Aylesbury. Turn left at the 4th roundabout into Lane End Road and then continue straight down this road. Cross another roundabout and into Hillbottom Road. The ground is down at the very bottom of this road. On my last visit I noticed that there were a number of AA road signs labelled 'London Wasps' which were helpful in pointing the way to the ground.

There is a fair sized car park located at the ground which costs £5 per car, or some of the industrial units provide match day parking (at around £3). As there is only one road that leads from the stadium, I have heard that it can be a nightmare leaving the official car park at full-time. I would recommend therefore, parking in one of the industrial units that line Hillbottom Road towards the ground. I did this and got away alright.

Alternatively the Club run a 'Park & Ride' scheme from the car park opposite the Cressex Cinema, by Junction 4 of the M40. Buses depart between 1.30pm & 2.30pm for Saturday fixtures and 6.15pm & 7.15pm for midweek fixtures. The bus drops fans close to the stadium at the bottom of Hillbottom Road. The cost of the service is £1 for adults and free for concessions. Buses return 15 minutes after the final whistle and then again after completing one drop off to pick up any remaining fans.

By Train

Wycombe Railway Station is situated around two and half miles away from the stadium and is really too far to walk. It is served by trains from London Marylebone and Birmingham Moor Street. You can either take a Taxi (costs about £8) or get the football special bus that runs from the station to the ground on match days. The Football Special (No.32) departs the Railway Station for the stadium at 13.55 on Saturday matchdays and 18.40 for midweek games (cost £2.50 return). The bus returns 10 minutes after the final whistle. Micheal Gerloff a visiting Charlton Athletic fan informs me; 'The shuttle bus was very crowded after the game and it took over 40 minutes to get to the station. We had to run to the platform to make the 17:57 train back to London'.

Programme

Official Programme: £3

Record & Average Attendance

Record Attendance: 10,000 v Chelsea, Friendly, July 13th, 2005.
Average Attendance: 2011-12: 4,843 (League One)

Ground Name: Huish Park
Capacity: 9,665 (Seating 5,212)
Address: Lufton Way, Yeovil, Somerset, BA22 8YF
Main Telephone No: 01935 423 662
Ticket Office No: Same as main number

Year Ground Opened: 1990
Pitch Size: 115 x 72 yards
Team Nickname: Glovers
Home Kit Colours: Green & White Hoops
Official website: www.ytfc.net

What's The Ground Like?

Yeovil is predominantly remembered for some classic 'giant killing' deeds in the FA Cup and the famous slope of the pitch. With the move to a new ground in 1990, that slope has gone, but the team have continued to impress. Generally the ground is a tidy looking one, in a pleasant setting, with lots of trees visible behind the stands. Both sides of the ground are similar looking stands and are of the same height. They are both cantilevered, covered single-tiered stands that are all seated. Each stand has windshields to either side. The only differences between these stands, is that the Augusta Westland Community Stand has some executive boxes running across the back of it, plus the dug outs and players tunnel, while the Screwfix Community Stand has a press box suspended from beneath its roof and a small simple looking electric scoreboard. At one end is the medium sized Thatchers Gold Stand Terrace, which is covered and for home supporters and again has windshields to either side. Opposite is the Copse Road Terrace, which is given to away fans. This is smaller and uncovered. Oddly the steel work is in place at the back of this stand to incorporate more terrace space, but the concrete rows have so far not been added. Perched above the rear of this stand is a large electric scoreboard. The ground is completed with a set of four modern floodlight pylons, one in each corner of the ground.

What Is It Like For Visiting Supporters?

Away fans are situated in the Copse Road open terrace at one end of the ground. This is uncovered, so hope for a dry day. Up to 1,750 supporters can be housed in this area. Additionally 300 seats are allocated to away fans in the Screwfix Community Stand, which is covered. However, tickets are only made available in this area to families with young children, senior citizens and ambulant disabled.

Normally a visit to Huish Park is enjoyable, and the atmosphere good. This is boosted by a very vocal crowd in the home terrace as well as the presence of a drummer and trumpeter in that end (on my last visit the trumpeter was even imitating an ambulance siren as the trainer ran on to treat an injured player!).

I found the large police presence in and around the ground perturbing. In my mind I was not at a high profile game, so I was somewhat surprised at the amount of local constabulary there. If Yeovil score then 'Glad All Over' by the Dave Clark Five blasts out around the ground.

Where To Drink?

There are three pubs within about 10-15 minutes walk of the ground, The Bell, The Arrow and The Airfield Tavern. Richard Reardon, a visiting Carlisle fan adds; 'The Arrow is only 10-15 minutes walk away. The weather was excellent so most of our substantial following sat outside at a number of picnic tables. Both sets of supporters mixed well, Sky TV for those that like that sort of thing. Police presence outside but it was all very friendly'.

Colin Jordan, a visiting Exeter City fan adds; 'We found the Bell pub on Preston Road (towards the Town Centre from the A3088 roundabout, rather than turning left towards Huish Park). It's a very large Greene King Hungry Horse pub, with a great deal of outside seating, and as with most of Yeovil it seems to be away fan friendly. Usual Greene King beer fayre, plus good quality food. It is though at least a 15-20 minute walk away from the ground'.

Directions & Car Parking

The ground is located on the very outskirts of Yeovil and is signposted from the A303. Leave the A303 at the Cartgate roundabout and take the A3088 towards Yeovil. Follow the road for around four miles until you reach a roundabout on the outskirts of Yeovil with the Westlands Airfield directly in front of you. Turn left at this roundabout and then continue straight on, crossing a number of roundabouts. As you pass the entrance to an Asda superstore, take the next left for the ground, which can be seen from the road.

There is a fair sized car park at the ground, which costs £2. Otherwise there is plenty of street parking in the area. Richard Reardon adds; 'Getting away from the ground was a bit of nightmare as there is only one road out of the official car park. It took 35 minutes to travel the half mile to the Preston Road roundabout'.

By Train

Yeovil has two railway stations; Yeovil Junction and Pen Mill Junction. Both of these stations are located quite a distance from the ground, with Pen Mill Junction just under three miles away and Yeovil Junction almost five miles away. From both stations it is advised to get a taxi to the stadium or alternatively if you arrive at Yeovil Junction, then you can catch the 'Hopper' minibus to the bus station in the town centre. I have been informed that for night games taxis can be scarce at Yeovil Junction, so if you intend going by taxi to the ground it may be an idea to look up the number of a local taxi firm and pre-book one.

John Midgley a visiting Huddersfield Town fan adds; 'Bus No.68 runs from both Yeovil Junction and Yeovil Pen Mill stations to the town centre. You can then take the regular First Traveller No.1 service (every 15 minutes), which drops you near the stadium at the Abbey Manor Park Housing Estate. The No.68 connects with the No.1 at the Lloyds TSB Bank, located on the town centre High Street (make sure you catch the No.1 with 'Abbey Manor Park' on the front).

Programme & Fanzine

Official Programme: £3
Onto Victory Fanzine: £1

Record & Average Attendance

Record Attendance: 9,527 v Leeds United, League One, April 25th, 2008.
Average Attendance: 2011-12: 3,984 (League One)

Ground Name: Bootham Crescent
Capacity: 7,872 (Seated 3,409)
Address: Bootham Crescent, York, YO30 7AQ
Main Telephone No: 01904 624447
Ticket Office No: Same as main number

Year Ground Opened: 1932
Pitch Size: 115 x 75 yards
Team Nickname: The Minstermen
Home Kit Colours: Red & Blue
Official website: www.yorkcityfootballclub.co.uk

What's The Ground Like?

The ground hasn't seen any major investment for a number of years now, which has resulted in it looking a little tired in places. However, it does have character, something that a lot of newer stadiums lack. On one side of the ground is the Main Stand. As you would expect it is the tallest stand at the ground, but only runs for around two thirds of the length of the pitch, with open corners to either side (one of which houses the supporters club). It is a covered all seated stand and to the rear it has windshields to either side. It also has a number of supporting pillars running across the middle.

Opposite is the Popular Stand. This is a simple affair, being small and covered. It too has a number of supporting pillars this time running across the front. On its roof is a rather basic looking television gantry. At one end is the David Longhurst Stand, which is a fair sized covered terrace, which has a row of supporting pillars across its front. Opposite is the open terraced Grosvenor Road End, reserved for away supporters. The ground is completed with a set four modern looking floodlight pylons.

What Is It Like For Visiting Supporters?

Away fans are placed in the open Grosvenor Road Terrace, where just over 2,000 fans can be accommodated. A further 300 seats are made available to away supporters in the Popular Stand, which unlike the open terrace is at least covered. After paying to enter the terrace and going through a line of stewards who seemed on my visit to be searching most fans going in, you can then pay a £1 transfer fee to go into the seated area. Away fans in both the seats and terracing share the same refreshment kiosk and toilets. The latter for men seem to have been there since the ground opened. The urinals are open air and are of the 'stand up against a brick wall variety', while women have a portakabin affair. On my last visit the refreshment kiosk was doing a brisk trade of meat pies & mushy peas served in a tray. On the whole I found York to be friendly and the supporters get behind their team well, making for a good atmosphere.

Daniel Scullane a visiting Bath City fan adds; 'The atmosphere was quite sedate on my last visit. Maybe it is something to do with the fact that away fans are extremely isolated inside. The layout of the ground is such that the away fans are about

30 yards from the nearest home fans on the popular side, and the grandstand is split from the away fans by about half the pitch. Still an enoyable visit made all the better by a cracking night out on the town afterwards!'

Where To Drink?

There is a supporters' club on the corner of the ground that overlooks the away end. When I went they were quite happy to allow away supporters in and there was some pleasant banter going on between both sets of supporters. The Club also serves a real ale, sometimes supplied by the local York Brewery. Otherwise the nearest pub is the Burton Stone Inn which you should see on the A19 as you near the ground. On my last visit this was very popular with away fans and this was helped by a large screen showing SKY television in the back room. However, it was very crowded, but the front room of the pub was more bearable. Going back down the A19 (away from the city centre) on the left there is another pub called the Old Grey Mare which sells Theakstons and was a lot quieter. More or less opposite to this pub (on the other side of the road) is a sandwich shop which sells hot pies for a bargain price.

If you have a bit of time on your hands then you may embark on a 15 minute stroll up the A19 and into York City Centre, where there are plenty of pubs to be found.

Directions & Car Parking

A1 From The South:

Take the A64 to Scarborough and York. When you near York, join the A1237 Ring Road and continue on it until you reach the junction with the A19. Turn right at the junction and take the A19 towards York City Centre and keep going until you get to a pub on your left called the Burton Stone Inn, at which point you turn left into Burton Stone Lane. Then take the first right into Grosvenor Road for the ground.

A1 From the North:

Take the A19 and follow the directions as above. If you arrive early enough then there is street parking to be found in a number of side roads off Burton Stone Lane. Otherwise you may have to travel a further distance away from the ground as there are a number of residents only parking schemes in operation in the general area, or you could seek out a pay and display car park in the city centre and walk back out to the ground.

By Train

York mainline railway station is a good 20 minute walk away from the ground. Walking route from York station thanks to Ninety-Two Club member Dave Dansie: From the car park attached to the station (there is no need to go through main station exit), take the new pedestrian footpath that emerges close to the Post Office building. Turn left, turn left again when you reach the river and cross the Ouse on the footbridge alongside the York-Scarborough railway line. Once over the bridge, turn left at the Abbey Guest House into Marygate car park and follow the footpath, the railway is to your left. At the far end of the car park, the footpath goes under the railway, turn right into Bootham Terrace and walk up the rise to the main road. Turn left, cross the road and Bootham Crescent is the first turning on the right.

Programme

Official Programme: £3

Record & Average Attendance

Record Attendance: 28,123 v Huddersfield Town, FA Cup 6th Round, March 5th, 1938.
Average Attendance: 2011-12: 3,117
(Blue Square Premier)

Capacity: 90,000 (all seated)
Stadium Address: Empire Way, Wembley,
London HA9 0WS
Postal Address: Wembley Stadium, P.O. Box 1966,
London, SW1P 9EQ

Year Ground Opened: 2007*
Pitch Size: 105m x 68m
Main Telephone No: 0844 980 8001
Official Website: www.wembleystadium.com

What's The Ground Like?

Unlike a number of new stadiums that have been built, Wembley Stadium has its own individual identity and character. From the moment you see the Arch towering over the stadium in the distance, then you know that this is going to be something special, and special it is. Plus unlike a number of other stadiums around the world that host a number of sporting events including football, Wembley is primarily for football and is the home of the England team. No wonder that it is labelled the 'Home of Football'.

The stadium is totally enclosed and comprises three tiers, with both sides of the stadium being slightly larger than the ends. These sides are semicircular in construction and although on a larger scale are reminiscent of the similar designs at the Emirates and City Of Manchester Stadiums. Both these side stands have large upper and lower tiers, with a smaller middle tier sandwiched in between. This middle tier overhangs the large lower tier and has a row of executive boxes at the back of it. At each end there is a large video screen, which is moulded into the third and hence is an integral part of the stadium. The stadium has a complicated looking roof that initially appears

retractable and could if necessary be used to enclose the stadium from the outside elements. However, just over one third can be moved, so that the pitch will always be open to the elements. Unlike the old stadium whereby the players would enter the field of play from a tunnel at one end, the players now enter the field in the conventional way, onto the halfway line from the North Stand, where the Royal Box is situated.

The most striking external feature of the stadium is 'The Arch', towering some 133 metres above it. It comprises of white tubular steel that can be seen for many miles across London and looks particularly spectacular at night when it is lit up. Oddly you can't see much of the Arch from inside the stadium. A bronze statue of Bobby Moore, is situated in front of the stadium. The legendary England World Cup winner gazes down on fans coming up Wembley Way.

What Is It Like For Visiting Supporters?

Seeing Wembley for the first time, you can't help but be impressed with the sheer quality of the place. From escalators to transport fans up to the top tier, to the landscaped concourse, you can see that no expense has been spared. Although not the most generous of leg room that I have come across, it is still more than adequate and there is good height between rows. Add to this that there literally is not a bad seat in the house (even seats at the very top of the upper tier have excellent views) and with the roofs of the stadium being situated very close to the crowd, then a full house should generate an excellent atmosphere. The top tier (Level 5) is particularly steep, which may cause a few to be a bit short of breath as they reach the top, but at least this angle ensures that the spectators are kept as close to the playing action as they possibly can be.

Apparently there is one refreshment till per 100 spectators inside the stadium and this seems to work well, with queues being acceptable. Food and drink prices have always been historically expensive at Wembley and the new stadium certainly follows in the same. The concourses themselves are mostly fairly spacious, have betting facilities, a number of flat screened televisions, as well as programme (nicely put in a carrier bag for you to carry home) and merchandise outlets.

Where To Drink?

There are not many pubs located close to the stadium. The few pubs that are close by such as; J.J. Moons (Wetherspoon), the Green Man (both near Wembley Stadium station) and the Torch (near Wembley Park tube station), are usually heaving many hours before kick-off. In addition, I should point out that most of the pubs mentioned above will designate themselves as only allowing entrance to their premises for fans of one club or another who are playing at Wembley on that day. So if you intend going early and intend visiting one of these pubs, I would recommend telephoning them in advance to check whether your team's supporters are being allowed admittance.

Most fans tend to either drink in the centre of London before the game, or have a drink near one of the London Underground stations located north of the stadium such as Harrow on the Hill or further afield such as Watford Junction or Ruislip. I have tended to drink in Harrow on the Hill, which is three stops away from Wembley Park on the tube and has a handy Wetherspoons and an O'Neills outlet, plus a number of other pubs and eating places.

Directions & Car Parking

The stadium has been labelled as a 'public transport' destination, meaning that there is limited parking available at the stadium itself and there is also a residents only parking scheme in operation in the local area. The stadium is well sign-posted from the end of the M1 and M40. I would recommend parking at one of the tube stations at the end of the Metropolitan line such as Uxbridge, Hillingdon or Ruislip or at Stanmore on the Jubilee line and then take the tube to Wembley Park.

By Train/Tube

The nearest underground station is Wembley Park which is around a 10 minute walk from the stadium. This is served by both the Jubilee and Metropolitan lines, although it is best to take the latter as it has fewer stops. Wembley Central is slightly further away from the stadium and has both rail and underground connections. This underground station is served by the Bakerloo line, while the railway station is on the London Euston-Milton Keynes line. The nearest train station is Wembley Stadium which is on the London Marylebone-Birmingham line.

Programme

The cost of programmes vary from match to match, but expect to pay in the region of £7.

Record Attendance

Record Attendance: 126,047 West Ham United v Bolton Wanderers, FA Cup Final, April 28th, 1923.

* Wembley Stadium was originally opened in 1924. That stadium was demolished in 2000.